RIVERS
OF SAND

RIVERS
OF SAND

FLY FISHING MICHIGAN AND THE GREAT LAKES REGION

Josh Greenberg

GUILFORD, CONNECTICUT
An imprint of Globe Pequot Press

Lyons Press is an imprint of Globe Pequot Press.

Project editor: Staci Zacharski
Text Design: Sheryl P. Kober
Layout artist: Melissa Evarts
Map by Melissa Baker

Library of Congress Cataloging-in-Publication Data

Greenberg, Josh.
 Rivers of sand : fly fishing Michigan and the Great Lakes region / Josh Greenberg.
    pages cm
 Summary: "An exploration of the unique techniques needed to fish the waters of Michigan and the Great Lakes region, and a discussion of (and paean to) the region itself"— Provided by publisher.
 ISBN 978-0-7627-7811-9 (pbk.)
 1. Fly fishing—Michigan. 2. Fly fishing—Great Lakes (North America)
 I. Title.
 SH509.G74 2014
 799.12'4—dc23

                                                                          2013035495

Printed in the United States of America

10 9 8 7 6 5 4 3 2 1

TABLE OF CONTENTS

INTRODUCTION

The Lower Peninsula of Michigan, like most places, has had its good old days. And, judging by the pictures, the good old days were pretty good. While a part of me pines for the good old days, the rest of me hightails it around the state with an arsenal of rods and reels, boxes and briefcases of flies, a GPS, a tattered atlas, and a sense of awe. I came to the Lower Peninsula first because of the trout fishing on the Au Sable, and I have lived near that river and fished it, and guided it, and lived off of it with the determination known only to desperate trout anglers trying to connect their livelihoods to their loves. But I have also had my fun on the other rivers, the small streams, and the still waters as well.

The Au Sable had enough allure that my parents bought a summer cabin on its main stream when I was in my mid-teens. I was already crazy about fishing. Now I became crazy about fishing the Au Sable. I got a summer job at the local fly shop, Gates Au Sable Lodge, tying flies and working a few shop hours. I read the history of the river. I knew that Au Sable meant "of sand" in French. I knew about the logging. The extinct grayling. I learned all the local patterns, of which there were hundreds. I just couldn't catch a decent trout out of the place.

In fact, the Au Sable was the first river that really whipped me. Not that I was a great angler. I wasn't. But I'd fished out west and could catch fish there. And I'd fished in the Smoky Mountains in Tennessee and caught fish there. And I'd fished on the Battenkill and though I caught nothing there, no one else was catching anything either. No, the Au Sable was different. The little fish were pretty easy to catch. They were eager brook trout and rose well. But the guys at the fly shop were catching bigger ones than I was. Lots bigger. And they were using the same flies as I was. I chased after their success. I became addicted to it. And I quickly dismissed almost every other river and every other type of fish as of secondary importance to the trout on the Au Sable.

I read books by the old river sages with names like Doug Swisher and Carl Richards. I begged information from my boss, Calvin "Rusty" Gates, or my fellow shop rats, or any of the guides that I had courage enough to talk to. I cared for one thing and one thing only: catching trout on the Au Sable. I remember when my friend Kyle told me about a great hatch he'd hit on a nearby creek, and all the wonderful trout he'd caught. He invited me to join him the next night. I refused, despite the fact that the trout he described were of greater quality and quantity than I'd caught all summer. The Au Sable was no longer a river to me. It had become a sort of eternal video game. And I devoted every cell in my body and second in my day to defeating it.

I got better. Perhaps a lot better. But my enjoyment was disingenuous. I fretted all day about where I'd fish that evening, and then, once I was done fishing, I fretted about why I'd been unable to catch that one fish up under the cedar that *seemed* to be eating spinners but wouldn't touch mine. Or I worried that I should have gone elsewhere. I literally measured myself based on the fish I could or couldn't catch from this one river.

And it's a shame I did this, because I loved the river: its sweeping cedars and towering pines, its inky mysteriousness at dusk, its clouds of fog in the mornings, its undulating water weeds. I knew I loved it for all of these reasons, perhaps more so than the trout fishing. But sometimes it's hard to recognize what you love most about something, especially when you're twenty years old.

It wasn't until I began guiding that I saw what the river really was, and what I was doing. I was making a living. I was doing what I loved. I won't say that I grew tired of the Au Sable. I didn't. I loved the river. Its puzzles had become familiar. What happened was, I began to enjoy the puzzles more than solving them. And, once that happened, I went looking for other puzzles to enjoy not solving.

I traveled to rivers I'd never bothered with, rivers like the Manistee, the Pere Marquette, the Muskegon, the Black, the Rifle, the Jordan, the Sturgeon, the Pigeon, the Little Manistee. I fished the inland lakes. I fished the Great Lakes, laughing as waves broke against my rain jacket, double-hauling into the blue surf for the quick shadows of coho salmon. I learned the fundamentals of Spey casting. I dreamed of carp on the fly. I watched copper smallmouth streak through clear water. I popped bugs for largemouth bass. I flung huge streamers from a tippy canoe for muskie. I watched silver steelhead shoot into the air on quiet winter days.

They were spectacularly different waters. For instance, hurling an indicator rig below the cofferdam on the Manistee among legions of people illegally snagging salmon was not like sneaking up on a trout rising in a backwater at dusk. There were big rivers, rivers whose characteristics had been shaped by the tails of spawning steelhead and salmon. There were small streams. There were magnificent deep lakes.

These new waters required new techniques, so I did what fly anglers do: I began to buy new shit. I bought all sorts of rods and reels, and bags of exotic tying materials. I bought two new boats. I bought books that directed me to new places. I bought gifts for my wife to distract her. I even bought a few guide trips. I enjoyed the new puzzles. I enjoyed the new waters. And, not surprisingly, I began to enjoy my time on the Au Sable more as well.

There is a wealth of different waters in Michigan, and they differ from each other in both their scenery and their fishing. The first thing I savored on all this new water was the newness. The new techniques, the new fish, the new scenery— just the exhilaration of difference. But that kind of thing doesn't last forever, and over time I came to appreciate the new water for the same reasons that I loved the Au Sable. All these new and different waterways were of the same ground. What I mean is this: I could easily mistake a picture of the Manistee for one of the Au Sable, or a picture of the Sturgeon for the Pigeon, and any lake for any other lake. But I would likely know that all the photos came from the Lower Peninsula of Michigan. It's the combination of land and water, the uniqueness of the area, and the haunting sense of mystery it holds that I loved, and love.

The rivers and lakes here share the same basic birth: that of spring water emerging from a huge mound of glacial sand on the northern interior of the Lower Peninsula. They share the same history: one of logging and, in many cases, the extinction of the native grayling and introduction of trout. They all flow into the Great Lakes. And much of their water is drawn from the same Great Lakes by cold winter winds, which falls as snow atop the same glacial sand, at which point the process begins anew. It's a unique cycle of water, and within this cycle swim some fish, and it's these fish, these waters, and the techniques of these waters that this book is about.

CHAPTER ONE

The Thin Blue Lines

Ask a hundred anglers to describe a small stream, and you'll likely get a hundred answers. I define a small stream as any waterway in which it is fruitless to fish *behind* someone.

My favorite description of *being* in a small stream comes from Thomas McGuane's novel *Ninety-Two in the Shade,* which describes a young guide wading a tidal creek: "He was descending into the permit's world; in knee-deep water, the small mangrove snappers, angelfish, and baby barracudas scattered before him, precise contained creatures of perfect mobility. The brilliant blue sky was reduced to a narrow ragged band."

This is creek fishing. It's a gateway into a world more precise and contained than the world around it. A creek is small, which consequently makes you enormous. Scale plays a factor in every facet of the small-stream experience. You are huge. The stream, the trout, and usually the equipment are not. Somehow this change of scale has an effect on the human spirit. We may become frustrated, the proverbial bull in a china shop. We may snag on tag alders and break tippets and rods and storm from the stream. My friend Kyle once hooked the same oak tree four times. He finally broke off his fly and sat down on the bank.

"What are you doing?" I asked.

"I'm in time-out," he said.

It happens.

On our best days, though, we adjust to the stream. We work precise, contained casts within the narrow confines, exploring upriver. Our enormity makes us move

slowly. Spook one trout, and it will spook another. A small stream is a row of dominoes, each ready to topple the next. A small-stream trout is a claustropho-bic trout. They have survived in these streams not because they are selective, but because they are perpetually scared to death.

I wade upstream in these creeks, and I wade cautiously, as if feeling for land mines with my feet. I try to imagine that I'm matching the speed of the creek. The slower the water, the slower my movements: You can blast through a shallow riffle, but you need to sneak through a big quiet pool. In a small stream you have the same impact that Godzilla would have wading up the Mississippi. You are a traumatic event within the delicate tunnel of a small stream. Every move you make disturbs *something*.

I think there's a feel to small-stream fishing, though, that goes beyond just being careful. You have to resign yourself to the terrain. Forget fond memories of drift boats on big rivers. Forget chugging around some endless riffle, or catch-ing dumb hatchery rainbows. You must account for not only yourself, but also your shadow, the shadow of the rod and line, the sound of your footsteps, and the force with which you try to unhook a fly snagged on an upstream alder. On a small stream, your presence stretches further in every direction than you might presume.

Because of the inevitable disturbance a wading angler creates in a small stream, I throw relatively long casts. I try to stand in one pool and cast to the next pool. I always try to put a water characteristic between myself and the trout. That is, if I'm in the tail of a pool, I cast over that pool and into the riffle above the pool. If I'm in the riffle, I cast over the tail of the pool into the dark water, and so on. I strive to use the features of the stream—depth changes, logs, or broken water—to conceal my presence from the trout

It would seem that because the small stream angler is moving deliberately, because she is hiding behind the old muck banks and the piled corpses of trees, that she is fishing slowly, or in place, but she isn't. Ideally, the angler is fishing as fast as possible while still doing it slowly. Deer hunters call this still-hunting.

The perfect terrestrial bank has draping vegetation, a cut bank, and a few overhanging trees as well. This trout ate a beetle on a rather long cast, though it might have eaten any number of flies. A fish eating terrestrials is a fish that can be reasoned with, especially in northern Michigan.
ADOLPH M. GREENBERG

In still-hunting, the hunter moves deliberately between objects that provide him cover. He goes from spruce tree, to old stump, and so on. To the wandering eye, the hunter appears still. Yet he's always in a slightly different place, enjoying a slightly different vantage point. The small-stream angler is the same. He moves from one casting position to the next, adjusting to the ever-altering landscape of the stream. Roll cast. Cross-body cast. Sidearm cast. Steeple cast. On a small stream, a cast is not so much an action as it is a *reaction* to the topography, or character, of the stream.

The best practice for fishing a small stream is to go into the woods and walk around throwing casts. I've never seen anyone do this, and I hope no one has ever seen me doing it, but it's actually pretty fun. It's also something to do when you're stuck in southern Ohio, you're sixteen, and you'd much rather be fishing.

In the Lower Peninsula of Michigan, most of the small streams are lined with tag alders, a gnarled little deciduous shrub with cones that release seeds like a pine tree. The alder is a firm catcher of flies, but the branches are very flexible and can be bent to retrieve a hook. In some places the alders will form into a shadowy tunnel and casting will be impossible. The alder flourishes in wetlands, particularly old beaver floodings, and often extend for hundreds of yards. You can become lost in them.

These streams are most often soft-bottomed, slow, and clear. They flow through areas of flatlands, through huge ancient, drained beaver ponds, and through fresh beaver ponds as well.

There is no force more influential on a small stream than the beaver. I could say that beavers and streams go back through generations, but that wouldn't be entirely true. The beaver was nearly eradicated in northern Michigan—and across the country—in the mid-1800s by extensive trapping. It's hard for me to believe this fact. The beaver does not live in easily accessible places. It creates its own mess of bogs and swampland. It lives far up small streams, moving between stair-stepping dams of its own design. To trap beaver, the old trappers had to hike into these places with traps and supplies and then hike out with traps, supplies, and beaver skins and their castor glands, which were sold for perfume. This was boggy work. It was cold work. They sank into muck. They fell through ice. Traps snapped

Often a curse and always an inconvenience, beaver dams do provide deep water both above and below their structures. The fish below the dam enjoy the oxygenated plunge pools and spillways and are often less wary than those occupying the flat water above. Here an angler is using the dam as cover to make long searching casts upstream.
ALEX CERVENIAK

shut on their fingers. But it was profitable. Still, the fact that humans were able to impact beaver populations seems almost impossible to me. Bison, yes. Beaver, no.

Beaver meat is actually surprisingly good, particularly on the grill. Pioneering Catholics in the New World were allowed to eat beaver during Lent, under the guise that they were aquatic and fishlike. It's a rich red meat, best marinated with garlic and red wine. The back legs and back straps are the best, and the rest should be used in stews. The tail, which is covered in reptile-like scales, was a delicacy back then, and is still considered so today by a few people. It's grilled until the skin can be peeled away, and then grilled again. It's fat, almost as rich as pork fat. And in the north woods, where food is often lean, a few ounces of fat went a long way toward staying alive.

Over the last few years, pelt prices have plummeted and the beavers trapped now are for nuisance reasons: because they have destroyed someone's forest, or dammed someone's creek. There are some malcontents that shoot beavers on sight, others who enjoy the beaver as a component of northern pastiche. Among fly tyers, beaver fur is considered dubbing par excellence. It sheds water well and, if some guard hairs are left in, offers a buggy look exceeded only by squirrel dubbing.

Nowadays the beaver is once again abundant. Across the country, diminished populations of fish in streams have been linked to the loss of beaver activity. Beaver ponds strain silt from the river. They provide deep waters, which are used by fish as wintering spots in small streams, where cold winters wreak havoc. They offer cover for young-of-the-year fish as well as mature fish. They trap organic matter, which feeds insects, which feed fish, which feed bigger fish, and so on. They increase the biodiversity of an area. And, despite all this, they are vilified in northern Michigan by anglers with the sort of fervor normally reserved for aluminum canoes and for poachers.

One reason for this vilification is that a beaver pond creates a wide, muck-bottomed pool that acts as a solar panel, increasing summertime temperatures. Another reason is that beavers have a tendency to block culverts and flood roads and whatever else happens to be in the way. Beaver dams may break and send huge sediment loads down creeks, which cover spawning gravel. Or they may cut flows to a creek, isolating populations of fish. But most of all, beavers create change, and change is always difficult to swallow. More than once I've arrived at a creek only to find that a beaver colony has made a lake out of the creek. Unlike out west, where many streams are in open areas, allowing anglers to fish beaver ponds, our Michigan streams are wooded. When a stream is flooded around here, the water goes into the woods. This leaves little chance to fish these ponds in anything other than a small boat, and even then, casting is only possible from the original stream channel.

But beavers can and do create some pretty great trout cover, and in extreme cases can make a good section of trout stream into a great one.

"Is this the dam that he was talking about?" my friend Matt said.

"Not sure what else it could be," I replied.

We rubbed our sweaty necks and looked for excuses to stand in the water and cool off. We had fished for three miles, starting at the lowest bridge on the creek and working upstream. Though we were told to come here, it just makes good sense to start at the lowest bridge. Either it will be good at the bridge or it will show signs—significant flow or gravel—that there is better water upstream. If you start at the highest bridge and don't catch a trout, all you'll know is that you didn't catch a trout, and that it *might* be better downstream.

The fishing had been fine despite a slow start as we worked through water that bore the signs of other anglers. We were in search of an old, dismantled beaver dam, above which the creek purportedly became deeper and slower and held large brown trout—or so we were told. So far we'd found the brown trout, but not the large ones. In other words, we were having a normal, wonderful day on a small stream in Michigan.

This creek wasn't lined with tag alders, though they grew in a few localized spots. The bottom of the stream was not sandy in the least. The creek was fast and clear and flowed over reddish rocks, through hemlock and cedar shadows, the sunlight rich with pollen, and the trout were in even the fastest water. Matt fished a Patriot Skunk; I had tied on a Rat-Faced McDougall. When I caught a fish, I told Matt that I caught it on a Rat-Faced McDougall. So far, the joke had not worn thin. We fish these flies on creeks for a reason. Their hackle is tied in the round, meaning there are hackle fibers in front of the hook, which act as a deflector against snags. Small streams are one of the best places to fish the flies that nobody fishes anymore.

Eventually we found the dam. It was broken in three spots, where the water gushed through in foamy torrents. Many of the branches and sticks had tumbled off the dam and into the stream below. A dark, narrow pool had formed at the spillway. Beaver-sharpened sticks crisscrossed through the shadowed water, white as bones. We couldn't see much beyond the dam—it was taller than us. Purportedly the secret meadow was somewhere above it, with its big, secret brown trout. I noted an absence of trees on the near horizon.

"There's an opening up there," I said.

"I see that," Matt replied.

We threw some casts at the bases of each of the three waterfalls in the broken dam, and pulled trout from two of them. Matt's was over ten inches and it pulled for the white sticks on the bottom, but wasn't strong enough. Matt turned the fish with the rod and brought it to the gravel at our feet. He unhooked the fish and blew on his fly.

Then we picked our way over the ruined dam and the meadow was before us, a great wide sweep of land—nearly a half-mile of open space, so rare in the huddled north woods. Dead trees stood emptily, having drowned in water when this was a lake, and everything we saw was underwater.

"This is amazing," Matt said. The meadow was beautiful. There were yellow butterflies bouncing around yellow flowers.

"Well, he said there were even bigger trout," I said. "But he was fishing at night. I thought we might find one or two during the day."

Matt considered this. "He came up here *at night?*"

"With Skip," I said. "I saw pictures."

"Nice fish?"

"*Big* fish," I said. I felt the need to apologize, though I didn't know why exactly. I figured that taking someone to a small stream is sort of like taking someone hunting with your dog, and if you're not careful you'll become a hopeless apologist for the dog, how it's not her day, and so on.

Matt shook his head. "I can't believe he came up here at night."

The meadow was huge. The drought had baked the bare mud until it retracted and cracked. The grass, though, was very green. The drowned trees, now bare and broken-branched, stood like gothic, petrified cheerleaders as we progressed up through the glary water. A thin, skin-like haze had covered the sky, and the water was almost not cold enough to cool us.

The mud on the banks had dried in places, but in other spots it was baked into a crust that our feet broke through, kind of like a crust atop deep snow. Unlike snow, the mud beneath the crust was sticky, and it was hard to get our feet free from it.

The mud was nothing more than silt that collected when the beaver pond was still a beaver pond. A beaver pond acts as an enormous silt trap, which is fine until the dam breaks and that silt-load is released all at once into the river below. Fortunately this dam had broken naturally, and in such a way that the water slowly lowered back into the original channel, leaving behind banks heaped high with mud. In some spots the mud was four feet above the original bank, visible from the creek as a single defined line between dark substrate (the collected silt) and much lighter substrate (the original stream bank). The new stream had heaped mud into small sloping towers on the bends.

Soon, I thought, tag alders and poplar trees would grow, replacing the grasses and flowers. The banks would stabilize in some spots, and erode in others. Slowly this stretch of stream would fill in, and in a dozen years the big browns that supposedly lived up here would die off and be replaced by the same small, healthy browns that we had caught downstream of the dam.

This massive, mud-caked meadow differed from the densely forested streams that we were used to. We threw long casts, but the stream had become deep but calm and the fish in the flat water were nervous. We caught some trout in the meadow, but only in the faster water, where the fish reacted more quickly. We decided to use the meadow to our advantage, and we got out of the water. I headed upstream, walking far from the creek so as not to disturb Matt's fish. We concocted a plan. I'd fish up from the big dead pine, where the stream meandered toward a cedar stand and hopefully the trout were less spooky in the shadows. Matt would fish up to the big dead pine, and then hopscotch above me. We'd stay out of the water completely, our theory being that our wake was spooking the fish well above our casting range.

I crouched as I approached the pine and then stood beside it, a hand on the bare wood, the bark long gone. Downstream, Matt was behind one of the odd mud statues, his line waving above it. For a second I mistook him *for* the hump of mud. Then his face popped up as he watched the drift.

I looked back at the water in time to see the rings of a soft rise in the shadows. Brook trout often *prefer* the sun. These browns, though not as cover-oriented as the Au Sable trout, wouldn't shy from the cool shade on this hot day, especially in the openness of the meadow.

I stripped line from my reel, shook the spare line into the water, and let the current pull it straight below me. Then I lifted it from the water and cast side to side, away from the fish, the spray hanging where the fly snapped, farther each cast, until I'd worked out all the line. I threw upstream and above the rise, but short. The water bulged as the fish turned toward the fly. It took from upstream and I struck too early. I cast back quickly—short. The fly landed in the sunny water. A shadow broke off from the shade, a long, slender, accelerating form that overtook the fly. I set, and had him. A brown, fourteen inches, thin, and not much of a fighter. I leaned over the bank to release him and he ducked under the overhang of the earth, into some old beaver tunnel I supposed.

I pulled three more fish from the shade on the far bank, none nearly as long as the first. Matt came walking past me and told a story of a fish he took from a thin, fast side channel that he figured was over four feet deep but only a foot wide. He headed upstream. I kept working the long shallow run, far into the shade with the Patriot Skunk I'd switched to. The long casts and bulky fly had begun to twist my tippet and I contemplated changing the tippet for one cast too many. A good fish took against the bank, and I broke it off on the hook-set.

After retying, I moved up to where a limpid riffle fed the flat water. A few caddis had begun to gather there, and I realized that the light was now evening light. Nothing rose in the riffle. I knelt on the edge of the bank and worked the riffle from right to left, raising two fish but missing both of them. Then, upstream, there was a loud yell. I turned in time to see Matt drop his rod, put his hands on his hips, and stare profoundly at me. I held my hands up, six inches apart, as a joke. He countered with his hands twenty inches apart. Then he strode across the meadow to tell me about it.

"I saw one of those big fish," he said. "I thought he was a log at first but then I realized it was a trout. He was just sitting over the sand, in a foot of water. No, not a foot. Less than a foot. His fin was damn near out of the water. I thought I saw him too late, but he didn't spook. God, he was just sitting there. I threw a cast over him and he came over and I *thought* he had it and I struck, but he must not have had it. I struck too soon. Then he took off."

He lit a cigarette and studied the meadow.

"I guess you'd really have to be here in the evening to see what's in here," he said, resignation in his voice. We had no flashlight. I had a wife, and he had a girlfriend. "It could be spectacular in the evening."

We fished through the rest of the meadow. The stream accelerated, and soon we were out of the meadow and back into the forest, where the water was shallow and fast and the fish were small. The hemlocks were tall and the shade was now thick. We came to a small private bridge and turned around there, ignoring the growing number of caddis. There was a small spit of state land and we hiked through that to the road, and followed the road back to the bridge. By the time we got to the truck, the sun had gone and the sky was ablaze.

≈

When it comes to having success on small streams, finding a good one is definitely more important than being able to throw a curve cast with a $700 rod. Some good creeks come easy. Others don't. Some, like the creek Matt and I fished, come by way of scuttlebutt. There's a good stream full of trout over yonder. You go. You fish. Sometimes they are good, sometimes not. If it is good, you vow to keep your mouth shut. You don't. No one does. And so the creek develops a following, hopefully small. A creek is to the garage band as the Au Sable is to the Stones.

When it comes down to it, the most efficient way to find a stream is to beg a friend to take you to his favorite one. This works well, but only with your best friends. A mere acquaintance won't do. With a mere acquaintance, it can be tense in the weeks and months afterward, as you wonder whether or not it's prudent to return to the creek by yourself, let alone with someone else. This kind of faithfulness can eat at you, especially when the going is tough on your home water and, dammit, that creek would be fishing so well. You may end up calling the guy just to see if he wants to return to the place he took you. He will know that you just want to fish his creek. Relationships may or may not fray, depending on how well you know each other, and what secrets you have to offer for barter.

I much prefer to find a good stream myself, so that it is "mine" and I can fish it when I want to, without feeling like I'm double-crossing someone. This method has several stages, like a science experiment. The first thing you need is a great notion. The great notion is usually: I wonder if so-and-so creek has any trout in it? Or, I'd really like to fish some small streams this year. Or, if this creek has fish in it, I wonder if there are any others around here that do as well? After that, it's best to turn to a map.

I'm not a map fiend, but I do like to get my hands on a good one. The ideal map has topography, roads, and a hint at the geographical features of an area (bogs, plains, woods, etc.). The best I've found is a contraband military map from a friend, though calling the US Army for a favor (map request re: fly fishing) probably won't result in maps of other counties.

A small stream offers nearly every river situation imaginable, often within a span of a hundred yards. Casting prowess is at a premium, but so too is an awareness of the surroundings and a respect for the wariness of the trout.
ALEX CERVENIAK

A regular gazetteer will do, though you'll want a separate topographical map, if possible, along with a county plat book. The topographical map tells you what a stream does by showing the gradient of the banks and surrounding area. Hills and valleys usually mean faster water and a gravel or rock bottom.

The plat book will tell you where the private land is. In Michigan we can wade any navigable stream. We can even get out on the banks to avoid a blockage of some sort (deep hole, logjam, etc.). But private land is private land, and finding a slice of public land in order to cut into the "club water" can mean the difference between fishing where everyone does, and fishing where no one does.

Map open, it's time to explore it for clues. Finding a small stream is a treasure hunt, and there is little in fly fishing that can compare to it. We are looking for what my old boss Rusty Gates used to call the thin blue lines. "Just find the thin blue lines," he'd say to someone who came into the fly shop looking for that mythical little stream. As if he'd just tell them!

Yes, we're looking for thin blue lines: those skinny, meandering lines that seem to go up away from their source. In fact, I always think in this reverse way, as if the streams leave the main river on their own accord and head for the hills. In reality, though, this is what I wish to do: leave the big river and follow the stream to where it's going, even though where it's going is actually back to the big river. A stream doesn't really mean to do anything, but that won't ever stop us from thinking it does. Anyway . . .

Index finger on the map, stream under my finger, I start the virtual fishing. I'm watching it bend and pinch between hillsides (fast water). Watching it straighten out, maybe go under an old bridge or some old weir (culvert? hindrance to fish passage? deep water? probably some combination of them all). Following it upward into what suddenly seems unchartered and brimming with possibilities. And with every mile *it keeps going*, the more optimistic I become. It's not that a short stream can't be a great stream, but the longer the drainage, the more water it's carrying. The more water it's carrying, the better the chance that it is suitable for fly fishing and has some nice fish in it, with a self-sustaining population of wild ones.

Many nights, friends and I have spent hours just staring at maps of Michigan, following tributaries down through their convergences, watching with our mind's eye as they grow in depth and volume, picking up groundwater, filling pools, turning in riffles, and, eventually, harboring trout. A good stream will likely be represented by no less than five miles on a DeLorme map, and many are much longer.

Where do I look around here? Well, everywhere, from the tip of the Mitt down through Grand Rapids, across to Bay City, and on up the east coast. But if you want the odds in your favor, pay particular attention to the headwater and tributary streams of the major trout rivers. That is the very best way to ensure that you're in trout country, and if you're in trout country, it's likely that any fair-size creek is a trout creek.

I don't always start my search looking for the tributaries to trout rivers, but it's a good bet. If the river is a trout river, your odds of finding a decent trout creek attached to it are good. It's also more likely that your newfound secret stream isn't so secret after all, though it seems, at least up here, that even the best small streams are protected by the simple fact that there are bigger fish elsewhere. And thank goodness for that.

Whether or not the prospective stream on the map has trout in it relies not only on what river it flows into, but also where it comes from. Though a bit obvious, the following example suffices for now. The Au Sable has heaps of trout in it and it begins within five miles of another stream, the Manistee. Though the rivers are unconnected, it's safe to assume that if there's trout in one stream emerging from those highlands, there's trout in the other as well. This is kind of like trout-stream genetics. If one kid is smart, you assume his sister is as well.

The farther you get from trout country, the harder it is to tell from a map whether a stream is worth your time or not. I remember one real winner of a creek—a beautiful, fast, gravel and rock stream that flowed into a big river down where the big river could no longer support wild trout (hardly any trout at all, actually). I would have overlooked it, but my friend Kyle didn't. He found, on some old map, where a hatchery had once been located on that very stream. Was it a trout hatchery? We didn't know. But it might have been, and if it was a trout hatchery, then the creek was probably a trout creek.

Neither Kyle nor I ended up fishing it first. Another buddy, Andy, did. And Andy took our friend Greg and me there on his second trip. We cut across the state land we knew from the map was there, and came in just above the steep valley before the stream entered the main river. I was hot from the walk in but the stream was screamingly cold, and this was in August. In fact, that stream was the coldest, most shadowed stream I've found up here. It had rainbows, browns, and brooks. They rushed through the frothy whitewater for big foam bugs. They sipped our ants along the banks in those dark shadows, their rise forms so faint I had to be on my knees to see them. There came a point—a series of horseshoe bends—where the fish were everywhere they were supposed to be and nowhere else. Where one good cast would produce one good fish. We never saw a single fish rise that day that wasn't rising to our flies.

There was something misty and reverential about that stream that I've not had duplicated in Michigan, or anywhere else for that matter. I've not returned. To me, fishing a great small stream is secondary to the pleasure of finding one. And once you find a treasure, sometimes just knowing it's locked up safe is better than rolling in it every afternoon.

But even a long stream can be a barren one. We need all the information we can gather before we spend money on gas. So we begin to ask questions. Does the stream flow through swampland? *Yes, in a few spots.* Is there gradient? *Yes.* Does the river flow in a straight line or does it bend often? *It bends often except where it rushes into the main river.* Is it in known trout country? Meaning, do the streams and rivers around it contain trout? *Yes.* Does it drain or feed a lake? *Yes.* Is it a trout lake? *Don't know.* Does it feed a trout river? *Yes.* Does it have numerous tributaries? *One mile below the lake, there's a major tributary.* Is there a hatchery on it? *No, but this is always a good sign.* How many road crossings? *Six.*

The gazetteer has gotten us this far, but now we go online. Google Earth shows a stream with hills and a serpentine course. These are good things. But Google Earth also shows that the lake this secret stream drains has houses on it, and is larger than the map seemed to indicate. Searching the Michigan Department of Natural Resources website, we see the lake is stocked with walleye and is not a trout lake. This is a bad sign. If it's draining a warm-water lake, it may be a warm-water stream. A couple of my friends once spent two hours on a known trout stream catching bluegill and one small bass from the point where it left a small pond. Several miles downriver, below a few unseen springs, this same stream is an excellent brook trout fishery.

So now our search on our hypothetical stream turns outward. Where are the tributaries to this stream? Do they come from other ponds, or from swampland? Some ponds and swamps are cold, but most are warm, particularly in the summer. Remember, no one factor completely disqualifies a small stream. We are looking for the likelihood that the thin blue lines on the map are filled with trout. In the case of this secret stream, there is a high point to the west and several tributaries are born from these highlands.

This particular stream feeds a famous trout river, but it enters the river downstream of the famous water. All told, from the upstream pond down to the river itself, there are nearly fifteen miles of stream. There are six bridges, but the county plat book reveals that two are private. A Forest Service road parallels the stream and connects the two lowest bridges. You put a big X at that point, develop a cough on Monday, call in sick on Wednesday, and hit the road before the sun clears the eastern horizon.

≈

Now that I think about it, a good small stream doesn't always look like a good small stream. There are those that are nothing more than flowing bogs that have excellent trout populations, and others that seem to have everything a trout could desire except the *trout* themselves. I have followed hot leads to nowhere: stagnant cesspools crawling with snakes and frogs and chubs. I have stopped at streams close to towns that I've never heard mentioned that were great. One stream flows through a gated community and I caught so many nice, wild trout under the community bridge I parked beside that I wondered if anyone in the gated community ever bothered to fish the thing! I guess the point is this: If you want a good stream, you have to do the legwork yourself.

But I think that when a stream shows promise, the fun really begins. One stream in particular comes to mind. I'll call it Cedar Creek because not only is this *not* the stream's name, but there are seemingly dozens of Cedar Creeks in Michigan. I knew about Cedar Creek because it flows into a river that I have often floated. At the mouth of the creek it looked like the worst kind of mucky stream there is. But—and this is a big *but*—it had exceptionally cold water, and during the Hex hatch the fish lined up and rose at the mouth of the creek.

I heard enough rumors about the creek that I decided to explore it. I called my friend Kyle—a Pennsylvanian who knows how to keep a secret, even if we didn't actually yet have a secret to keep—and we spread maps all over my kitchen table along with vises and boxes and spools of tippet, and began to plot our game plan, and drank more beers than two brave explorers ought to do.

The map showed a creek that began and ended in two vast bogs, each comprising several square miles of space. Between the bogs the map showed a stream with a defined channel. We did not search it out on Google Earth—I'm not sure if Google Earth even existed then—but in retrospect I'm glad we didn't. If we had, we probably wouldn't have gone there.

Below the bridge culvert at Cedar Creek, the stream quickly entered a massive stand of cedars and the air went dark and smelled of moss and, well, cedar. The stream narrowed at the head of the cedar forest and then went *underground,* disappearing and reappearing between the thick mat of cedar roots and decomposed tree matter. A pool would appear as nothing more than a single square foot of water that seemed to boil, though it was only the current upwelling into the opening.

We walked through the forest, discombobulated. Then we heard a strangely familiar noise. It was the sound of a riffle . . . flowing under the ground beneath our feet. We stopped to examine the sound, and by peering through a crack in the earth, we could see a quick rush of shadowed water through its hidden cauldrons and magical dark pools.

"There could be grayling under here," I said.

Kyle—ever pragmatic—sat down Indian style, as he does, and consulted a fly box.

"Could be," he said.

Nowhere was there room for a proper presentation. The stream spread out across the entire cedar forest, appearing here and there as quiet pothole pools, reflecting the cedars above them, glinting just enough to discern them from the shadows. Around the water, ferns grew nearly three feet tall. I had never been to a spot like this one, and I thought of where it entered the main river—wide, shallow, mucky, flat—and marveled at how, only a mile upstream, it lived fast and free beneath this forest. You can never truly know a creek until you've waded the entire thing, tip to back.

Kyle had his little five-foot rod, and I had my seven-footer. We would have been better off with ten-foot cane rods with four feet of 5X attached to the tip. But this is what we had, and a creek angler must be versatile. We rigged up, Kyle with an ant, figuring that a fish living under a forest would likely eat plenty of ants. I tied on a Patriot Skunk. After that we spread out among the forest, chasing one pool, and then the next. The stream was lousy with brook trout. And not just any brook trout, but the prettiest, darkest, earthiest brook trout I'd ever held. They came slashing from the shadows, appearing milliseconds before they crashed into the fly as a single tannic bolt of movement, a quick streak through the boiling water.

We found some good holes many yards from where it seemed the stream actually was. These were dark-water spots that seemed like the mouth of a well. The sun came soft through the cedars. There was the sensation of being drugged, as if we'd stumbled into *A Midsummer Night's Dream.*

We often fished with only a foot or two of line and five or so feet of leader while hiding among the cedar trees. I remember looking to my left and watching Kyle catch three trout in a row. I could not see the water he was fishing. It seemed he was pulling the trout directly from the earth.

We were exalted. We left the stream with a *real* secret to keep.

The next day Kyle traced Cedar Creek up from the main river, and after a few hours of wading through knee-deep black muck, he came to a massive, unexplainable hole filled with about fifty brook trout, all very much spooked. I could not go that day, and I grilled him that evening. He said that there was nothing up there but muck and that one good pool. Maybe, he said, if you were at that pool during a hatch . . . But no, there was nothing there.

The following week he waded above the culvert bridge upstream of the cedars. He caught a few small trout, but soon the stream became wide and shallow, tag alders in every direction. He tromped back to his truck and tried to find another upstream crossing, but there was none to be had. The stream had only that one magical underground half-mile. That was it, he said. That was all there was.

I love the guy, but I studied his face, looking for an eye tic, or hidden smile, or some other sign that he was lying. He looked tired, sunburnt, but not completely dissatisfied. There was a moment where I wondered if he had more to tell, if he hadn't found a secret of his own. After all, a good trout river is a monument many people visit, but a creek is loved with what borders on jealousy.

Small-stream fishing tackle and attire is as simple as the fishing. I wear sandals, long underwear if it's cold, shorts if it's not, a fishing shirt with pockets to fit a box of flies, a lanyard with nippers, and an Arcticreel to keep drinks cold. I usually wear socks under my sandals to keep the leeches out, but then I'm severely take-me-to-the-hospital allergic to leeches, and chances are that everyone else in the world is not.

I bring only three spools of tippet—4X, 5X, and 6X—and a spare leader in case the other one is ruined beyond repair. I never fish a leader over nine feet on a small stream, and tend to prefer something right around seven and a half feet. Fluorocarbon is good stuff because it doesn't twist up, but for the money, Maxima Ultragreen is stiff and doesn't seem to stretch like other monofilament tippets. It's the perfect small-stream leader and tippet material, and is much stronger than the pound-test it's rated.

I don't stress about fly choice on a small stream, but you don't want to hit a Trico spinner fall with a box of hoppers either. First, you'll need some well-hackled attractors in #10 to #16. Think Adams, Irresistible, Patriot, Griffith's Gnat. The Patriot Skunk, a Michigan adaptation of the Pennsylvania original, is a small-stream fly par excellence, and I use it almost all the time now. That and several other rubber-leg bugs, including the olive Foam Skunk. A Skunk, by the way, is a traditional Michigan fly with white rubber legs and a black chenille body, hence the name Skunk. Many Au Sable anglers now call just about every rubber-leg fly a Skunk.

I also bring imitations of what may be hatching. You might actually need them. There was a day in early June on a small stream where if it weren't for a Marinaro-style sulphur spinner and 6X, I wouldn't have caught the eight-inch brook trout that, after twenty minutes of me not catching it, absolutely *had* to be caught. I bring a few flies for each major hatch that you may see, including some that have already hatched on the big rivers. I wouldn't bring midges. I wouldn't bring six styles of BWOs. Just a few good working patterns that float high and that you have confidence in.

But in my mind nothing is more suited to small streams than the terrestrial. A small stream has more bank per *square inch* of water than does a river. Think about it: A stream may be one-eighth the size of even a modest trout river, yet it has the same amount of riverbank. That means, at least to me, that there are more terrestrials per trout in a small stream than in a river. Creeks are *great* for terrestrials. We have a few grasshoppers, some crickets, a beetle here and there. The ant, though, is king.

Kyle is from Pennsylvania. He first came to the Au Sable in the month of May because that was when Vince Marinaro came here. I hope that there are still college kids who count among their idols Marinaro. Over time, Kyle became a part of the culture up here, tying flies by the dozen and fishing when he could afford to go. It wasn't long before Kyle insisted that we try chumming up some big fish with grasshoppers, as Marinaro and Charles Fox famously did on the Letort Spring Run.

It took nearly half a decade to finally get around to doing it. We purchased little insect nets and spent two hours running around his girlfriend's horse pasture, diving and swooping for grasshoppers. We deposited them in a plastic bucket with a slit in the top that we could push the insect in without fear of them climbing out.

With about two hundred grasshoppers in tow, we headed to the headwaters of the Manistee, where the water is narrow and deep, a luscious, dark stretch of creek.

I crouched downstream with a camera, and Kyle, far upriver, began feeding the hoppers down. The response was immediate, and violent, and within minutes we had some decent fish feeding. I called him and he asked, "Is it working?" and I said, "Oh, hell yes it is." Then, very quickly, the trout quit rising. Hopper after hopper swept around the bend, drifting over the dark slot, kicking next to cover, resigning to the current, drifting over the tail of the pool, and floating downstream below me.

I called Kyle again and told him that nothing was rising.

"The big ones aren't out yet," he said. "I'm saving all the good grasshoppers. How about now?"

"Nothing."

"Now?"

"Still nothing."

Once he was out of grasshoppers, he came trundling over to me and sat down. We sat there and smoked some cheap cigars and thought about what had happened. Were the fish full? Were they suspicious? Did they even know what a grasshopper was?

We shrugged and went fishing up through the same hundred yards that the grasshoppers had drifted through. In those hundred yards, Kyle caught no less than six trout on a #16 flying ant, including a twelve-inch brook trout, from the same spots—the dark slot, the logjam—where nothing would touch a grasshopper. Clearly the grasshoppers were not a food source in that stretch of stream, or at least not as great a one as flying ants. That, or the fish were sick of people chumming them with grasshoppers.

I always have ants, but rarely do I fish the simple dubbed-bodied one with the one black hackle. I usually tie them with rubber legs, and parachute wings, and laid-back wings, and so on. I tie them in cinnamon and black, and sometimes I'll make one hump of cinnamon and the other black. The key, I think, is to match the body shape. The rest of these modifications just add floatability. There are ants everywhere, both on the ground and, at times, in the air. In late summer, particularly after rainstorms, they leave their numerous mounds and take flight. They look like smoke leaving a small volcano. If you are on the stream when this happens, you will not forget it.

When it comes to flies, I bring one box of them. I may add a few nymphs, and a streamer in the fall.

Even a half-foot in rod length can make all the difference in casting under overhangs. A short fly rod is simply easier to use on a small, brushy stream.
JOSH GREENBERG

I have searched for the perfect small-stream rod since I began fishing small streams, and I now own three that are *only* fished on small streams, and I have a fourth, a bamboo, currently under construction. My go-to had been a seven-foot two-weight built on a Winston IM6 blank, but my new honey is a five-foot three-weight glass rod that is surprisingly stiff, and can even fish a large grasshopper pattern or a small streamer. Longer rods are okay, maybe better than short rods, on streams that don't have a canopy. But most of our streams do have a canopy, and after a day of catching the tip of your eight-footer on branches, you'll pine for something shorter.

My other small-stream rod is a six-foot glass rod that I hardly ever fish anymore. The thing is just too slow. On a creek, there is nothing worse than having a rod that is too slow. There's too many trees and behind an angler for a full cast, and most small stream backcasts are abbreviated and must be compensated by a fast, snapping forward cast that overloads a soft rod and destroys your loop, depositing your fly halfway up the alder branch the fish is rising under. Roll-casting with such a rod is also a struggle. I think many people like the idea of fishing wispy little wands on wispy little creeks until they try to catch a trout on one.

There is nothing constant about a stream. They are small, fragile things that magnify not only us, but all the trees and boulders, ponds and dams, and other such "threats" to what we like to envision as *our* perfect little stream.

Some changes are dramatic. The East Branch of the Au Sable, for instance, has been overdeveloped with houses and new road crossings. It has been dammed by beavers and warmed in places to a point that precludes trout survival. A fish hatchery on the East Branch prevents fish passage from the main stream of the Au Sable. Many years ago, locals considered the East Branch to be some of the finest trout fishing on the Au Sable system. In fact, when my dad and I first came to fish northern Michigan, Bob Smock Sr., who had a fly shop in his garage, sent us to the East Branch. We traveled with high hopes, but aside from a few small brook trout, we caught nothing but chubs. I had a few leeches on bare shins as well.

Not all changes may be so dramatic either. A small stream is a fragile thing. Even a single, big tree can fall into the creek and become a dam, and a simple landslide can become the kind of current diversion that can alter many yards of creek. A culvert may be plugged. A family of otters or greedy human anglers might move through. An ice dam may form, or there may be anchor ice. One of the tenets of island biogeography is that the smaller the island, the greater the ease with which species are extirpated from it. A small stream is a small island, an isolated population whose survival depends on the small quantity of water in which they live.

For years my boss Rusty would tell me about a small stream that we'll call Gator Creek for lack of a better name. Working the shop, Gator Creek was the creek that he winked about. Best brook trout creek around, he'd say. Brook trout everywhere. Man, you wouldn't believe the brook trout fishing in that creek. So, once I found out the true name of Gator Creek, I broke out my maps, traced the thing, and went fishing.

Gator Creek was a long creek, and it had once had a fish hatchery on it at its very upper end. There were five bridges on the thing, one just above where it emptied into the main river. The first time I fished the creek was with a fellow shop employee. We left after work and drove across two counties. By the time we got to the second-lowest bridge, the sun was setting and the white millers were hovering over the stream. No rises. No sign of fish. The stream slowly weaved through an endless bog of tag alders. We got in and went shoulder-to-shoulder upstream, taking turns on likely spots. The bottom was sand and decomposing wood. We fished for several hours. The first brook trout came from the tail end of a logjam and was over a foot long. The second was just under. And that was all we caught. No small trout. No actual rises that weren't to our flies.

"Brook trout everywhere," I said, holding the bigger trout.

"Yep," my friend said. "That's a *nice* brook trout, though."

A few years later I returned to Gator Creek, determined to find the plethora of brook trout that Rusty spoke of. This time I went to the lowest bridge to see if things were different there, and at first blush they were. The bottom was completely stone, and broke quickly from riffle to pool and back again. It was completely opposite of the stream several miles upriver.

It was late September, the start of the fall cool-down, but grasshoppers fled from my footsteps as I walked down to the stream. I tied on an olive Foam Skunk and waded in. I'd heard this was a brook trout fishery, but the water was warm. My second cast was over a gravel hump and toward a deep chute. The fly went over the chute without a take, but as it approached the gravel hump, a fish I'd not bothered to look for rose up, rested beneath the fly, and refused it. I cast again and this time the fish ate, and I missed it. The fish shot into the chute and was gone.

It was a good fish. A brown. Huge for such a creek.

I waded upstream with more care, my rod pointed behind me. There Gator Creek had cut a trench in the earth, and it was clear by the massive logs stuck into the clay hillsides that this creek could and would flood very quickly. There is a stream in New Zealand, Kendall Creek, that is merely a bed of boulders fifty yards across. Strange that it's considered one of the most dangerous crossings in the entire country. It lives in a canyon of sheer rock walls. Peak to base, nothing but rock. All the rain that falls in the valley proceeds directly to the creek, which becomes a river, and moves boulders down it with the sound of the footfalls of a giant.

A character of a river is often revealed by its high-water mark. Clearly this stretch of Gator Creek had something in common with Kendall Creek. The river had scoured passages through oxbows, receded, reopened old passageways, ad infinitum, throwing logs and rocks far up into the woods. It had cut this sharp gorge, and now the gorge aided the creek in flooding. Everywhere sticks poked up to catch loose line. At times the water disappeared completely beneath timber. Once I broke through a jam and caught myself with my elbows and my feet were barely wet, the water was so far below me.

I eventually came to a big pool. A great pool. A deep trench of water that broke against a high clay bank on the left. This part I remember very clearly. It was a long, narrow pool with a wide bubble line that bounced and swirled off logs that had been buried in the clay. This was a stream that flooded in a big way. A stream that rushed through this steep valley with incredible force, scattering whole trees, crushing them, folding them into the soil on the banks.

I stood atop the bottommost jam, the one the pool ran into before it was swept beneath the logjams behind me. Several mosquitoes found the back of my neck. The sunlight was scattered by the big leaves. I had a shadow-casting moment—the kind you have when no one is around and you get to let some line out. I cast way too far up into the bubble line. A greedy cast. I began stripping line back as my fly bounced down the bubble line. The line I stripped back was swept beneath the logjam under me and I stooped in mid-float to untangle it, and that was when I heard it.

Bloop!

I lifted and struck and in doing so somehow freed my line from the logjam, and a great big gold-colored brown trout twisted deep through that scattered sunlight and ran hard for the clay bank and the catacombs beneath it. I leapt from my log perch and began running upriver with my rod low to my side. It was pretty heated for a moment, with that fish digging for that far bank and my rod tip in the water trying to keep my line underneath the overhang.

The trout really had no good answer after that first rush. It was no great battle. I'd been lucky to hook it and that was all, and I beached it on the sand on the inside of the bend. Twenty inches, I thought. It wasn't. But it was very close. It was a female fish. Big and deep-bodied, in perfect condition, not very dark at all. I held her several times to the rod for measurement. I don't know why. Just to get the story right, I guess. Then I pushed her back into the water and almost quit right there. A big secret, I thought, a big secret tiny stream. Trophy brown and brook trout. Dry flies. Right here in Michigan. Or maybe, I thought, there'd be some evening fishing here. Big rising trout at dusk. Who knew what else was in this pool?

I'd keep fishing, I decided. Just to scout it out for a return trip, learn the water a bit more. I straightened myself up, hooked my fly to the cork, took maybe ten steps, and saw, in the shallow riffle that fed the pool, in twelve inches of water, waving its tail, swooping left and right for nymphs, its long sinuous shadow following it, a *monster* trout. Dark green in the back. A broad-shouldered fish.

I thought, better than twenty. Way better. The kind of fish that, catch it or not, affects the rest of your week. I dropped immediately into what I hoped was a predatory crouch. Blew on the fly. Then, fearing it wasn't enough, shook the fly in desiccant. I thought to myself that I'd just spent two summers in New Zealand catching trout of this size in streams of this size and this fish was no different. Except, of course, that it was. This was an enormous Michigan trout made all the more enormous by being in this tiny stream. It was not this one fish that might not ever happen again: It was this *situation* that might never happen again. So I breathed deeply and savored it.

The trout was no lazy fish, and it swung across the riffle with grand control, the way a greedy king might work the dinner table. It did not hold or return to a common spot after it fed, as most trout do. This fish was all over the riffle, though it favored the inside of the bend, and it would swing nearly to shore and eat before coasting out through the broken water—it shadow distorting over the rocks on the bottom—nearly to the middle of the creek, to feed once again.

I remembered then a trout on a little river in New Zealand. It was Kyle's turn to fish. The trout was feeding at the head of a fifty-yard pool that was maybe thirty feet wide, just below a modest cataract. It was rising to large gray mayflies, and it would cover the entire width of the pool, moving as much as thirty feet to take one. The trout never rested or paused. It fed with a fluidity that belied what the books said about trout vision. It was as if its movements determined where the next mayfly would be, and not vice versa. Kyle caught the fish, or at least hooked it. I can't remember. In the end, the landing of such a fish wouldn't matter. He fooled the trout not by casting at it, or even leading it, but by casting as far to the side of it as he could—across the river from it. The trout's rise procedure started from twenty feet away, and when it took the fly we all yelled, if only to exhale the pent-up servitude we had to a localized, unbelievable drama.

This trout, on this mysterious little Michigan stream, in the day, in the sunlight, was priceless in the way only nature can be priceless. A deer hunter would feel the same to witness the battle of two great whitetail bucks on the opening day of rifle season. I worked out line, letting it lay in the current below me. I breathed. I cast. My fly landed where I wanted it to—off to the side of the fish, just ahead of it. I thought it was a great cast. The fish went rigid in the water, as if I'd shot it. It stayed put, though, so I cast again, knowing full well what a spooked fish looks like. And I cast again, knowing what futility looks like. And, finally, the trout turned and swam past me—looking very large and missile-like—and disappeared into the deep green depths of the pool.

I cursed.

I then stormed upriver for probably two miles looking for another. And there were more great pools but no more fish except for one tiny brook trout and a handful of chubs. I ended up so far upriver that I climbed the ridge through private land and bushwhacked to the road—which, of course, took much longer than simply walking back downstream to the bridge. But I wasn't done yet. I walked past the truck and followed the road to where it crossed the main river, and spent two more hours fishing down the main river and then back up the creek to the bridge, thinking with every cast of the fish I'd landed, and the one I'd spooked, and trying to discredit the growing notion in my head that what had just happened, and where it had happened, probably wouldn't happen again.

But what had happened to the great brook trout stream Rusty had sent me to? Was it a myth? Was this creek a diversion to protect the real brook trout stream? I don't know. I don't think so. What I think happened is that somewhere in the

The prize is not measured in inches or pounds. Some of the best fish can't be quantified. As such, the story of a day on a creek is often left to vague (but emphatic) adjectives.
ALEX CERVENIAK

creek, *something* had changed. A beaver pond. A human pond. Groundwater pollution. Groundwater withdrawal.

Trout streams have a tendency to wink out at times. This can happen all at once, as it did recently on the Pigeon River, a fine trout river in northern Michigan, when a massive silt flow from an improperly managed private dam flooded downstream and turned the river to fudge, killing fish and sending conservation groups to court with the hopes of having the dam removed (that was the *third* time such an event had occurred because of the dam). Other streams, like the East Branch, change over time due to development and blockages to fish migration. Such streams are not beyond reclamation, and even on the East Branch, a large-scale habitat project has already begun to help what was a waning trout population.

I know that as anglers we should not only participate in conservation causes, but also be personal stewards of these secret streams. If the water of your favorite creek seems unnaturally low, call your local conservation group or the Department of Natural Resources. Tell the field biologist. It could be nothing but a drought. Or it could be that an upstream dam—the one that forms the resort-happy lake—is cutting off flow.

And if you see other cars parked at your secret creek, or the trout seem small one year, or fewer in number, or skittish, then, well, go somewhere else. Leave the fish alone, and let them feed unmolested for the season. Such personal choices will pay off in a few summers when the trout are back, fat and bright, and slashing at every fly you throw.

CHAPTER TWO
Making a Day of It

Part I: Summer

The Au Sable used to be a summer destination for me. My parents, both teachers, bought a camp along the river, and we vacationed there in July and August. So I missed the glory months of May and June. I first learned the Au Sable as a river of summer, with morning and evening hatches of tiny bugs, and long dry afternoons during which you were forced to work the water hard just to catch a trout. My average fish was around six or seven inches, at least during the day.

The normal routine, as explained to me and practiced by me, was to fish the cover with attractor flies: Michigan Skunks, deerflies (imitated using Rusty's Secret Rubber Bug), ants, and a host of attractor patterns. On one hot float in August with my Ohio friend Bob, we stopped in at the Gates Lodge on the way through. We were in our late teens at the time.

"They quit rising for our dry flies," I said to Rusty. "Should we fish nymphs?"

Rusty's eyebrows lifted. "Just fish closer to the wood."

"No nymphs?"

He stared at me.

"Just hit the wood," he said slowly.

Rusty was once featured in a book where he had to give his three favorite flies: dry, streamer, and nymph. He wrote "parachute anything, leech, what's a nymph?"

I was always pretty swayed by Rusty's opinions, especially when I was younger, but it didn't take me long to realize that there were days when one could never be close enough to the wood to catch a trout. I had spent much of my youth with my dad fly fishing the Smoky Mountains, as well as the split-shot-happy states of Montana, Colorado, and New Mexico. So I began fishing nymphs on the Au Sable and quickly learned from others who did so as well.

The Au Sable is a tricky river to nymph-fish. It is shallow, especially in the famous upper reaches of its three branches, the pools short and scattered about. In the Smoky Mountains, or out west for that matter, I usually just tied on a nymph and caught some fish. Here, no dice. The summer trout couldn't have cared less. It wasn't until a day in October, during a three-day weekend getaway with my dad, when I finally found some success with the nymph.

It was a sunny and warm day for October, and the fish would have nothing to do with a streamer. We switched to what we considered a standard nymphing rig: indicator, split shot, and a couple of bead-head nymphs. I worked a dark chute and, well, I had a moment of extreme confidence. The mysteries of the sunny day dissolved. The fish were not in the open water spawning. They were not in the cover hiding. They were at the bottom of this deep hole, right where my nymphs were.

And they were.

Upstream, my dad caught a lovely fish in a cut behind a logjam. It was a pool he came to call the Stick of Butter Pool. I don't know why he called it that, but now that's what I call it, too.

We left the river that day with what we thought was a secret. I went nuts all winter fantasizing about catching big Au Sable browns on nymph rigs. Different pools I'd try. New approaches. New flies. I arrived at the ready, and spent the first half of the summer fishing nymphs . . . and caught nothing. Well, not nothing, but very few trout, all small, most of which ate the nymphs as they were swinging at the end of the drift.

I kept my ears open and listened to the guides, and the customers coming in and out of the shop, and I began to pick up some tricks. After a few years, I began to get some fish. By the time I started guiding, I had learned at least one truth: The Au Sable doesn't nymph well. But parts of it do. And not always where I was thinking. And from there, I began to chisel away at what worked, and what didn't, and where. I began to tie a bead-head nymph off the bend of my dry fly. I learned that you could catch fish even if they weren't rising to dry flies. And I learned that the best times to be on the river—those famous hatches—are relatively short. They don't call it the "magic hour" for nothing. Which leaves a lot of time for us anglers to try and make a day of it.

≈

It begins with reading the water. And by reading the water, I don't necessarily mean the obvious honey holes: the bubble lines and main seams and logjams and big deep bends and riffles. Those are easy to see. I mean the little things: the shelves, the inside seams, the sandy soft water, the summer weed beds, the submerged cover.

Take something as simple as bottom composition. Oftentimes a river is divided by substrate size, with small stuff on the slow side of the river and larger, more immovable stuff on the faster side. The line where these two bottom substrates meet will likely extend down the river for miles, alternating sides as the river picks up speed here or loses speed there. All our rivers have this, usually divided nearly down the middle: half sand, half gravel. The Manistee and Pere Marquette are particularly good examples of rivers that have a strong, obvious division in their bottom composition. Trout will sit somewhere near this line, easing in and out of the slower and faster currents to feed or rest, depending. In the summer, they tend to sit over the gravel (faster water). In the winter, they love the sand (slower water).

Shelves and drop-offs can be very obvious, or they can be minute. An obvious shelf often leads directly into a pool or deep water. These are winter spots, and they are easier to see. Just stand next to a pool and look down. A less obvious shelf will occur within a riffle and can be nothing more than a slight depression or pocket. There's one downstream of the lodge, well below where the South Branch comes in, that is within a riffle and well concealed. The drop-off isn't much, a foot of extra depth at best. But it is a killer spot. You won't usually catch big fish off that shelf. Who cares? On a day when you can't catch anything, a trout is a trout. Even a six-inch fish is bigger than nothing.

More than any other river characteristic, shelves and other little fast-water pockets are tailor-made for fishing a dry fly with a trailing nymph. Around here, we call it "fishing the bead."

I truly, sincerely, and perhaps guiltily love fishing a dry fly with a dropper attached to it. When you tie on a dropper, you are immediately adding a third dimension to the river. It reminds me of what my friend Marvin described when he first began fly fishing. He came to the sport late, after many years of serious, high-level canoeing. Marvin said that what he found initially most pleasant about fly fishing was that the things he never noticed when he was canoeing—bubble lines, sweepers, drop-offs—were now what he noticed most. We live in an existence of infinite matrices and most of what we call hobbies are really turnkeys into them. Which is why kayakers see the whitewater, and we see all the dark water around it.

Not only do I enjoy fishing a dropper, but I love everything that I now associate with it. I carry a small pack and a box of junky dry flies heavy on foam and rubber legs and flash, and another box of tiny, glittery nymphs. There are spools of fluorocarbon (always fluorocarbon) and shades and sunscreen, and if the river is warm enough I'll wet wade, and I love that, too. The trout are normally small, and twelve inches is a good one. But it is pretty fishing, and somehow cleaner to me than the magical evening rise. No DEET. No waders. No flashlights. Just you; a nice fast, light, long graphite rod; and a bunch of perfectly formed, small, wild trout. The fact that no one is doing it makes it all the sweeter. You fish slowly and break down the river, making multiple casts through good spots. To me, the addition of the nymph is kind of like the difference between scooping the icing off a cake and getting a whole slice.

When I'm fishing a dry and dropper rig, I will wade both upstream and downstream. Each has its advantages. Wading upstream you are much less likely to spook fish. If you aren't spooking fish, you have more fish to cast to. To me, wading upstream is for those days where I want to meditatively pick apart the river. Those are the advantages. The major disadvantage to wading upstream is that it's tiring. Less because of the current on your legs than because of the current on your line, which you must strip in and then recast repeatedly.

Going downstream you will get longer drifts, simply because the limiting factor is how far you can feed line out, as opposed to wading upstream, in which you are limited by the length you can cast. The downstream approach also allows you to work the face-side of logs, which tend to slant away from the bank. Unless you are an expert curve caster, it is very difficult to work a logjam properly with a dry and dropper from downstream of the logjam in question. It's best to be above it, where you can better control the drift, and keep your flies close to but out of the cover.

But working logjams is a small part of dropper fishing—maybe the smallest part. What I'm really looking for are changes in depth, specifically areas that go from shallow (up to eighteen inches) to mid-depth (twenty to thirty-six inches). There are very obvious spots, and then there are spots that aren't obvious at all. Just a few inches of depth change can hold several fish, or one good one. This change of depth can exist on its own or be part of a larger river characteristic.

For instance, there are many big, deep holes that have more subtle depth changes away from the deep water. These depth changes usually exist as color changes: from sand, to white gravel, to orange stones, and finally into the pool itself. These color changes reflect the different currents that exist within the pool, and the size of the particles that these currents can move. You'll catch more fish on the dropper from the inside of a deep bend or pool than you will working the heavy bubble line that runs through it.

As spring gives way to summer, massive beds of weeds grow in some of our rivers. Working the churning pocket water between the weed beds is a great way to spend a sunny summer afternoon. There is one great patch of weeds upstream of the lodge that I escape to after work if no one is around and the canoe traffic is light. The weeds grow downstream of a huge willow branch that has split from the main tree but hasn't detached completely. Between the weed beds are swirling little pools, some no more than a few square feet. These pools are loaded with fish. It is excellent dropper fishing, and good ant fishing as well. Consequently, fishing a buoyant ant with a bead below it is great fun.

On the Au Sable River the most effective dropper distances range from sixteen to thirty inches, and every inch within that range matters. I typically start at around twenty to twenty-four inches and go from there. The higher the water, the deeper the dropper. I've never done well with a dropper fished less than twelve inches behind the dry fly, even when the water is low and clear.

I like bead-heads, and when it comes to any sort of nymph fishing, that's what I typically use. I just say "beads," and almost always in #16 to #20. This fly selection applies to the bulk of our trout season, from April through October. Our list of preferred dropper flies is unexceptional, but the top two seem to always be a bead-head Pheasant Tail or some variation thereof, or a Copper John, usually

A selection of summer flies is known collectively as "junk," and a day spent blind-fishing such flies at the banks is known as "pitching junk." They are not subtle or elegant, but well-tied attractors such as these are durable and high floating.
JON RAY

a red one. Other popular choices are Trigger Nymphs, Prince Nymphs, Psycho Prince Nymphs, and a variety of local patterns, most notably the Tank's series of bead-head nymphs.

One mistake people make, I think, is to fish unnecessarily large dry flies to float their nymphs. I often fish #16 bead-heads beneath #16 dry flies. This is especially effective in August and September, when the fish seem to respond to smaller dry flies, especially during the noon hour. A parachute Patriot, a parachute flying ant, an Adams, a Borcher's, the Awesome—all medium to small flies—have plenty of mass to float almost all bead-heads that are the same size or smaller.

Why bead-heads? I think the answer is equal parts flash and speed-to-depth. A bead-head sinks very quickly, which means it's in the "zone" for a longer period of time. The flash helps. But how much it helps is hard to tell, and clearly, during the dog-days of summer, the flash can hurt. In fact, we're finding that in August and September, when the water is clear and full of weeds, that fishing a lightly weighted, standard Pheasant Tail or similar fly is the way to go. Without the weight of the bead, the fly doesn't go as deep. Instead of getting pulled under by the take of a trout, the dry fly will shoot up or to the side. Set the hook!

And setting the hook, or not setting the hook, is where most people go wrong with the two-fly rig.

I once guided a husband-and-wife couple—she was there to take pictures, he was there to catch trout on dry flies. I begged him into fishing a dropper because it was sunny, and August, and noon, and I *knew* they'd be on the nymph. And as soon as I begged him into fishing the nymph, I instantly regretted it. He was so convinced that the nymph was catching on the bottom every time his dry fly sank that he wouldn't set the hook. I'd yell *strike,* and he'd say *nope.* That went on for a couple of hours. Finally his fly went under and I yelled *strike* and he said *nope,* and I dropped anchor, went over to where his fly had gone under, and measured the height of the water on my leg. I then marched over to the boat and held up his rig against my leg, illustrating that his nymph was at least a foot from the bottom (more, actually, because the nymph is rarely straight below the dry fly; instead it lags behind in the slower bottom currents). He watched me carefully, nodded his head. His wife took a picture of me, for some reason. My impromptu diagram did nothing. Finally I quit yelling *strike* like an umpire, and he suddenly started setting the hook. His wife took pictures of his fish. Lesson learned.

Still . . . *strike!* Just set the hook every time your fly goes under. One way to look at it is this: If your dry fly goes under, you'll have to recast anyway. So, every time your dry fly goes under, gently begin the motion of backcasting. If there is a fish on there, that's great. If not, well, you're already halfway into your backcast. This advice, like all advice, can backfire. I once told a beginner to start his cast every time his fly went under. I did not tell him that there might be a fish on it. I thought this was a clever little trick to ensure that he was focused on technique instead of catching fish. About an hour later his fly went under and he did his backcast and slapped down his forward cast and never noticed the four-inch trout that went rocketing into the cedar trees and beyond reclamation.

On most days, trout quit eating nymphs sometime in the late afternoon. I don't know why this is, but it is. Usually the cut-off is around 3 p.m. The exception to this quasi-rule is in the time leading up to a late afternoon or evening hatch. This most often happens in May. Like the day we caught Elvis.

It didn't look like such a great day in May to me: cold, clear, east wind. We were between hatches. Let me rephrase that: We were between *major* hatches. In fact, there were lots of different kinds of bugs hatching but not a lot of any one kind. The density of bugs just wasn't enough to distract the trout from the oodles of nymphs still in the river. It amazes some people how stingy the Au Sable trout are about rising in the spring. But if you think about all the bugs left to hatch—the ones living as nymphs—we're lucky they even rise at all.

I thought that perhaps the sulphurs would get going. We hadn't seen them yet, but it gave me something to be optimistic about.

I met my clients in the parking lot—Dan and John, son-in-law and father-in-law. They were full of grins and caffeine after bombing up from Indianapolis that morning, which meant they'd been up since about 3 a.m. Nice guys. Had fished out west, which of course spurred me, the anxious Midwest guide, to make sure their expectations were in order before the boat was even on the trailer. To their absolute credit, they allowed me to establish the boundaries of expected and exceptional, and they operated within those parameters all day. Midwesterners tend to understand this type of thing.

I remember the day started slowly—but then again it almost always does after a cold night in May. I had them fish Hendrickson dries at first just so they could get a feel for the boat and the river, and I could get a feel for them. They were good anglers, plenty good enough to go to a two-fly rig. I tied on a Mattress Thrasher stone, attached twenty inches of 6X fluorocarbon to the bend, and then a #16 Quasimodo (really just a bead-head Pheasant Tail on a curved hook, hence the hunchback reference). I figured that even if the sulphurs weren't really going *yet,* they would within a few days; the nymphs had to be active, and when it comes to a fly imitating a mayfly nymph, it's hard to beat a Pheasant Tail, and when it comes to catching trout, it's hard to beat a bead-head. We began catching a few fish in all the normal spots you catch small fish on bead-heads in the Au Sable: shallow water pockets, shelves, thigh-deep seams.

There is always a lull on a guide trip, it seems, when the conversation switches away from fishing. I kept waiting for this to happen, and it started to at times, but then Dan would hook a fish. Then John. Around noon, we began getting the browns, and not just the little browns, but the ten-inch fish, the twelve-inch fish, even the fourteen-inch fish. All on the nymphs. We had not yet seen a rise. We stopped at the fly shop on the way through so I could grab a dozen more Qua-simodos. It was already late in the day, and I wondered if the good nymph fishing foretold an even better sulphur hatch.

I gave a customary fishing report to the shop guys.

"They biting?" Steve asked.

"Yep," I said. I rattled the complimentary fly box. "*Beads.*"

To Steve, nymphs are bait. He scowled. I left.

We floated downstream and came to a large, artificial wooden wall that had been in the river for a long time. An artesian well emptied from a pipe protruding from the wall. I anticipated a fish or two along the wall and one under the cedar farther down. I decided that, given the day, we would get out and wade for a bit. Dan and John got out; I sat in the boat and began pre-rigging some more dropper rigs. They fished for a while—I think John caught one—and then returned to the boat.

Just before I pushed us off, there was a great whitewater explosion along the wall. We turned in time to see a small fish porpoise out of the water three times *toward* us, and a climbing wake behind it that dissolved into the form of a brown trout on the hunt. It was a great brown, and it circled after the small fish but missed it. We were silent. The brown paused, and then it settled right down behind a rock in no more than eighteen inches of water, less than fifteen feet from us. I couldn't believe it. No one said a thing.

"Dan," I whispered. "Cast at that fish."

Dan, in the middle seat, pivoted quietly and threw two perfect casts. On the second cast, the fish rose subtly—an inch—and opened its mouth and took the nymph. I was yelling *strike* before the stonefly sank. Dan set. The fish bolted. The reel screamed. And Dan's first words were those of helplessness:

"It's only a three-weight!"

The fight went fine at first, but then the fish got wrapped up in the top fly and was then hooked in both the tail and the mouth. Now with leverage, the fish pulled hard downstream toward a submerged, human-made log raft, an old fish hide from the 1930s. I could see it twisting down there. By then I already had my net in my hand, but I wouldn't need it.

A landowner across the river, Ed, emerged suddenly from his cabin in hip boots, carrying what looked to be a salmon net with a basket at least three feet wide and a telescoping handle. He had the look of a hungry man chasing a chicken.

He stormed across his own yard and leapt off the wood wall up to his waist—hippers be damned—and slogged down the center of the pool, giddy as hell. I wanted to warn him off the fish. But I, the guide, was suddenly inconsequential. This was Ed's deal now.

Ed chased down the fish (which is *not* the way to do it) and dug the brown off the bottom (also a no-no), then hoisted the huge net high, our trophy brown reduced by the scale of the apparatus. He let out a victory whoop that drowned out our own. We slapped hands. Ed was breathing heavily.

"You caught Elvis," Ed said.

"Who's Elvis?" Dan asked.

Ed pointed into the net with his free hand. He was still catching his breath. "That's Elvis."

"What's so good about Elvis?" John asked.

"Elvis is the goddamn son-of-a-bitch that we can't ever catch," Ed said. "But you caught him."

"He took the nymph," I said, hoping to clarify in case Ed though we'd hooked Elvis in the tail.

Ed ignored me. "I saw the whole thing from up there," he said, pointing back at his cabin. "He's been chasing trout all morning. Just *slamming* them into the wall."

"Why do you call him Elvis?" Dan asked.

Ed reached down and rolled the fish over. The top jaw had been shortened years ago, an obvious hook-related injury, and the resulting mouth had an unmistakable sneer. Apparently, from Ed's side of the river, in the right light, they could see the characteristic scoff of the King himself as he moped in the bottom of the pool, waiting to attack. This fish would be five or more years old. A big old angry brown who, for one single second, forgot all about six-inch brook trout and decided to eat a #16 Quasimodo nymph in shallow water.

Our good nymph fishing carried right into the full-blown sulphur hatch I was hoping for, which tailed off into a blizzard of hendrickson spinners, which lasted until well after dark. It was one of those unbelievable days that the Au Sable tends to spit out now and again, just to let you know it can. But it would have been somewhat less memorable if it weren't for the dropper fishing through the first half of the day, which culminated in Elvis, which, in ten years, will be the only thing left of the story.

≈

And sometimes, in some places, you leave the bead-heads at home and throw junk. That's what Matt and I were doing on the Pere Marquette River this past summer. Throwing junk. And I mean junk. We're talking foam, and more foam, all glued together and lashed on a hook, with a tangle of rubber legs and huge poly wings. We fished fast nine-foot rods and heavy floating lines with what line manufacturers like to call "aggressive front tapers." We bombed the banks from the fore and aft of guide Jeff Hubbard's drift boat.

We were exhausted, and not from the fishing. The night before, we hungered for steaks to grill over the campfire. Every store in Baldwin, Michigan, was closed at 10 p.m. except for two gas stations, one of which had prepackaged steaks, the kind of meat that sits in a bath of what smells like embalming fluid. We ate the steaks and commented that they were terrible. We sat around the fire. We enjoyed

The downstream presentation allows the angler to feed the line—and thus the fly—beneath the overhanging vegetation. Here Matt works the shade on the Pere Marquette with a large foam fly.
JOSH GREENBERG

the stars. By the time we hit the sack, it was well after midnight. We couldn't have been in bed for five minutes before raccoons were in our campsite. We chased them away. They returned. We hid our garbage in the truck. They found our beer bottles. We removed the beer bottles. It began storming.

We showed up at a hotel at 9 a.m. in the morning, and the owner graciously allowed us to check in about six hours before the official check-in time. I'd hardly finished my first cup of coffee before Hubbard showed up ten minutes early with his squeaky-clean truck and elbow-polished boat while we ambled around shaking sand from our hair and whining about raccoons.

It was already hot and getting hotter. The forecast included the possibility of a heat-induced thunderstorm. In fact, Jeff had asked if we wanted to reschedule, but for Matt and me, who make our hay in the summer, a day off is planned a year in advance and that date is non-negotiable and contains just a hint of guilt about not working. Not enough to ruin the day, just enough to make you feel like you're joy-riding in the company car.

The plan of attack was simple. We were going to fish huge foam dry flies. We'd not only fish the banks and the cover—as we do on the Au Sable—but we'd also float our flies down the big seams and over the huge deep holes of the Pere Marquette, trying to tempt up a big brown or rainbow.

I'd heard that the Pere Marquette, or PM, as it's known throughout the state, is an excellent hopper river where you *really can* catch big fish on dry flies in the daytime, something that very rarely happens on the Au Sable. Then again, Matt and I speculated, we very rarely fished flies this big on the Au Sable.

The Au Sable is a shallow river—much shallower, on average, than the PM. It is spread out over an even bottom. It drifts beneath cedars, and is littered with fallen trees and other such cover, underneath which our big browns sit, rather protected. A good daytime attractor dry fly will typically be somewhere in the #14 to #18 range. The Awesome (an old-school deerfly pattern), an Adams, an ant. A parachute Patriot (of which one of our guides Joe Guild, has said, "If they ever stop biting the Patriot, I'll have to quit guiding"). A big fly would be a #10 Skunk. We happily catch a small trout, rarely over a foot long. Hubbard, however, had us fishing #6s, and was telling us a story of the twenty-three-inch brown one of clients caught a few days earlier. On a dry fly, in the early evening.

We started out slow. The overnight rain had stained the water a bit. Jeff figured the fish had gorged before dawn and were full. We pitched frumpy casts at the banks. We cheered and jeered. We were actually fishing terribly. The flies were much larger than we were used to fishing on a long cast. You really have to accelerate hard on the forward cast, and then come to a nice, sharp stop, to turn those big bugs over. I kept trying to sneak casts under branches by under-powering my forward casts, the result of which looked like some old president throwing out the first pitch at the World Series.

"Twitch the fly," Jeff said.

We twitched the fly. There's a fine line between twitching the fly and retrieving the fly. It's not a streamer. Not a popper. Just a little twitch. I had a tendency to get twitch happy.

"Just a little bit," Jeff coached.

As the day heated up, the fishing did, too. This happens sometimes in the summer. All of a sudden, we began getting into some fish. They weren't explosive rises either. The fish just sort of sucked the huge flies under, a disturbance not unlike someone turning on a handheld vacuum an inch below the surface.

Well, one fish did explode. It came near the tail end of one of those long drifts only possible from a boat. The spot was a typical Pere Marquette hot spot: right where a big logjam leaves the bank, where the current hits the logjam and backs up on itself. We were all watching Matt's fly when the fish bombed it. Matt struck. His tippet separated.

"Did I strike too hard?" he asked.

We shrugged. "Sometimes you lose them," we said.

Yeah, Matt, you struck too hard. That's why the tippet broke.

It can suck, fishing with two other guides.

As advertised, the fish were larger than we caught on the Au Sable, though not as numerous. The upper Au Sable is as fine a nursery stretch for trout as there is in the country, but it has only trout. The PM is different. It is connected directly to Lake Michigan and hosts huge runs of wild salmon and steelhead. These lake-run species nourish the resident trout in the form of flesh, eggs, and offspring. There are very few brook trout in the PM, though there are oodles of baby steelhead, known as smolts, which had a tendency to come up and nibble at one of the dozen rubber legs on Jeff's flies. Sometimes a smolt would actually pull the fly

A perfect scenario: a backwater with just enough flow along a slow undercut bank. Line control is at a premium when fishing over a variety of currents, and a longer rod allows the angler to circumvent many of them.
JOSH GREENBERG

under. Or, sometimes, it would *look like* a smolt had pulled the fly under. "Smolt," we'd announce, as if we'd fished the river our whole lives, only to see the flash of a good trout. We struck too late. Jeff groaned and back-rowed.

The PM differs just enough from the Au Sable to know that you are on a completely different river. Its banks are not lined by swamp. It is a river of high banks and deciduous trees, mixed in with small patches of cedar and hemlock. It flows fast in spots, and there are even a few fast riffles you'd have to call rapids. Its banks are sandy, but they are much more fertile than the Au Sable, and there are good populations of grasshoppers even close to the river. The general flow of the river is different, featuring a scalloped gravel bottom worn into such a shape by the tails of generations of salmon and steelhead. The river will drop sharply into pools and beneath undercuts. The best trout runs are typically of mid-thigh depth.

In fact, all of these west coast rivers look different from our rivers. Just northwest of the Pere Marquette, the Pine River—an astoundingly beautiful river of big clay banks and real, true rapids—flows faster than any river in the Lower Peninsula of Michigan, and offers summer dry-fly fishing similar to the PM. Like many west coast rivers, it tends to flood as well, sometimes viciously. The last time I was there the water was high and stained, and while we caught a few fish on dry flies, we did much better on streamers. Near the end of our float, we came upon a rescue mission involving two kayaks, a volunteer fire department, and a hovercraft. We pulled over into a backwater and waited until the hovercraft passed us. It did so at a very high rate of speed, the driver sporting the sort of shit-eating grin that evidently comes with driving a hovercraft.

As expected, the fishing on the PM picked up right before dusk, and we caught our best fish then. They came in the faster water, on the major seams. Not as tight to the cover as they do on the Au Sable. Jeff told us not to twitch the fly at dusk—that the fish already knew what they were looking for. So we stopped twitching. Matt caught a rainbow that was just shy of nineteen inches, a fine highlight for the day. At dark, the fog came. We call it the "killer mist." And the river went dead and stayed that way, and we rowed out.

Part II: Winter

The winter is different fishing, and enjoyable because of it. In the winter, just discovering the woodstove has coals from last night's fire is a euphoria topped only by the cup of coffee to enjoy beside it. Life stands out in sharp contrast to winter's backdrop.

Fishing in winter indulges this contrast. You notice every heartbeat along the river, and you pursue the cold-slowed ones of the trout. You fish methodically, carefully, conserving the heat in your body, especially your hands. Ideally you match the pace of the trout, and your surroundings. I'm not sure if this is a mythical musing or just common sense, but I find that I do best in the winter when I take a very long time to perform every step of the procedure well, from sorting out flies, to considering the depth of them, to attaching the proper amount of weight, to checking my knots, to warming my hands once again, and so on.

Winter up here is serious business, as they say, though I find the most serious part of it probably has more to do with alcohol and love triangles and depression than it does the weather. Still, it gets cold here, sometimes as much as thirty below, and so getting out on even a mild January day has a pleasant sting to it.

Winters are a good excuse to wear good clothes. I don't have oodles of winter fishing clothes: I have one set that I trust and have become attached to. A good winter outfit consists of some combination of the following: polypropylene, wool, down, fleece, Gore-Tex. To this ensemble, I'll usually add a gaiter or balaclava of fleece or wool. A hat with a brim that covers your ears is nice. Some hats do both, some don't. If you don't have a hat that does both, you'll need to wear two: one with a brim, and one that keeps your ears warm. A good winter hat is windproof. I find wearing a simple knit hat allows the wind to rattle my eardrums like an arctic clipper heading down an alleyway.

In the winter your hands are the most important part of your fishing equipment, and should be treated as such. As a guide, I was always careful never to "lose" my hands to the cold or the wet. This meant bringing a spare pair of gloves, as well as having a pair of thick rubberized mittens with a wool lining to use while rowing, or more often around here, poling. Chemical hand-warmers are a welcome luxury, and they are cheap. There are also chemical warmers for your feet. Even a big one that you stick to your midsection. I've not tried the latter and probably never will.

Though I rarely remember to bring one with me, a good thick towel makes sense, especially if you're in a boat. Being able to get your hands dry, and then warm, can be the difference between a two-hour day and a six-hour day. I think I've remembered a towel only a half-dozen times, always on guide trips, and it was great to have.

Boot-foot waders are next to necessary for winter fishing, though sadly the breathable models are very hard to come by as of 2013. Orvis still offers boot-foots, and they are pretty good ones, though a little thin for rugged wear. Patagonia, Simms, and Dan Bailey do *not* offer boot-foot waders (Simms has promised one soon). Many seasoned winter anglers use neoprene boot-foots. Neoprene is warm in the winter and durable, but it does not breathe and can become clammy, especially if the temperature jumps during the day. If it sounds like I don't think there's a good option in winter waders, that's because I don't. I remain hopeful with every sales rep meeting that something is in the works for the following year, though I doubt it. The wading boot business is, even in the piddling industry of fly fishing, a big one.

Aside from clothes, I don't carry a lot of winter fishing stuff. At its best, winter is a season of simplicity. There's something clean and tidy about it. You put a pack, a net, and a rod in the back of your truck. You drive to your fishing spot, and you huff and puff through the snowdrifts. And that's the only thing you hear: the sound of you breathing. There's a satisfaction to this. You are on an expedition. You may even daydream that you are on an expedition, your mind recalling several documentaries on alpine expeditions, the audio nothing more than the crunch of snow, the breathing of the climbers. But then you come to the river, and you hear that instead.

There's no room, amidst all the clothes, for extra junk. The forty-pound vests are hung in the garage, waiting for complex hatches and mosquitoes. Having to dig through an overstuffed vest in the winter produces an effect similar to shopping in a hot, crowded mall. A winter day is short, and it can be frustrating enough managing all your crap. Chances are you won't need the emergency blanket and the signal beacons.

I like fishing bobbers. I always have and I probably always will, and now that I like fly fishing, I like fishing bobbers on a fly rod. We call this indicator fishing. It's funny, but I get a fingernails-on-chalkboard sensation when someone calls a fly rod a pole, yet calling an indicator a bobber is fine with me. But I'll call it an indicator, or a float, just so I don't make anyone barf.

An indicator does two things. The first is that it lets you know when a trout has taken your fly (or you've snagged the bottom). We call this having a "bobber down." We'll even say we had a few "bobber downs" during an afternoon, which is another way of saying we didn't catch anything, but maybe should have. But then again, maybe not.

The second, and perhaps more important, function of an indicator is to suspend your flies at whatever depth you desire. In the winter, this is typically very close to, but not on, the bottom.

I hate getting hung up on the bottom, even if I get my flies back. Getting hung up on the bottom is like repeatedly passing a semi-friend in the aisles of the grocery store. Once is okay, maybe a little catch-up. The second time is self-consciously more involved—you really should get together sometime and have a beer. But the third time is just plain awkward, and the fourth time must be avoided at all costs, even if you didn't get to use all your coupons.

At its best—that is, when you get your flies back—getting hung up means that you struck at something that wasn't there. At its worst, it means you spend time re-tying your flies, which means you're not fishing. The whole "if you're not getting hung up, you're not nymph fishing" business is just plain silly. The best nymph fishers will adjust their depth almost continuously to get as close to the bottom as possible without really touching it.

My rig is simple and has changed slightly over time to reflect my time fishing with steelhead guides, who fish indicators for a living: It involves eight feet of straight fifteen-pound Maxima Ultragreen, which connects the fly line to a small swivel. Instead of clipping off the tag end of the knot attaching the swivel, keep it on and tie an overhand knot in it about an inch from this swivel. This is where you put your split shot; the overhand knot keeps them from sliding off the tag end. I use lead-free weight and personally think everyone should. Lead does bad things. Tin and tungsten do not. People who know anything about lead don't use it.

From the swivel, I tie twenty inches of fluorocarbon tippet, usually 4X, and attach my first nymph. Off the bend of the hook, I tie another twenty inches of tippet, usually 5X, and my second fly, which is almost always smaller than the first. I only recently returned to tying off the bend of the first hook, mostly because a guide friend told me that he foul hooks fewer fish with the flies tied off the bend than through the eye. I hate foul hooking fish, so I switched too, though I haven't been doing it long enough to notice a difference.

I have a short list of go-to nymphs, and they are very recognizable: Prince, Psycho Prince, Copper John, Pheasant Tail, Squirrel Nymph, Lightning Bug, and Tank's nymphs. All with gold, silver or copper beads. There are other nymphs, of course, and playing around tying new ones is part of the fun. Most are between #10 and #18. When the water is high, or warming, as in March, I'll sometimes fish a #6 or #8 bead-head Woolly Bugger with rubber legs and knock them silly on it. On the very coldest days, small and shiny seems to be the way to go.

It was one of these very coldest days in February a few years ago when I decided to give a new, prototype shiny fly a try. It was a day that a cadre of buddies spent all morning trying to convince me to go steelhead fishing with them. I abstained because I had some work to do around the place. They went. I shoveled the sidewalk or whatever it was I had to do. Come 3 p.m., I sprinted into the garage and dressed in my thawed waders (I've learned the hard way to store *all* my winter gear—especially waders and boots—in a warm place or it'll freeze solid) and ran down the river to what I now call the Rainbow Hole.

There was probably an ancillary motive to my decision to even go fishing that day, which was to catch a big old trout to show off in case my friends didn't catch any steelhead. I'm not a competitive angler, but the guys were really razzing on me.

The Rainbow Hole is the perfect little nymph spot. It's not even a pool, really, just an innocuous little pocket on the backside of a long gravel riffle. The river peels off the gravel shelf on the south bank, gathers speed, and pushes into a solid logjam. The water then tails out in the shadow of a huge, majestic white pine, that day heavy with snow and heaving in the northwest wind. The sun was already setting through the lake-effect clouds, staining the sky an apocalyptic yellow, and a few dry snowflakes were falling almost as an afterthought of what was surely a snowstorm west of Grayling by Kalkaska and the snowbelt there.

I quickly rigged a nymph setup and tied on a big fly and then, as a second fly, the new little bug I'd been working on: kind of a Lightning Bug without a tail. I guess I could call it a Lightning Midge. It was easy to tie, which is all I tend to care about, and was very sparkly. The kind of fly your daughter picks out in the fly shop and announces "I like this one!" Rainbows tend to have a thing for glitter. And while we don't have many rainbows in the Au Sable, we do have a few, and some of these few are big. They are a phantom race of fish, these big rainbows, ascending the river in midwinter and early spring to rest in such pools as the one I was fishing before they spawn and seemingly disappear for the rest of the year.

Thinking I didn't have time to muck around adjusting for depth, I went deep immediately, and got snagged on the log that I remembered was there *after* I'd cast. I gave it a few hard yanks and walked upstream and downstream, trying to wrestle it free. Nothing. It broke above the split shot, of course, and so I retied the whole rig, trying to avoid the urge to slap on a streamer in the name of efficiency.

By then I was mumbling. Something about swinging for the fences and striking out. You only get so many at bats on a short winter afternoon.

I did it right the second time, or as close to right as I know how to do it. I started on the lip of the drop-off and worked the inside water, the slow stuff that trout tend to sit in when they are actively feeding. I catch many more fish on the insides of the bends than I do in the heart of the pool. Almost all bends on all rivers show a color gradation—usually going from silt, to sand, to gravel, and so on. Fish will sit on the sand, to be certain. But for the indicator angler, it's the deeper drop-offs that are of interest. And having nearly blown my entire foray by being hasty, I worked the shallow shelf-line, allowing my drift to sneak under the leaning white pine, then letting it swing out.

There's a rhythm to this fishing that grows on me. A commitment to the mechanisms of the motions: Flip the rig upstream, throw a powerful roll cast, throw a less powerful roll cast—a stack mend, Doug Swisher calls it, on some ancient but very good 3M video—that relocates the fly line and indicator (but not the flies) upstream of where they landed, throw a traditional mend, another mend, and then feed it down. At the end of the drift, allow the flies to swing slightly. Let the current lift the split shot and flies toward the surface. Then fling them upstream, and repeat those steps by rote. With every cast I become more dedicated to the procedure. And, on that chilly day at the Rainbow Hole, more anticipatory. And then . . .

The yellow sky began to fade. The wind quit, and a hard, still chill settled down within the river valley. I paused to crunch the ice from my guides between my fingers. I had to pull hard on the handle of my reel to get it to spin. My breath fogged my glasses, and I removed them. It would be cold that night. Below zero. It was the deepest of the winter months. Too cold to be dreary. Snow was heaped everywhere, but not fresh snow. It was an old snow by now, at least the bulk of it, with a centimeter of fresh powder arriving every afternoon in a brief, lake-aided cloudburst. The days ran together, each beginning with me adding wood to the stove, and ending much the same way. And I became melancholy or even pissed off to think that it would end soon. That this laid-back, wonderful, repetitive, breathtaking season would give way to March, and I would have to rush to put my boat back together and get my paperwork done, and before I was ready, back in the boat and propelled headlong and manic through the summer once again.

And just when I was wondering which of my casts would be the last for the day, just as my line began to swing out in the dark water beneath the leaning white pine, and without me *feeling* it, a great wild, twisting rainbow leapt straight in the air, as unexpected as fire, and then the line was taut and the fish leapt again, and again, toward me, the line bowing in the direction of the fish's first upstream run as I realized, with my cold, slow brain, that I was hooked to it.

I tried to turn the handle of my reel to catch up to the line, but my reel had once again frozen solid. My fingers were very numb—too numb now to get a solid grip on the reel handle—and so I gave up on it and began stripping in line until I was neck and neck with the fish, I in the shallow water, the fish in the deep. Then the fish turned and raced downstream and I let the line go through my fingers. I cursed the frozen reel. Normally after a few showy jumps, I'm ready for the fish to get off. Throw the hook. Go free. A jumping trout in thirty-three-degree water is enough satisfaction. But I wanted this one. And so, out of slack, I sprinted downstream after the fish.

It stopped its run just short of a very wide, shallow riffle and turned and began to wander slowly upstream. I held my rod low and brought the fish at an angle toward me. It flashed at the surface, ran, but not too hard, and came to the surface again, twisting, the current sweeping it below me, and I began to pray that it would not come off, this suddenly important fish. I wasn't thinking of my friends and their steelhead, or my own braggadocio. I just wanted the goddamn fish in my net. Succumbed. Captured. I stripped the line through my guides that were now clogged with ice. The line would not come farther. My net, now in my hand, wouldn't reach. I pirouetted. I pranced about. I lunged. The line was stuck. Frozen solid. The nail knot was safely imprisoned in my top eyelet. I couldn't get the fish any closer than this, and *this* wasn't close enough.

I thought, *to hell with it.* I threw my rod into the water and grabbed the leader. The fish went away from me, but slowly, and I ran it down and netted it. It was a messy deal, and I was breathing hard and even sweating. I charged toward the bank, net and fish in hand, rod dragging in the water behind me. I crouched by the shelf ice and held the net in the water and threw the rod onto the ice. I got out my camera and took a picture. It was a female rainbow, wildly spotted, beautiful, and long. The little Lightning Midge was hooked in the corner of its mouth. I tried to remember what the picture wouldn't: the flare of its pectoral fins as I held it for release, the way they caught the plane and held the fish even in the water. Then the kick of the trout—the acceleration across the gravel, and the way the green of the pool I now call the Rainbow Hole evaporated the fish from me.

I stood and smiled. I just stood there smiling, with my hands tucked up under my jacket. Smug. Ecstatic. Remembering the rainbow now, I'm just as smug and ecstatic. Only in the fishing of artificial flies, I think, do we so completely fool an animal in its world, and then, for a short exciting while, tether it to ours.

A trout "on the fin," as they say in New Zealand. It sits in the depression behind the largest rock in the frame. The sand that has collected below the trout is an indicator of the same hydrodynamics that the trout is enjoying.
JOSH GREENBERG

I don't always indicator-fish nymphs in the winter. In fact, what I prefer to do, if I have the time and the gumption, is to sight fish to trout with long, fine leaders. No split shot. No float. Just fly, leader, line, and a good pair of shades.

When I returned from New Zealand, I was *really* into sight-nymphing trout. I saw it as the highest echelon of trout fishing. It had all the elements of dry-fly fishing, with the additional element of being unable to know for certain that the trout ate your fly. Plus, of course, you were seeing the trout. And just seeing a trout means to a trout angler, especially one that doesn't live in trout country, that they have arrived. When I was a kid, I remember my dad and me sneaking up on the big green pools of the Little River in the Smokies and my dad, who has great fish eyes, spotting one after another, and then hoisting me on his shoulders so I could see them as well. To a trout-crazy kid from Ohio, a trout is *the* emblem of beauty. That was what attracted me to New Zealand. And that was what I loved about it there.

Once I became a full-time resident of Michigan, I remembered very quickly that Michigan is *not* New Zealand. It is Michigan, and its big trout *do not* come out during the day unless it is raining, or the water is high, or there is a great hatch of insects. Or, I learned, it is winter.

I can't remember my first day of sight fishing the Au Sable, though I'm sure it happened somewhere on the lower Holy Water section of the main stream. I do remember how much more difficult it was here than in New Zealand. A New Zealand trout is a big, spooky fish that often sits—at least in the summer—on the insides of the bends in shallow water. They are not generally picky. They do require good casting, though sometimes they'll oblige a very poor cast. A winter trout in Michigan won't oblige anything.

In fact, there's one bend just down the road from my house where I can spot at least two or three fish every day in the winter, and I've yet to catch one of them. I'd say I've tried everything, but I don't know what everything is. I walk quietly up the near bank, and the fish sit on the sand. If the light is right, I can see them from thirty or forty feet away. I fish a long leader and a small nymph. On even my most perfect casts—the fly landing three feet above the fish, and inches off to one side—the fish flee into the deep water, and I curse and try the next one, and the next, and so on, until I'm out of fish to try. I don't know what else to do.

What's worse, sometimes the fish won't spook because of my cast. My fly will drift right toward them. And then, just as my heart flutters with hope, they bolt. This sort of abject rejection of the flies that I tied hurts profoundly.

To make matters even worse, there is another wade—a series of pools—where the fish are anything but picky. Spooky, yes, but picky, no. Here I've had days where I catch six or more fish in an afternoon of sight fishing. These are big bends with huge sandy insides, and like clockwork the fish are there, their tails wagging—a sure sign of a feeding fish. Once, last year, while using a two-nymph rig, I saw two fish sitting beside each other and caught both of them on one cast.

This easy stretch is less than four miles from the impossible pool, which makes the fish in the impossible pool all the more impossible. A part of me wonders if I'm not just psyched out. That in my quest to fish longer, finer leaders and smaller, more realistic flies, I'm missing something obvious. Like a #8 Woolly Worm on a seven-foot leader. This kind of psyching out does happen to anglers. The literature of angling is full of such tales of ignorance. I think Hemingway said something to the effect of *after the original mistake, the errors tend to compound.* The chances are that my failure has less to do with the length of the leader or the size of the fly, and much more to do with where I'm casting, and the way the water brings food to the fish. In other words, I overlooked something easy way back at the beginning, and everything I'm doing to recover from the original mistake makes the situation more complicated, and puts me that much further from actually catching a fish.

This winter sight-fishing business is relatively unknown. I've never seen anyone else doing it, though I know some who do. It is not as hard to spot trout on the Au Sable or Pere Marquette or the Manistee as people think it is. After spawning season—roughly October 15 to December 1—the trout move quickly into new water. What was once a game of gravel becomes a game of slow, deep pools and quiet, sandy backwaters and inside bends. The fish in the deep pools are not only hard to see, but easily confused with the menominee—a bottom-hugging whitefish-type non-trout. I have seen many anglers fishing to these menominee, frustration and lust all over their faces, and once I even advised an angler that they were whitefish and would be difficult to catch. Bad move. You never ask a woman if she's pregnant, and you never tell anyone mistakenly fishing to menominee that they are mistakenly fishing to menominee.

The easiest way to differentiate between a menominee and a trout is by color and shape. If you are close enough to see what color it is and what shape it is, then it is a menominee.

The most important tool in the arsenal of any angler trying to spot any fish is polarized sunglasses. I learned this lesson while broken down on a small bluff overlooking a trout stream on New Zealand's North Island. Our car had been overheating more or less on every mountain pass, so we took a break before starting another. A nice Kiwi family was having a picnic on the bluff and the dad was watching the river, so I went and stood next to him and watched the river, too.

I stared for a while and didn't see anything in the pool beneath the bluff. This was a famous river up in its headwaters, but down here, in the lowlands, it was considered to be a middling fishery.

"Well, I'd have both of those by now," the man said.

"Both of what?" I asked politely.

"Those two big blokes down there," he said, pointing straight down beneath us. "The one has to be seven or eight pounds."

"Hmmm," I said, blind. "Yep."

"And the other is five, five and a half."

I craned my neck.

He pointed more vigorously. "Right there."

"Yeah?"

"You don't see them?"

"Nope." It was harder for me to admit this than it should have been.

"Try these, mate," he said, handing me his sunglasses. I put them on. My world went from amber to crystalline.

"Behind the big orange rock," he said, and I could tell he was embarrassed for me. Which was fine, because I was embarrassed for myself. "See him?"

And then I saw him, the big fish, deep down in the pool—ten feet or more. A great big whopper of a trout, the smaller one behind it and closer to the shore. And I instantly, and I mean instantly, thought of the three months I'd been in the bush with the other sunglasses, and how many fish such as this I'd walked by under the illusion that there were no fish to be seen.

The brand name of the glasses was Strike, and I immediately bought some at the first hardware store I came to. I went through two pairs during my time in New Zealand, never mind our limited fortnightly stipend. The lenses weren't yellow, like the lowlight glasses here in the states. They were a kind of bright gray, if that makes sense, and they had the effect of making water disappear. Even on the brightest days, the Strike glasses somehow blocked as much glare as dark glasses, while still seeing deep into the shadows and dark spots of the river. Sadly, Strike is a New Zealand company, and I can't imagine that they'll export too readily to the US. I left mine in a hostel somewhere in Wellington only days before our return flight home.

Since then, I've been enjoying a pair of yellow lenses from Smith, though they are still a tad too dark for winter sight fishing on dark days or late in the afternoon. I remain on the lookout for anything resembling the Strike glasses, though so far these pale yellow lenses are as close as I've gotten.

The best winter sight fishing is typically between 11 a.m. and 3 p.m., and really by 3 p.m. much of the river has been usurped by shadows and can no longer be sight fished, at least not easily. Because there are many fish in our rivers, I don't spend a lot of time trying to see into water that is occluded due to poor light or glare or shadow or dark river bottom. In other words, I don't worry about walking past a fish. In New Zealand, walking past a fish could mean a half-mile before your next one. In Michigan, there'll likely be another fish within fifty yards. So spooking a few here or there won't be the end of the world.

I've become pretty good at spotting fish, though some folks are much better than I am. I don't have great fish eyes, but I've been looking for trout for most of my life and so I know where to look for fish. In the winter, forget troughs, shelves, bubble lines, undercuts, and every other piece of fishy water, and focus on sand—at least around here. Our fish love to sit on sand. So did the fish in New Zealand—that, and atop white rocks. In fact, in New Zealand we often found fish sitting atop the brightest rocks in the pool. Now I know this would seem to be a bias—that fish sitting atop bright rocks are easiest to see—but many of these pools were so clear and so relatively shallow that we wouldn't have missed another two-foot-long fish in them. No, there has to be a reason why fish sit atop bright rocks and bright bottoms, and it's definitely not for camouflage. My best guess is that the brighter bottom reflects light upward, allowing a fish to better see if that thing floating down the river is a stick or a cased caddis.

Kyle working a huge sand flat for a sighted trout. Stalking such fish is the epitome of the sport. The trout sits just out of sight of the camera, on the sandy drop-off to the left of the bottom vegetation. These fish don't tolerate mistakes. In fact, they often don't tolerate seemingly perfect casts.
JOSH GREENBERG

The best sandy spots on the Au Sable are the long sand flats on the insides of bends, preferably with some submerged cover and some humps or swales in the sand to break the current. Just recently, in very late November, Matt and I worked our way up some newly opened water that is just tailor-made for spotting fish. Rather than give a blow by painful blow—the fish were out, but not actively feeding—let's just say that we found one large, lumbering brown sitting in a sand divot about ten feet long and two feet wide, its tail brushing the logjam behind it. This is the ideal spot. Fish love to sit in *front* of cover. This fish was doing exactly what it should have been doing, which was slowly sliding into the faster water to feed and then returning to its divot. Unlike the other fish that day, we got within fifteen feet of the trout and took turns casting at it. But like the other fish that day, we didn't catch it.

What quickly becomes apparent in the winter is just how different a season it is from the others. The trout move away from the current instead of into it. Even our winter streamer fishing is done differently, often casting at what seems to be the wrong side of the river: that shallow, sandy, woody crap with no depth and little in the way of overhead cover. When you're streamer fishing the sand, you rarely if ever see the trout before they go on the attack. They just appear. But all of those fish chasing streamers were once sitting in the sand, waiting, and that's what makes the sight-fishing game so fun.

I don't look for any one portion of a fish. I know some books tell you to look for the tail, or the white of the mouth, and so on, and this is probably sound advice, so by all means, if John Goddard suggests looking for the tail of the fish, look for the tail of the fish. I generally look first for anything facing directly upstream that is the shape of a trout. Then, upon seeing such a shape facing in such a direction, I'll stare at it until I decide if it's alive (trout) or dead (waving stick, weeds, bikini bottom). Most often a trout presents itself as something paler and more translucent-looking than any wood in the river. A long, dark shape is almost always *not* a trout, especially in winter. But when they are . . .

I don't generally fish in temperatures below twenty degrees, but even then you can find fish sitting in the open, sometimes nearly under the shelf ice that grows from the banks during our coldest nights. Speaking of ice, there are all sorts of purported remedies for clearing ice from the guides of fly rods. PAM. Vaseline. Some stuff from Loon Outdoors. They all claim to work. I've tried PAM. It didn't.

But ice in the guides won't impede the sight fisher the same as it will the streamer or indicator angler. Whereas the indicator angler succeeds through quantity, the sight fisher relies on quality. The sight fisher is a hunter, sneaking along the bank or in the shallow water, rod strung up, pausing here or there to cast, sighing, and moving yet farther upriver. You might make twenty or less casts in a *great* afternoon of sight fishing. There's a pleasure to this, though. Compared to streamers, or a two-fly indicator rig, fishing one fly on a ten- to twelve-foot leader and a nice nine-foot four- or five-weight rod is liberating. This is real casting, not just target practice. And I learned this lesson quickly both in New Zealand and in Michigan: Don't cast right at the fish!

Even in the dead of winter, a trout on the feed will move for a fly, sometimes as much as three or four feet. This is to our advantage for two reasons, the first being that we don't have to cast right at the fish to catch it. The second, and more important, reason is that if you hit the trout right on the nose with a nymph, it might eat the fly and spit it out without you noticing a thing, especially at thirty feet and directly downstream of the fish. Instead, throw your cast just slightly to the side of the fish. If the fish moves toward your fly, wait until the fish straightens out, or begins to return to its original location, and set the hook.

≈

It wasn't really winter anymore, but it should have been. It was very early March and we were having one of those spring-cleaning warm-ups that would have been wonderful, but I was very sick. I'd had the flu first, and then, after kicking the flu, I developed streptococcus in my cheek and jaw muscle and couldn't open my mouth more than one finger wide. The doctor told me to keep sticking my fingers in my mouth. One finger was now the baseline. If I couldn't eat one finger, I was to go to the emergency room "immediately."

His "immediately" was in my head that very beautiful day in early March as my wife and I drove to the Manistee; me for some fishing, and she for a nice run on the dirt roads over there. Of course, we assumed for some reason that the roads would be dirt. They weren't. Just slush. And there was still snow everywhere—five or so crusted inches of it. Of course there was. Somehow I'd assumed, with my feverish mind, that the roads would be cleared of snow and the ice melted to dirt.

We drove through the slush silently. I parked where I meant to.

We'd have to leave, I thought. She can't run in this. And it was too late for me to go elsewhere. The day was lost.

But Katy stared at the road with her even gaze and then shrugged and went for a sloshing run. I made my way down the road from where I parked—watching her trot off into the distance—and cut into the piled roadside snow and slid down the hill, into the river.

The river was alive. It had to be. It was nearly sixty degrees and the wind was from the southwest and *warm*—a great rushing, tree-rattling wind. There were stoneflies hatching, both the #16s and the big ones, the #12s. They are called black stones because their bodies are such, but in the sun they looked nearly amber. I stood there watching the big, slow flat above me, jamming a finger in my mouth and then taking some snow from the bank and rubbing it on my very sore jawbone.

And then I didn't know what to do. There was nothing rising, and the water on that part of the Manistee is deep and sandy and hard to wade. There are few pinch-points to indicator fish, and the wading is too difficult to cover much water with a streamer. I stared for a while, begging a fish to rise. And finally, up by where I parked, one did.

I started to wade upriver but I was way too sick to make it, so I cut onto private land and found a deer trail through the cedars. I walked up that way thinking that if anyone stopped me, I'd explain about the streptococcus and the one finger and the "immediately" and that would be enough to grant me access for the day.

I got roughly across from where I'd seen the rise and crouched in some tag alders, waiting. The fish rose twice more. I looped on a fresh leader and tied on a fresh fly and realized that I had no floatant, or nippers, or anything else that was on the lanyard that was in the truck, which was on the other side of the only rising fish I was likely to see that day. The river might as well have been a moat of crocodiles. So I chewed through the tag of tippet with, if not a howl of pain, then a loud whine, and I blew on the fly though it was already dry. Then I waded into the river and made two terrible casts—the first dry-fly casts of the year—and caught the trout, a ten-inch fish. While I was playing it, another fish rose, behind the first. My eyes wanted it to be bigger. It wasn't. I blew on the fly and it floated, and the fish rose and I set the hook.

After I landed that one, I looked far down the slow water and saw a few fish beginning to rise just above where I'd entered the river. I got back on the bank and walked the same deer trail downstream, realizing, again too late, that I'd not gone to the truck when I could have, and now I'd probably have to change flies. I wondered how far Katy had left on her run. She was training for a marathon, but I've noticed that the time a runner a feels while running is different than the time an angler feels while fishing. I'd already been on the river over an hour. Maybe longer. The roads were slush. She'd be returning soon with wet, cold feet. We'd have to leave these rising fish.

I waded in across from where I thought the fish were rising, but they had quit, or were very intermittent. I tied on a fresh fly and stood there. A cloud—a single, lone cloud—had obscured the sun and the stoneflies had quit. All stoneflies seem to like the sun, none more so than the early black stones of March and April. I stood there. I stuck a finger in my mouth. I looked back upriver toward where I'd caught the two fish, thinking maybe there'd be more. There weren't. I casually looked upstream about twenty feet, and saw something big swimming in place. I took a step forward. It was definitely swimming. I found a hump in the sand and stood on it. It was a big brown.

I locked up. I stood there just locked up. Already the day had given me more than I wanted. Katy's run would be good, and I would be happy with the trout I'd caught. I'd be beat, and I'd go home and sleep with the windows open. That was my plan. Now I had a different plan, which was to catch this big fish, this March gift, my karmic dividend.

There wasn't much else to do but go for it. I threw the black stone over the fish just as the sun popped out, and already there were stones again fluttering all over the place. The big trout didn't care for the stones. Or my stone. It just sat there wagging its tail slowly, which is what the Kiwis call being "on the fin." This fish was on the fin. I decided to try a #18 Pheasant Tail on 5X tippet. I cut off the stone and tied on the tippet and the fly. I breathed. I cast, and not too badly. It wasn't a bad cast at all. The fly drifted just to the right of the fish, and just when I thought it was past, the fish turned and followed it downriver. I stood there hunched slightly, retrieving line. The fish swam toward me, the little Pheasant Tail evidently right between his eyes.

It followed the fly to my legs before turning away. My nymph actually got stuck to my waders, it was that close! The brown swam back upstream. I fought the urge to immediately recast. I pulled the fly from my leg and held it in my hand, squeezing it softly. The brown returned to where it had been.

Okay, I thought. I cast again. A flub, as I recall. There might have been several more of them. I don't remember, because the memory of it—and my notes from that day—are obscured by what happened next. I cast just to the right of the fish, and again it turned and accelerated downstream after the nymph—a very inefficient trout—and this time its mouth opened and shut, and as it swung around I lifted and it leapt immediately. And then, well, the fish basically quit fighting and I reeled it in. It had been a long winter for both of us, it seemed. The fish was over twenty-one inches long. A big-headed, skinny-bodied fish. A fish Matt and Kyle would call a "Barney," a name they developed in New Zealand for unhealthy male trout with big heads.

I yelled for Katy, now wanting her to return as badly as I'd hoped she wouldn't minutes before. The camera was in the truck, with the lanyard. Then the fish kicked in my hands, so I let it go.

I waded across the river and climbed up through the snow, wheezing and hacking. I walked the road back with a finger in my mouth. I looked back down the road, and I could see her trotting towards me. She finished by me and walked around with her hands over her head.

"How was the run?" I said.

"It was awesome," she said.

CHAPTER THREE

The Rise

It was 8 p.m. on the Big Sandy by the time I dragged the one-man canoe across the abandoned campground and got the anchor tied up, the boat bag where I wanted it, the net where I thought I could reach it, the bright flashlight in my top-right shirt pocket, the headlamp on my head, the bug spray applied, my leader fixed, and a #14 Borcher's tied on. This was not unfamiliar water to me. In fact, it was and is my favorite water. But it was the first time I'd done this float by myself, and the first time I'd launched from this campground.

Well, I'd actually meant to launch here another time, with a friend from Ohio. That was back in college. We drove up together—some eight hours—and arrived in Grayling at 9 p.m. We grabbed a canoe and hurriedly lashed it to the top of my van, drove to the campground, and dragged the canoe to the river, hopped in, reached for our paddles, and . . . we'd forgotten the paddles. By then it was too late to go back. We tried to borrow some from a group of campers. We reasoned with them. They reasoned with us. Then we argued with them, and they argued with us. Finally we left them and went wade fishing instead.

But that was June and this was May, which is why I was at the campground at 8 p.m. and already there were sulphurs on the water and spinners in the air, in great dancing columns, and I was selfishly glad to be alone, to know that every rising fish would be mine to cast to. The spinners were Borcher's Drakes, a mayfly that seems to like the slower water of the lower river.

The canoe trip didn't begin well. I pushed off and nearly tipped the boat trying to figure out how I, in the only seat—and squarely in the middle of the canoe—was to retrieve an anchor attached to the stern. The canoe was so tippy, the procedure so impossible, that I swung back to the shore and put the anchor in the boat and then pushed off again. It was early—the big fish waited for the shadows—so I spent some time seeing what the boat could and couldn't do. It could go fast and straight, but it tracked too well. I practiced spinning it and found myself fighting the length and keel of it.

Then I realized that there was nothing else I could do but go fishing and figure it out along the way.

Paddling this stretch of river was like walking into a familiar restaurant. First I passed old Wayne, who was anchored in his old square boat fifty feet from his house. He was listening to the Detroit Tigers game on the little silver radio that sat on the railing of his porch. I went around two bends and saw a boat ahead, and I slid to the south side of a young man who turned out to be Wayne's grandson. Further down was Mark, right where he always was, his drift boat anchored within easy casting distance of the gravel shelf where the fish were already rising.

"You again!" he said. "Alone?"

"You again!" I said. "Yep—solo mission."

We spoke just to pass the time between my coming and going. Once I passed him, I leaned back in the canoe and looked up into the now colorless sky and saw spinners of all sizes: sulphurs, March browns, bat flies, *Siphloplectons* (the bug everyone thinks is a brown drake but isn't), and hordes of Borcher's drakes with a few gray drakes thrown in. The spinners, indifferent of species, were flying upstream in bobbing waves, a mass of them mirroring the width of the river below.

Fly fishers are notorious for fiddling with even the smallest things. I think it's because fly fishing isn't so much a hobby as it is an activity that relies on hobbies to make it work. Not all fly fishers tie their own flies, for instance. Or build graphite rods. Or wood rods. Or fix reels. Or make hand-tied leaders. Any one of these hobbies can become a passion that actually overwhelms the act of fly fishing itself. Art Flick, the famous trout guy, quit fishing for three years just to study bugs. I respect that kind of commitment, but to me, that's like quitting dating just so you can practice kissing in the mirror.

There are some fly fishers who would go nuts first identifying the mystery fly (or flies), and then tying entomologically perfect replications of them. They would catch fish on their new flies at roughly the rate I can catch them on the Borcher's. So much of the groundwork of the sport has already been laid. When you come across a secret that is also a mystery, you tend to become romantically attached to it.

For a long while the flies that were fished in our streams were simple, because the fish here were grayling and they were simple to catch. Most folks fished a brace of flies, and it wasn't uncommon, if you can believe the old fish stories, to catch three fish on one cast. I know a lot of people pine for the old days, and I'd trade my house to catch a native grayling on the Au Sable, but that kind of express-lane fish catching doesn't even sound fun. I never root for extinction, but I think the introduction and propagation of trout was, in this case, a very happy end to what truly was a tragedy.

And it was because of the trout, and their selective nature, that the flies of this part of Michigan underwent such a rapid transformation from classic wets to idiosyncratic dry flies, the heritage and techniques of which are hardly equaled in North America. Flies such as the Cornie's Quill (which used the quill of a California condor) and the Barber Pole, to name only two, have come and have either gone or are going (though they still work, even if you have to find a substitute for the condor). But other flies, like the Borcher's, the Skunk, the Roberts' Yellow Drake, and most notably the Adams, have not only stayed in use, but are still the most popular flies in the bins of our fly shops.

These are attractive flies in their own way. For instance, the Roberts' Yellow Drake uses pheasant for the tail, a natural deer-hair body crisscrossed with yellow thread, a white deer-hair post, and brown hackle. If you tie it in a #16, it works for the sulphurs. A #14 is a can't-miss March brown. In a #10, it's a perfect brown drake. And a #6 Roberts' Yellow Drake is just fine for the Hex. Tied well, it is a perfectly balanced dry fly, with a natural class that would make it at home on those old metal signs of up north pastiche, along with duck calls, wood rods, and English setters.

We now tie this fly in a variety of colors, either by varying the color of the thread, the color of the deer hair, or both. The most popular fly in our fly shop, for instance, is the Rusty's White Knot. It is a Roberts' Drake tied with a custom-dyed deer-hair body that is the color of very dark red wine and wrapped with dark brown UNI-Thread. It has moose-hair tails and a dark dun hackle. I have no explanation for the name. I asked once, but Rusty gave me a secret smile, which could have meant that I didn't want to know or, just as likely, he didn't want to remember.

I'm jumping ahead, though. The Roberts' Yellow Drake was a fly of the 1950s. To me, it's representative of the old Au Sable River. I'm not suggesting it's outdated, just that it stands as an example of one type of fly: a fly that is suggestive of several different insects. One could include the Borcher's Drake and the Adams, which originated on the nearby Boardman River, in this category as well.

In 1971, some twenty years after Clarence Roberts introduced the Roberts' Yellow Drake, two astute anglers, Doug Swisher and Carl Richards, introduced their tome *Selective Trout*, which reflected vast amounts of research that they conducted on the Au Sable River. These guys were indicative of a new race of anglers. They studied the trout, to be certain, but they also studied everything around the trout, especially the insects. In a nutshell, *Selective Trout* was intended to revamp ideas of trout selectivity and bug imitation. It did so somewhat concurrently with Vincent Marinaro's *A Modern Dry-Fly Code* and *The Ring of the Rise* (I'm speaking in decades here), along with a wealth of other articles and publications and, just a bit later, videos, all extolling the value of being something just less than a professional scientist on the river.

Anglers adopted these new techniques. Everyone had a travel fly-tying kit. Everyone tried (and most failed) to tie Swisher and Richards No-Hackles, the ones with the sweeping mallard wings that, if tied only slightly improperly, will spin a tippet into a Slinky. I think it was these new anglers that created the basis for the stereotypical fly fisherman, the guy who carries the bug seines and the magnifying glasses and speaks in Latin and smokes pipes and so on. Thanks, guys.

In Michigan, all these new flies sort of spilled over and intermingled with the Roberts' Drakes and the Borcher's, creating a unique melting pot of flies that is as rich and as diverse as any anywhere. Locals tended to fish their traditional favorites. Downstaters and out-of-towners—lumped under the local label *trunk slammers*—came here armed to the teeth with the new flies and techniques. Both caught fish, though I suspect the locals probably caught more than their fair share.

Some of these locals were guides, and their secret flies were nothing more than the old-school flies fished to trout that had grown tired of getting hooked with No-Hackles. One guide—one of the best handlers of an Au Sable riverboat that there probably ever was—has a secret for big rising fish that won't eat his Roberts' Yellow Drake. He puts the eye of a second one through the hook point of the first one, and fishes them tandem. Calls it a "trailing shuck."

The first good fish I saw rising that night on the Big Sandy was in the middle of the river. The fish was not rising in one spot. It was cruising around very slowly, rising scattershot, showing a snout and no splash.

I was at least seventy-five yards upstream when I first saw the fish rise. As I closed the distance, slowing myself with the paddle, it quit rising, and then started again downriver, working its way up. I watched it feed five or six times, each rise-form upriver of the last, before it once again disappeared, only to begin again lower down. I slid the canoe into the weeds and began to push my way through them, digging the base of the paddle into the muck. I was not hiding myself in the weeds, just my wake.

When I was even with the fish, I got out of the boat carefully and sunk to my knees in muck. It wouldn't matter. I had no plans on moving until I caught the fish or spooked it.

The fish appeared to be eating sulphur duns. In the flat water I could see the individual flies but not if the fish was eating them. I couldn't tell from my station in the weeds if there were spinners on the water or not, but they were still in the air. It could be spinners, I thought. A classic masking hatch. The fish was fifty feet away, rising in slack water behind a half-submerged stump. Classic spinner water. I stared until my contacts ran dry. I saw sulphurs standing pert on the water. I saw them bouncing. I saw them taking flight.

The Borcher's Drake—a classic Michigan pattern—is a beautiful fly, with its moose-mane tails and wrapped turkey-tail body. But it is brown. Dark brown, in fact. There's nothing *sulfur* about it. So I nearly clipped it off. But then I remembered all the times a Borcher's had worked during the sulphur hatch. And I also remembered that I didn't *feel* like changing flies. If the fish refused the Borcher's, at least I'd know exactly what to do next. Tie on the sulphur. If I were to tie on a sulphur and the fish refused it, I'd be faced with at least a half-dozen reasonable choices, one being a *different* sulphur.

This is not intended as advice. It's merely a failing of mine—the result of carrying too many flies.

It wasn't an easy cast, and ideally in this sort of quiet water, at least when it was still light out and the fish were spooky, I'd have rather been upstream farther so I could land my cast well above the fish and feed the drift down. But there were tag alders upstream, and one big white pine. And being downstream of the fish wouldn't work. It was too light out. The drift too difficult. Maybe Doug Swisher. Not me. The fish would spook.

Not that I thought the fish was very big. I liked the subtle rise-form, but there wasn't a bulge ahead of it, which is the result of the water displacing as the fish lifts toward the surface to feed. The bigger the fish, the more water displaced, the taller the bow wave. Some trout down here take all the mystery out of it, and will show everything: head, dorsal, tail. One huge trout that my friend Joe and I worked above Wayne's was seemingly standing on its tail to rise. It broke the water, mouth already open and perfectly perpendicular to the water, as if it were rising at the first stars above us. We watched its jaws shut with seductive slowness. We heard the click of them close. We could see its nickel-size eye. I did some quick calculations in my head, enough to know it was a big-ass fish rising at 8 p.m. So early. I was shaking. I cast once. The fish never returned.

This fish I was about to cast to wasn't a knee-shaking fish. But in the slow water it was still a bit tense, as my first acceptable cast hung up in the slower water and I quit trying to mend upstream and begin tossing mends downstream, an acknowledgment that my drift would soon go to hell, but maybe not before the fish ate it.

This trout was a mover, and I'd already pegged it for a rainbow. It fed a foot away from my fly and I waited, but its next rise was two feet upstream, and my fly was already dragging away.

I took a deep breath and stripped in the line and piled it into the weeds. Change flies? Don't change flies? Swisher and Richards said that it *wasn't* all about the drift. The fly had a lot to do with whether or not a fish ate it. Rusty said he would "force-feed" a fish, meaning that he'd *make* the fish eat by presenting the fly perfectly. It was the classic case of presentation versus imitation. Of carrying a vest full of flies, or a mind full of tricks.

I made three more casts, but the fly kept landing behind the trout's next rise upriver. I stopped casting and took a moment to reflect. The fish began rising at Point A. It passed through Point B. It rose up to but not beyond Point C. It then

"Hurry up and wait" is the unofficial dictum of dry-fly anglers on the technical waters of the Au Sable and Manistee Rivers. Spending time in observance is crucial for those trout that rise around the wood cover on the banks of the river. Such fish may rise so subtly that they are only identifiable by the small stain of water they leave along the log adjacent to their position.
ADOLPH M. GREENBERG

disappeared for ten or twenty seconds, before once again rising at Point A. It seemed simple: Quit casting at Point A!

I worked out the line and stood there false casting. When the fish rose at Point A, I hauled off a cast ten feet upriver of it. By then I had the drift somewhat figured out, and I began feeding downstream mends into the current almost immediately. A downstream mend fed slack into the drift. An upstream mend just kept the fast water from messing with my line. The problem here, though, was the quintessential fly-fishing conundrum: too much fast water between the fish and the angler. I couldn't throw a large enough mend without moving the fly. So I just fed slack into it. It occurred to me that an upstream mend was for the optimist, as in "I could make this a *perfect* drift." A downstream mend was for the realist: "We're all going to get screwed eventually, but not just yet."

By the time the fish took, I had almost all my line out. I set the hook with a grandly awkward downstream sweep of the rod and the fish leapt, ran quickly across the river, pulling out backing, and jumped again. It was a perfect moment. An airborne twisting trout at sunset in a big, flat, empty river. The fact that it was in my backing was a bonus. A convenient tagline for the story.

It came in easily after the initial run. A beautiful rainbow, hard-bodied and healthy, fat with the spring mayflies, and getting fatter. Our fish grow fastest in May and June, and a fish like this might grow another inch by the first of July. The sweet season was short for both of us.

The trout kicked off well, and I stood and blew on my fly. The spinners were now on the water, some holding their wings still upright. It wouldn't last long. Never long enough. Those memories of dusk that last the longest were, in fact, some of the shortest.

The best time to work in a fly shop is the morning after a wonderful night on the river. Just after 7 a.m. the shop fills with coffee-hungry, bed-weary, bug-bitten anglers, and they all stand around and tell stories. There was the big fish on the South Branch that was swimming upstream with its mouth open, letting the spent flies pour in. And another fish, on the main stream, doing the same. There was the one that got away. There was the one that was caught. Digital cameras make the rounds.

The worst time to work in a fly shop is at 3 p.m. on a rainy day in early May when the hendrickson duns are wing-to-wing across the river and everyone is fishing except you.

While the Au Sable to me will always be the river of the evening rise, there is hardly a time more popular and more storied than the afternoon hendrickson hatches of late April and early May.

I say late April and early May as if the hendricksons were that reliable. They aren't. They can begin hatching on April 4. Or they can begin hatching on April 24. Timing the first hendrickson hatch is like predicting a great viewing of the northern lights. The northern lights tend to be most prevalent in the fall. And hendricksons tend to hatch sometime in the spring.

But, unlike the northern lights, once they get going, the hendricksons will usually keep going, come wind, hail, snow, rain, or sun. They are a sturdy mayfly,

The hendrickson is our first major hatch of the year. It's a mayfly that hatches undeterred by weather. But the spinner, pictured, is as picky as a princess, and many nights are spent staring upward at the clouds of spinners that ultimately decide their time is better spent elsewhere.
ALEX CERVENIAK

and beautiful, grayish tan with a hint of pink. The warmer the winter, the earlier in the season they'll begin hatching. The warmer the day, the later in the afternoon they'll hatch (or, if it's very warm, they'll hatch once in the morning and again in the evening). They are preceded by the #18 olives, and succeeded by the #16 mahoganies. They are masked by the black caddis hatch, also known as the Mother's Day caddis, and later by hatches of popcorn caddis. They are dotted with small irruptions of stoneflies. But, for the most part, the hendrickson is king.

This hatch is loved because of its determination. Any true Au Sable angler has a story that involves snow, wind, and the heaviest hatch of hendricksons they'd ever seen. The best hatch I ever saw occurred between lake-effect squalls of hail. My cronies and I were taking turns leaving the shop to go fishing, standing under Stephan Bridge to avoid the hail (and to remain hidden in case Rusty showed up), and making sidearm casts to the trout rising along the fence line in front of the shop.

A fine daytime brown that was eating hendrickson spinners along a grassy bank in the early afternoon. Its blue cheeks are characteristic of the browns of the lower Au Sable.
JOSH GREENBERG

Though this brown was caught in early April, it was an obvious benefactor of a warm winter and early spring.
JOSH GREENBERG

The second best hendrickson hatch I've experienced was on the South Branch, during what was clearly the best season of hendricksons I've had in Michigan. It was three or four years ago, back when I was guiding full-time, and I had one of my favorite clients in the boat, a man from Georgia named Roy, who is a good caster but, more importantly, a great fish-catcher. Roy catches fish because he repeatedly gets good floats where fish are either rising or should be rising. Instead of casting right at the logs, or right at a rise, he starts his drift well above the fish and feeds the line down. More than anyone else I've floated or fished with, Roy applies a system to the river, and that system, it's very clear, works.

Some of this success may be due to the fact that he is just so precise. He uses the same leader system—one nine-foot Orvis leader with two feet of tippet attached to it. He greases his flies once and then uses the powder desiccant the rest of the time. Over the time I've guided him, I've seen him make only a few subtle changes to his system based on something he saw work, or a fly he tried that caught fish, and so on, but the general principles of it have stayed the same.

It makes sense when you think about it. For instance, if his leaders are always the same length, then he's going to be more accurate with his casts. If his flies are always treated in the same manner, he knows that his fly will be floating properly when the fish of a lifetime is rising. Over time, these little advantages of confidence tend to add up.

And he may also be very lucky. In fact, our head guide, Jimmy Calvin, who has floated Roy for years, once said of an upcoming week, "You know it's going to be good fishing because Roy's coming in on Monday."

It's the dream of every guide to have a great angler in the boat on a great day, and that's what I had that day on the South Branch. I don't think we caught a fish until lunch. It was cold and clear when we started, but a northwest wind was blowing some clouds in off the lake. When we stopped for lunch, it briefly flurried. As we sat there eating a sandwich, we saw a few hendricksons start, and a few fish rise. Roy stood up on the old dock we ate on—a huge, lilting monstrosity of a dock installed by the Department of Natural Resources—and, still chewing his sandwich, caught a seventeen-inch brown and a fourteen-inch brown and lost another teener while I ran all over the humps of the dock with my net.

We finished lunch just as it began snowing, and launched into what was clearly going to be a massive hatch of hendricksons.

"Those bugs can't get off the water," Roy noted.

"Yep," I said. I thought about it. "I think it's about to become awesome."

We came upon a big fish rising just as the snow squall quit and another big wind came blowing in from the northwest. These winds are colder than the water of Lake Michigan. They draw water from the lake and leave most of it in Kalkaska County. By the time it gets to us, the clouds are broken and fading fast, so our precipitation comes in spurts. The difference between being in the snowbelt and not being in the snowbelt can be as little as ten miles, and the difference in annual snowfall can be fifty inches or more.

The same wind that was rattling the treetops was blowing all the hendricksons along the bank. The fish was sitting tight there, rising lazily once for every fifteen bugs going over him. And that was the easy part. There was no backcast to speak of so we tried roll-casting, but the wind flung our fly, leader, and the better half of the fly line far downriver of the fish.

"Back on up," Roy said.

I backed on up.

Roy ended up not casting to the fish so much as holding his rod in the air and letting the wind flutter his fly like a #14 kite. When the fly was where he'd want it, he'd drop the rod and feed down line and then, holding his rod far to the side, drag it out of there and repeat the procedure. In the time I'd repositioned the boat, the hatch had gone from wonderful to what my peers like to call *epic*. The fish was letting great gobs of hendricksons float by, then it would rise three or four times in succession.

I believe fish do rise in a rhythm. Sometimes. But not all the time. I doubt a fish has an internal metronome. Like dogs at a bowl, they tend to take one bite after they finished with the last one. Some just seem to chew faster than others. Others will take a bite, wander around the house for a bit, and return for another. Fish respond to the criteria of their current situation. But they aren't robots. They do goofy things. Finding a fish doing something goofy, figuring out what's goofy about it, imitating it, and catching the fish is the highest echelon of the dry-fly experience.

This fish, we decided, was only eating individual bugs. It would let a big batch of flies go by, and then feed on the stragglers before the next big wave came through. So, we postulated, we'd cast behind the next big batch of bugs and be the first single fly coming at it.

Kyle spent two hours working this fish both from the boat and on land. It was a fine display of trout selectivity. Here, Kyle keeps his false cast away from the rise to avoid spooking the trout. This was the best test between trout and angler that I've witnessed. The trout was never touched and we left it—one of the only rising trout Kyle and I have ever left—in search of dumber ones.
JOSH GREENBERG

By that point we'd spent an hour on this fish between our failed casts and me dickering with the boat position (moving a twenty-three-foot boat around with a single wooden pole in a twenty-five-miles-per-hour wind is not easy). Obviously there were other fish around, and some would probably be just as big and a lot easier, but we wanted *this* fish, which, on this cold afternoon, had established itself as an adversary.

And that's when I heard the crack in the big white pine above us. We both looked up and saw that a branch had broken free from the white pine and was falling. And it was a big branch. Like twenty feet long. Probably a hundred pounds. A cartoonishly big branch. It hit a few other branches, bounced off, and gained momentum, landing butt first smack-dab atop the rising trout. It couldn't have been better targeted if it had been shot through the sights of a sniper rifle. We sat there for about five minutes, as if the fish would return. But, of course, it didn't. And I'm still wondering if it didn't get nailed.

The rest of the day was wonderful. The duns stayed frozen to the surface until dark, and maybe later. For all I know, there were fish rising at midnight. For all I know, there were bugs on the water in the morning. We caught our last fish just before dark and then, tired and cold, we bailed, paddling through a river of hendricksons. I loaded the boat quickly and we hopped in the truck, heater blasting.

"Well," Roy said, as we held our hands to the heater vent. "I sure would have liked to have caught that one got hit by the tree."

There are two underrated things up here when you try to discuss dry-fly fishing in northern Michigan. One is the gray drake on the west coast of the state, specifically the Muskegon and the Pere Marquette, but also many of the other rivers over there, including the Boardman and the Pine. The other is the *Isonychia* hatch on the Au Sable and Manistee.

I never get to fish the gray drake anywhere except in its limited range on the Au Sable, so I'm just relaying information when I say that it is underfished. The gray drake occurs just before our brown drake hatches over here, and right in the middle of our sulphurs. The gray drake hatch is no good, actually. It crawls out onto the banks at some mysterious time of day when no one is around. Fish do not eat gray drake emergers. It causes me some embarrassment, in fact, that I tied a bunch of gray drake emergers for my friend and guide Jeff Hubbard, only to learn that the gray drake doesn't really emerge, per se, and fishing a gray drake emerger makes as much sense as baiting deer with backstraps.

It's the spinner fall that is supposedly wonderful. And except for a few Au Sable gray drake spinner falls I've seen very few of the bug. But the pictures from the west coast tell the story. Of bugs so thick you can't false-cast without getting

There is no better seat in fly fishing than the front of an Au Sable riverboat on an evening when the fish are rising. Matt and I spun around and paddled upriver to reposition on a fish that was eating *Isonychias* along the far sunny bank. Alas, the fish rose twice to the fly, but refused it both times. It spooked on the second rise, the long red stripe along its side promising us rainbows in our dreams that night.
JOSH GREENBERG

dozens of them snared on your fly. Of big fish rising with aplomb. Of rivers devoid of anglers rivers. The gray drake is erratic. Perhaps more so than our notoriously erratic brown drakes over here. When does a good gray drake spinner fall happen? When it happens.

It must be good. And I'd love to fish it. My friend Tank Ron finds it more and more difficult to come north when the gray drakes are going on the rivers near his home in Grand Rapids. I've noticed this subtle change in his migrations. All of a sudden, there's these two weeks where Tank Ron just doesn't show. He hints around that it was his girlfriend, or work. Whatever. It was the gray drakes. They were on thick. And you were fishing them.

All things considered, the *Isonychia* is probably the Au Sable's best hatch. It lasts nearly two months—from the beginning of June through the end of July. It also reappears in the fall, though this fall hatch is not nearly as good as the early summer one. Every book ever written on bugs says that the *Isonychia* crawls onto the banks to hatch. This is wrong, at least on the Au Sable. The *Isonychia* hatches from very hard, fast riffles. It will emerge and leave its shuck in the middle of the river. I've seen this happen thousands of time, and every time I see it I get that smugness that comes from witnessing an event the books say doesn't exist.

The best *Isonychia* hatches are the very first ones, which typically begin either with or just after the brown drakes. The dun is an army-green mayfly with ivory-white legs. In fact, the Iso's street name is the white-gloved howdy, which may be the finest common name of all the mayflies. They tend to hatch heaviest just after dinner, and are best on nights that are too cold or crappy for a spinner fall. The best Iso fishing I've ever had was on the lower Au Sable with my friend Matt. The fish were blowing up in the riffles like they were chasing minnows. We'd drift through a slow pool of nothing and come to another hundred-yard riffle literally teeming with fish exploding through the roiled surface. Watching your dry fly drifting down the river had the same appeal as watching a seal swimming across the ocean during the Discovery Channel's shark week.

The best fly for the Iso, at least for me, is a mutation of Fran Betters' fly, the Usual. It's nothing more than a rabbit-foot tail, a dubbed gray body that we blend ourselves with a coffee grinder, and a thick laid-back wing, also of rabbit foot. We call it the Dust Bunny. It is a boring old fly but it is fun to fish, though it can get a bit waterlogged and requires both gel and powder desiccant to keep it from sinking.

If the popularity of a hatch is measured in the sales of flies, our two best-selling flies are Rusty's White Knot, which imitates the Iso spinner, and the Dust Bunny, which imitates the Iso emerger. But this is probably misleading. The Iso is a long-lived bug. It has its on nights and its off nights. In fact, you can go a week without seeing the actual bug, and then have two great days of it. The real reason it's such a popular fly is that it hatches amidst two marquee hatches: the brown drake and the Hex. You very rarely hear from people who take a week's vacation to fish the Iso. They are here for the brown drakes. And no sooner do the brown drakes come through a river valley like a three-day hurricane, than the reports show up online that the bugs are long gone, but "there are some Isos around."

≈

People chase drakes. They leave their campsites and bungalows and cabins and mansions after dinner—which is way too early—and they drive to the river en masse. If you do not fly fish, and are just on the river to canoe, you will wonder why these smoking, stinking people are appearing from the forest like desert creatures at an oasis.

The brown drake lives in muck all year. When it emerges—which can happen at any time during the day—it does so all at once. It is a fly of early June. It hatches at its best when the biting flies are at their worse. If you aren't near muck, if your boots aren't covered with filth, if you aren't getting bitten, if you aren't repeatedly staring at the sky to see if the spinners are out yet, if you aren't exhausted from a week of doing exactly what you're doing now, then you're not drake fishing.

The drakes around here begin on the upper North Branch and, depending on the air temperatures that week, will "move" rapidly to the South Branch, and then the main stream, and finally to the Manistee. If it is cold, this can take two weeks. If it is stinking hot, it can happen in a matter of days. We anglers are always a step or two behind the drakes. When the river is full of them, you'll know it. You'll see them dripping from the branches, hanging from spider webs, piled in the weeds. They are so enigmatic, though, that you may see a ton of bugs from the night before, or from that morning, and think you're in for a great night, only to find out that the detritus around you was from the last spinner fall of the year, and you really should have gone to the Manistee, because your buddy did, and his e-mail with all the photo attachments has clogged up your inbox.

But the very enigmatic nature that makes the brown drake so elusive can also benefit you. For instance, everyone fishes drakes at dusk, though the fishing is just as good at dawn. A cold day will hurt the spinner fall, but they'll hatch all day. Or, as happened to my friend Joe and me, you can be heartbroken, just paddling out after a lackluster night, and run into the best drake hatch you've ever seen. Those nights are hard to forget. Cold. Half-moon. After midnight. The once crowded river now deserted because it's clearly *way too cold*. You're nursing what was meant to be your victory beer when all of a sudden *something* hits you in the face. That's when the memory begins to focus.

"There's a good pool up here," I say.

"Was that a fish?" Joe asks.

And then the memory loses focus again, though you know there were lots of big fish rising, they were all yours, and you caught them. Joe hooked one—a big one—and lost it. He was about fifty yards upstream of me. I caught it in my spot a half hour later. The fish, after breaking Joe off, had swum all the way down to me and began rising to the emerging drakes as if nothing had happened. I gave Joe his fly back and let him hold the fish for the picture.

Then you try to forget the oil filter coming off your truck on the way home, and having to crawl into the trunk of Joe's brother's Camaro at 2 a.m. just to get back to bed.

That's a drake memory.

Too often, though, the drake is considered a night hatch. It can be, but not always. Not by a long shot. Once, at noon, on what should have been a normal June day—it was hot and sunny—there were drakes all over the flat water above my parents' cabin. They were hatching out of the muck so profusely that the river was muddy from it. The trout were actually swimming up through the mud flats, their backs humping the water.

I had to go to the fly shop to work. So I went. I told Rusty about the big drake hatch up at my parents' cabin.

"What are you doing here then?" he said.

I wasn't sure if he was testing me or not, so I stayed and worked. He didn't bring it back up, so I figured I'd done the right thing.

There's no certainty in hitting a brown drake spinner fall. The best method I've found is to go fishing two days after a big emergence. Sometimes this works, sometimes it doesn't. If it's very hot out, the drakes will spin the next night. Or they'll skip that night and spin in the morning.

Did I mention that they're hard to hit?

Temperature plays a huge role in spinner falls, and the drakes seem particularly responsive to it, which can be a good or a bad thing, depending on how you look at it. A sudden change in temperature, especially a thunderstorm, can bring the drakes out in a matter of minutes. In fact, drakes seem magnetically attracted to thunderstorms, which can make for a test of guts. Is this big fish worth it? And, how do I want to die?

One of my most frustrating days of guiding ever was on the Manistee, in a stretch we call the Swamp—a big, open sand flat that flows in and around islands and backwaters and would seem very much like a bayou if it weren't for the rising trout and lack of snakes. The fishing was slow, at least for June, until the thunderstorms began to build late in the afternoon. And then there were drakes everywhere and lightning everywhere and big fish rising everywhere and we paddled. For four hours we paddled, taking cover when the big dark clouds were over us and paddling when they weren't. The lightning, I should mention, never stopped. It's just that we'd become so used to the lightning that we were predicting which clouds seemed to pose the most immediate threat to our lives.

We hit the takeout at dusk, and the skies opened up and the rain poured down on us so hard we could hear nothing but it. By then there were thousands of drakes in the air. Maybe millions. And the rain knocked them into the river, and the lightning flashed, and the fish rose. My truck, it turned out, had not been moved by the car spotter—an event that seems to only occur on the longest, wettest days. I had to knock on the door of a permanent trailer to get a lift back to my truck while my client stood under a shallow overhanging roof. Clad head-to-toe in Simms, he looked very much like a raincoat and waders left to dry.

That's a drake memory.

The flies we tie to imitate the brown drakes represent the very best of Michigan tradition and innovation. Some are terribly ugly, made of old sweaters, and they work so well you'll only find them in the boxes of the guides. Others are beautiful extended-body flies, with bullet heads and a parachute wing, a fly that Doug Swisher made famous. Some people only fish a Roberts' Yellow Drake. Others carry a dozen or more different brown drakes, some with trailing shucks, some crippled, some spent, some with articulated bodies with the hopes they'll writhe like a dying bug. Some will swim nymphs before the hatch—the brown drake nymph is a strong swimmer.

My favorite fly is made of red yarn. It is tied by an old guy in Traverse City, and once a year he drives them out to us and I buy them and stock them in the shop. I use them almost without exception. They reek of mothballs and some fall apart after a fish or two, but the point is, they only fall apart after they've caught a fish, and I'm okay with that. They look nothing like a brown drake at all in your hand. But they are stupendous on the water. The old guy who ties them learned the fly from an even older guy, who apparently stole it from an even older guy, a succession of Yoda-like old men, each with bigger trout secrets than the last.

≈

After I landed the rainbow, the first spinners hit the water. The Borcher's drake spinners held their wings upright, much as *Isonychia* do, looking like clear-winged duns. They were followed by the gray drakes at dusk. But nothing prepared me for the enormous sulphur spinner fall and hatch that followed. There were sulphurs in my face. Sulphurs in the weeds. Sulphurs in the backwaters. Sulphurs in my fly box. I shined my light across the river and there were sulphurs from bank to bank. Not a single fish rose. It was like watching a volcano erupt but hearing nothing.

There are many frustrating events to the dry-fly angler. There are days where the bugs don't hatch and, subsequently, the trout don't rise. There are days where the bugs hatch but an outside factor—wind or bright sun—keeps the fish down. There are days where the spinners hit the water too early, when only small fish are interested. There are days where the bugs are on the water and the fish are rising, but for whatever reason are almost impossible to catch. But there is almost nothing as frustrating as a river coated in bugs and not a single fish rising.

Blind fishing becomes pointless. What would be the point in blind fishing a fly to fish that aren't eating the thousands already on the surface? There'd once been an evening downstream of the Big Sandy where the sulphur spinners were so thick in the backwaters that they were piling up like foam. Darkness came with nary a rise, and in desperation, I began fishing a giant Muddler tied on a 2/0 hook. Within minutes I hooked a huge fish from a shallow backwater and it went careening down the fast middle current, leaping wildly before finally throwing the hook. I was younger then, and foolish enough destroy a perfectly good leader so I could throw a huge fly on a four-weight.

I wouldn't do that now. I sat in the canoe and let the claustrophobia that accompanies a dark night wear off. I'd remained on the south bank of the river, and the glare was thick on the water when I looked upstream. Several years before, on a guide trip, a client named Tom had taken a good brown beneath a tall, leaning white pine a hundred yards upstream of where I now stood. We'd heard the fish once and had swung the boat around and got up behind the rise. Tom was an excellent angler, and after about fifteen minutes of nothing, I asked him to throw a cast with a little left hook to it. He complied. And the fish was caught. He thanked me for the advice on the hook cast. I thanked him for being able to throw a hook cast in pitch black with a twelve-foot leader and a #18 fly right between the eyes of a trout that was rising soundlessly.

I decided to sneak up the south bank in the canoe, paddling softly, and check out the spot where Tom had caught his trout

It was a classic, innocuous spot to find fish eating spinners late: a long tail-out from a huge pool. A gravel bottom punctuated by several softball-size rocks that the fish could sit behind and tip up and eat spinners. The disturbance from the rocks made identifying quiet rises difficult. And that night with Tom, I'd had to fight the feeling I had that we were casting at a current swirl instead of a fish.

I paddled quietly up through the weeds and stopped fifteen feet below the swirl of the rocks and waited. I heard a light popping sound above the rocks, toward the base of the big pine that shadowed the glare. I pushed up, digging the paddle blade into the muck. The sound came again, and—my heart rate increasing—I knew it was a rise. I pushed up farther, into the shadow of the pine, the nose of the canoe touching a log I'd forgotten about. I had to move the canoe a bit to pull up alongside the log. The current was enough that I held to a branch from the log to stay in place. The fish rose again, and I realized I was too close. It was just in front of me. Less than ten feet, rising almost off the bow of the canoe. The sound came from the shadow, the rings appearing in the starry glare below it.

Still holding the branch, I reached backward and grabbed the rod and put it in my lap. I removed the fly from the hook keeper—the same Borcher's that had taken the rainbow—and dropped it in the water. And then, fishing one-handed, I threw a cast that was nothing more than the leader upstream. The fish rose again; I set the hook and it was on.

I immediately—mistakenly—let go of the branch to get my hand on the reel and in doing so, lost any connection with the earth. The river pushed me away from the weeds. Realizing what was happening, I tried to put a foot over the side, to try to gain traction on the bottom, and nearly overturned the canoe.

The fish took off down and across the stream. Like the rainbow, it was full of the spirit of May, and its first run pulled drag determinedly. Not with the spellbinding speed of the 'bow, but with the dogged determination of a big brown with places to go.

I held the rod over my head as the canoe spun into the current and away from the bank. The darkness closed in, and very quickly I was discombobulated. The fish that was below me was now above me. Either it had changed directions, or

I had. There was little for me to run into. In faster river, this scene would reek of sensationalism. But no—this was a big, slow river. Even going down sideways in the dark was much safer than I'd be driving home from the river.

It would also be sensational to say the fish was towing me, but I like to remember it that way.

In memory, this went on for minutes. In memory, I floated in the dark forever, the fish in front of me and then behind me and then to the side of me, the reel spinning, the spray of the fish splashing a quick white flower in the dark. But that is in memory. And the whole thing undoubtedly occurred quickly.

When the fish was close enough, I turned on my light. I was well below where I'd hooked the rainbow—much farther downstream than I'd thought I'd be. I reached for my net behind me, but couldn't reach it and took on water trying to do so. I reached again and nearly flipped. I thought of paddling to the bank, but the idea of paddling with one hand in an unstable canoe seemed unnecessarily dangerous.

The fish lolled on the surface and hovered beside the canoe. It was a big golden brown—a trophy caught on a small fly. A female fish with a small mouth. I brought her alongside the canoe and cupped her side with my hand and with my other hand popped out the fly. She kicked away before I could take a last look.

Out west there are more moments such as this, and my own catalog of western memories is packed full of the type of fishing "you only read about." New Zealand even more so. Day after day of such adventures. Perhaps it is easier to connect to the fruits of the wilderness in those near-mythic places. But on my home rivers—humble and beautiful and languid and limpid—the memories exist more fully against the backdrop of heartbreak, frustration, and wanting. They stand like mountains on the plain. A rare place that one can venture to only rarely, and never according to a plan. On this river, we fish like worshippers, not waiting to choose but, it seems, waiting to be chosen.

CHAPTER FOUR

The Small Flies

The Tricos begin on the North Branch of the Au Sable just as the late-night Hex hatch is winding down for the season. Every night, fewer and fewer vehicles crowd the same old accesses. There are fewer boat trailers bouncing in the potholes behind my house at two in the morning. Sure, some diehards will continue chasing the Hex. They will follow the bugs to the coldest reaches of river, and then they will head to different rivers entirely. They will spread out among the rivers north of us. The Jordan, Black, Pigeon. They will chase the bugs through every secret spring and creek, or even more secret river mouths, where great lake-dwelling trout, wooed by the cold water, arrive to feed.

To some, the Hex has ended. To others, the Tricos have begun.

It's July. Even late July. We now must wake in the mornings. Mostly, we forego waders, even vests. There are no flashlights, or nets really. No boats. No jackets to guard against the cold. No tremendous need for bug spray. Our box of flies is small. We carry a few extra spools of tippet. We know exactly what's been forecasted for the overnight low, because this forecast determines at what time we set our alarms. A cold night means a long night of sleep, but also the possibility of wind, and a strong wind ruins our game entirely. A warm night and we're up before dawn.

The Trico is a small insect here, smaller than out west. The male and female differ in both looks and behavior. The male hatches in the middle of the night. Wet, their bodies look like the bodies of black flies. The duns have white wings, and the spinners have lovely white tails that look like the very finest rib bones of a small fish. The female has an olive-white abdomen and hatches in the morning.

After hatching, the females draw the attention of the males, and enormous glimmering clouds of the insects form above the riffles. After mating, the males fall dead upon the water. This is the earliest of the several different spinner falls an angler may enjoy during a decent morning. Fertilized females fly to the streamside brush, push out their little green egg sacks, and return to the river.

Apparently the female can then return to action, if she so desires, and the process can repeat itself. This makes for a prolonged spinner fall, and the frequent exclamation that the bugs are "coming in waves." All the flies that have hatched that morning are intended to mate and die, though, as with the rest of life, only the latter is guaranteed. The angler's heart falls when the wind blows during the spinner flight, and what was a dazzling swarm of insects—and several hours of prospective fun—is scattered among the ferns and houses along the riverbanks, lost to the morning and the trout and us.

Like the brown drakes, the Tricos on the Au Sable begin to hatch on the skinny waters of the North Branch near the unproductive Dam 2, and extend down to the very popular Dam 4. These are old logging dams, where water was backed up to provide locomotion to the logs being cut upriver. Once the dams

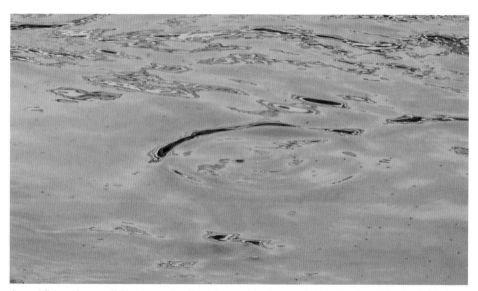

A good fish eating small flies leaves hardly a ring, and in the weed-choked water of the Au Sable in high summer, many of the largest trout rise unnoticed.
JOSH GREENBERG

were opened via explosives, a great rush of water and wood (and an occasional lumberjack) was unloosed downstream, hence the areas downstream of the dams are scoured and wide. During this time the river's utility and worth was solely its ability to move huge logs downstream. To this end it was manipulated drastically to exploit this potential. Grainy pictures of the logging days show unidentifiable lakes, on which float thousands of round pine logs. The sheer amount of human effort and noise that accompanied this era leaves not an echo in the ears of most Trico fishers.

The so-called Skinny North is very skinny. If the water is more than knee-deep, then "you're standing where you should be fishing." This is a favorite adage of the Skinny North sages, and it's rather true. Any little depression in the silvery gravel will hold a surprising number of trout. Some depressions, however, seem stocked full of them. Angling these areas reminds me of the stories I've heard of hunting doves in South America. On a good Trico morning, one can catch many trout from these little pools; sometimes dozens or more without taking a step in any direction. If you think you've caught enough, then you've caught enough.

The river here is glass-looking. Not glassy, but glass-looking. The silver pea-pebble bottom is never far away from the translucent reflection of the sky. The trout too are silvery, at least compared to the brook trout of the reddish South Branch. The trees are lush in July: oak, some maple, poplar, cottonwood, and a few civilized riverside willows. There are homes here, and other anglers. This is a place where people with their priorities straight come to retire.

One of the dominating features of the Skinny North—and the North Branch in total—are the number of old artificial sweepers and small islands. These are human-made trout hotels—the product of the Civilian Conservation Corps of the 1930s—that now host small gardens of baby's breath and black-eyed Susans, long grasses, dewy cobwebs, juvenile cedars. Franklin D. Roosevelt created the CCC to combat the Great Depression. I sure like his pitch, in which he said: "Most important, we can take a vast army of the unemployed out into healthful surroundings . . . [and] conserve our precious natural resources" for future generations. This was in March of 1933.

By 1935 the huge army of young men was transforming Michigan's landscape more profoundly than perhaps any generation before or since. They improved hundreds of miles of trout streams that had been gutted by commercial logging, and stocked over seventy-five million fish in their first three years. They built bridges, established wildlife sanctuaries, and contributed to numerous wildlife studies. They also formed one of the greatest fire armies in the history of Michigan, when a fire broke out on Isle Royale—an island off the Keweenaw Peninsula of Michigan's Upper Peninsula.

The fire began on July 23, 1935. It blew so much smoke to the Keweenaw shoreline—then a major shipping route—that vessels had to sound their horns to avoid running into each other. As the fire worsened, men from CCC camps in Michigan and Wisconsin were shipped to the island. Isle Royale is not like Grayling, Michigan. Here, the land is sand. There, it is leaf litter in various states of decomposition. Ben East, a reporter for the *Grand Rapids Press,* reported that the "land itself burns."

There were now 1,800 men fighting the fire on the one small island—perhaps more people than have been on the island simultaneously, before or since. They dug over one hundred miles of trenches by hand, with axes and shovels. They lived a life of equal parts sleep and toil, carrying lamps hundreds of yards inland toward the fire, passing men carrying their own lamps away from the fire to rest. Perhaps there is nothing as frightening as fighting a fire on an island in Lake Superior, kind of like having a fistfight atop Mount Everest.

All told, the fire burned 35,000 of the 132,000 acres of the island, though reporter East noted that without the CCC men, "some of the finest scenic spots on the island would have been laid bare."

I share this story only to convey the impact this organization had on the land and history of northern Michigan. They fought a fire on a relatively uninhabited island to protect "the scenery." Would we consider this frivolous? Or detrimental? Is it? I don't know.

North of Kellogg Bridge sits the foundations of one of the CCC camps, though there is nothing there now. The organization was dissolved by the second big war, which surely claimed the lives of many of the same young men who fought the fires, built the trout structures, and otherwise changed the face of the natural resources of Michigan, far more dramatically and, for the most part, positively than they may ever be changed again.

≈

Truly the Skinny North would be a crowded place if it was a big-fish spot, but it is not. The trout are plentiful but small, and they rise in bulk. Though the river is shallow, the trout are not particularly spooky. Apparently they've come to terms with their position in the food chain and will eat Tricos until they themselves are eaten.

I come here often with my wife. Six-inch brook trout are just right for her. I can sit on one of the CCC islands and crush mint leaves in my fingers and watch her catch fish continuously until one is hooked too stubbornly and needs my attention. Or we'll spread out and fish to our own pods of brook trout, nothing but our ankles wet, allowing our flies to bob between the happy white mouths.

I fish a two-weight, and she my favorite four-weight. Our leaders will be less than twelve feet, though they'll taper to at least 7X. The fish are not as spooky here as they are farther down on the North, or on the Main, and a long leader is too frustrating and too unnecessary to warrant the trouble. The fly line should be cleaned and dressed and must float high enough in the tip to avoid being snagged on the rocks and weeds inches below the river surface. This is the skinniest water one can fish, and snagging on the bottom while dry-fly fishing is both common-place and annoying.

But there are some big brook trout here as well. By big, I mean a foot or even better. This is not only a big Trico fish for this section, it is a big Michigan trout on a Trico regardless of species and location. These larger fish are usually loners and rise on the backside of the artificial wing dams and islands, occupying the deeper side channels and secluded pools away from the shallow main river. The only good way to cast to these isolated fish is from directly downstream.

The problem with this approach is that you're standing in the faster riffle water below the pool where the fish is rising. This creates drag on your fly line, which kills the drift almost immediately. There isn't a very good way to avoid this except to sneak as close to the fish as possible. A puddle cast doesn't work, as the puddle tends to land atop the fish. The cast, if it does go well, must land only a foot or so above the fish. Any farther upriver and the fly will drag over the fish.

To catch one of these rogues, the angler gets very close to the fish and then makes as few good casts as possible, and no bad casts at all. Robert Traver called this "hoarding the cast." There seems to be a correlation between the number of casts you make at a difficult fish and the number of seconds it takes for the fish to rise again. Three casts could mean fifteen seconds. Fifteen casts could be twenty-four hours. It's somewhat paradoxical, but when the fishing is tough, not casting is much more effective than always casting. This is Zen fishing, and the Skinny North is a Zen landscape.

Within a few days, the Tricos spread farther downstream, past Dam 4, past the dismantled CCC camp, past the old Sheep Pasture, and even past Kellogg Bridge. This is water and landscape of such diversity that an angler at Meadow Springs—a sleepy, deep bastard of a stretch of river—seems several states removed from the angler working the riffles below Dam 4 in the shadows of the bluffs to the west. The Tricos will hatch here for months (they are multi-generational, and hatches contain multiple species), on and off through September, before the frosty mornings of October put an end to the Tricos, and the summer, until the next year.

The main stream of the Au Sable is a different river entirely. Though often narrower than the North Branch, it carries more water between its banks. It's a cold, rich river. The bottom is in general rockier and far weedier—the elodea and water weeds grow in great underwater gardens that can stretch to the surface even in four-foot-deep holes. Springs, cloaked in watercress, enter continuously from the banks. Old cedars sweep out, are piled into by other logs, and form unfishable fortresses that hold hundreds of fish. It's a haunting but developed river: There are few areas that aren't owned by someone.

The Tricos come late here, sometimes up to two or more weeks after they've begun on the North. I'll know when they've begun at the lodge when small-fly guru Terry Warrington begins to hold court on the riverside bench behind the lodge. He always casts from a seated position, and will complain about his back and his age, while simultaneously sliding an 8X tippet through a #26 fly without bifocals.

I'd bet a few fly rods that the fish feeding off the bench are probably the most selective small trout in the world. Here the river slides low and clear across alternating patches of gravel and weeds, and to the eyes of a tourist, the rise forms can be impossible to distinguish from the curls of current. There have been conversations between Terry and visitors as to what exactly is happening before them.

"He refused it!" Terry will say gleefully.

Small-fly guru Terry Warrington on the Au Sable. The Trico hatch is most noted for its spinner fall and the persistence of its anglers. A difficult trout may require many dozens of casts before its rise is timed. I believe a trout rising during a heavy Trico spinner fall rises first to rhythm and second to targets, meaning that timing the rise is more important than the fly.
JOSH GREENBERG

"What refused it?"

"That little trout there," Terry explains.

"Refused what?"

"My fly."

"What fly?"

Over time, the eyes adjust. We are, after all, watching a spinner fall that is like any other mayfly spinner fall, only in miniature, like seeing a city from the window of a plane. As the eye adjusts for scale, the play becomes apparent. Fly fishing is just another lens with which to view rivers. And within fly fishing, there are many lenses as well. The streamer fisher, for instance, would see little of this. His river is measured in miles, big holes, good runs, submerged logs. The small-fly angler will stay rooted in a spot, like Terry at the bench, for hours. It's the same puzzle, but with different-size pieces.

A good drift in the river by the bench is very difficult and requires long leaders, puddle casts, and flies that remain floating in the swirling currents. The fish will take a sunken fly, but they won't take a dragging fly, and in most cases here, a drowned fly is one that the current has pulled under. You very rarely "accidentally" catch a trout while casting from the dock of the lodge in July. May, yes. July, no.

This spot also debunks the northern myth of "stupid little brook trout." Brook trout may start out stupid, but they sure wise up fast. Truly, I'm uncertain if brook trout are any dumber than brown trout; they just tend to populate more profusely. The more brook trout there are, the more likely you are to catch them. I have no data suggesting the truth one way or the other, but the river by the bench, which is 45 percent browns, 45 percent brook trout, and 10 percent rainbows (give or take), yields roughly these ratios to the fly angler. I once had a client catch nineteen browns in a row, in early July, on a small parachute Patriot. I cannot say the same has ever happened with brook trout on this stretch.

Regardless, by July there are no "stupid little brook trout" rising off the bench behind the lodge. Every trout resides at the epoch of selectivity. Getting worked over by a four-inch brookie can actually be fun—like a teacher smilingly absorbing an attack by a kindergarten thug—provided you have the experience to know that a wise young fish is more difficult to catch than a big dumb one.

The necessary cast from the bench is made by decelerating the rod on the forward cast, so the line and, more importantly, the leader land with good coils. So often people fish with leaders that land straight no matter how curved and coiled the fly line. For this reason alone, I'm not a great fan of braided leaders for this kind of fishing. They transfer energy too efficiently, land too loudly, and don't move well enough with the current. The only way to fish such leaders is to use a very long piece of tippet.

George Harvey's leader formula is, I think, the best, though I'll sometimes add length to every section, to extend the leader to twelve or even fourteen feet. I also know people who make their leader out of only four or five long sections, which achieves the same effect. In New Zealand many anglers eschew leaders completely, instead using a single long strand of tippet. In this case the "leader" can be shorter—even down to seven feet—and provided the fly is either a small dry or a nymph, a good cast will propel the fly sufficiently past the end of the line. Slack is the only the rule: All the rest are techniques designed to conform to the rule.

There are some mornings where a small crowd forms to watch Terry fish, or listen to Terry talk, or both. Terry never quits talking, though he does so quietly or at least in the right way. He likes people, but prefers reasonable people. His bumper sticker reads *The more you believe, the less you know*. He has retired here from the Upper Peninsula after a career as a professor of chemistry at Michigan Tech in Houghton. He lives only a mile from the lodge and divides his time between his garden and the river. His rod room has about sixty rods in it, a vise, and many fly lines that hang in loose coils from the walls. His fishing career has taken him all over the world, particularly in search of the Atlantic salmon of the Canadian territories, and he has caught hundreds of fish that I can only dream about. But his appetites have apparently grown far smaller.

He is a careful, quiet wader, and can be surprisingly up front about the wading of others.

"I'm going fishing with my friend today," he'll say.

"Good luck," I'll say.

"Oh we won't catch anything. My friend wades like a water buffalo. But we'll have fun anyway," he'll say.

His Trico success is simple: He gets very good floats over trout with the correct flies. To do this, he wades close to the fish, waits to cast, uses very long leaders—sometimes as long as sixteen feet, made with a combination of stiff Maxima Chameleon and loose monofilament, ending in a tippet of very fine (8X or 9X) fluorocarbon—and uses a rod he's built with a large cork grip, because that's how he likes his grip. He carries all his flies in an ancient green-fabric creel, the manufacturer's label long since worn away. His wading staff is his own design. He does everything his way. It works. Repeatedly. Like one of his chemistry experiments, I suppose.

Once the Tricos are going well, he'll slide into the river and head up to the fence line behind the restaurant. Here the weeds grow to the surface, and the trout rise between the swaying grasses, tight to the logs on the bank. Above the fish you *can* catch are trout that rise beneath a half-dozen tag alders that you *cannot* catch. They rise downstream of several branches that extend into the water. The branches bend heavily with accumulated weeds and sway back and forth. This swaying moves the bubble line, which moves the fish that you *can* catch as much as two or three feet within the space of ten seconds. They rarely, if ever, stop rising,

It's 9X! Terry fighting a large rainbow that ate a #28 Trico in a famous small-fly pool on the Au Sable.
JOSH GREENBERG

which makes them good targets for someone like Terry, who is always fiddling with something. Because of this, he's probably done more to change how we fish Tricos on the Au Sable than anyone else I know.

The average artificial fly is tied of natural and artificial components gleaned from a variety of animals and synthetics. The tail fibers we use may be the same sort of bristles used on some paintbrushes. The wings may be plastic (which is also used in carpet), or Styrofoam, or hackle (which grows on chickens), or any number of other organic materials, ranging from calf fur to deer hair. The hooks begin as steel, are heated, extruded, bent to shape, chemically sharpened, and shipped somewhere else. Many times the hooks are shipped to Thailand, or Sri Lanka, or India, where they are put in a vise and, using some of these aforementioned components, made into a fly named after someone in America, tied by someone who has never caught a trout, and so on. Each component of the fly probably comes from some distant land, uniting in an unlikely facsimile, designed to catch a trout unaware of all the miles and labor wrapped up into the diminutive artificial floating towards them.

I mean this not to poke fun at the fly-fishing industry, but to suggest that the teaming of unlikely materials is somehow at the very core of fly fishing. There is delight in deriving solutions from materials not only foreign to us people, but foreign to each other.

≈

Amadou is a type of fungus prepared in a specific manner. It is not a sponge, though it feels like a sponge. When you hold amadou in your hands, it is immediately unrecognizable. It doesn't tear easily—as would a sponge—but is more pliable and softer than animal skin. It is for sale in most fly shops, and costs a bunch of money. It has been popularized by Andre Puyans, among others. It is also known as "horse hoof fungus" and "tinder fungus." I like this excerpt from Wikipedia:

> *Amadou was a precious resource to ancient people, allowing them to start a fire by catching sparks from flint struck against iron pyrites. Remarkable evidence for this is provided by the discovery of the 5,000-year-old remains of "Ötzi the Iceman," who carried it on a cross-alpine excursion before his murder and subsequent ice-entombment.*

If it's prepared for tinder, it is pounded flat and soaked in niter solution. If it's prepared for drying flies, it is soaked in washing soda and beaten, from time to time, for several weeks. It is then laid out, let to dry, and then pounded flat with a blunt object. It is incredibly absorbent after this process is completed. In Romania this same material was also apparently used to makes hats, which makes me wonder if the hats grew exceptionally heavy during an extended downpour, and if those Romanians—fly fishers some, I hope—ever used their amadou hat to make right a sinking fly.

Cul de canard are feathers from, as they say in Michigan, the "ass end of a duck." They are located near the preen gland of the duck, which secretes some kind of natural Gink. They are soft, frilly even, and would seem, at first blush, to be the exact wrong kind of material to make a fly float. After all, we judge hackle based on the stiffness of the barbules. Good hackle should be dense, without web, and strong yet flexible in the stem. Cul de canard, or CDC, is none of these things. It's also probably the highest floating natural material in the world.

A number of years ago, Rusty brought in a new fly—a Trico imitation—from an overseas manufacturer. He rarely bought overseas flies, and normally we ignored them. This one, we couldn't. It was a Trico, but it seemed too large in the hook, too fat in the body, and somewhat poorly tied. It was also the fly that changed the way we tie and fish our small flies up here.

The new fly looked huge on the water. A white puffball, we said. If the new fly was a bobber, it would be a huge red-and-white catfish bobber. Compared to the invisible Tricos we were fishing, this was a piece of cake. Terry was the only one of us who took the fly seriously. And he took it very seriously. At the time, he was teaching all of the lodge's instructional classes, and between him and his clients, he began to empty the bin of the new Tricos. The males first and then, when the males were gone, all the females as well.

"Best Trico I've ever fished," he said, in his absolute manner.

We tried it. We headed out at dawn, to the big, slow pools where the fish eat Tricos in triangular formations, much like geese in migration, and threw the puff-ball at the head of the triangle. We watched it bob through the wakes of the rings of rising trout. We watched it disappear. We waited. We set the hook. The fly was an absolute winner.

So, fly tyers all of us, we fiddled with it.

First, of course, was the hook size. A standard #22 just wouldn't do. The switch to a smaller hook demanded a refined body on the fly, so instead of dubbing, we simply used thread. Better, and easier. Next we needed to address the wing. Standard CDC was too long. Terry solved this problem: CDC puffs. These are short fibers. If normal CDC was an uptown firework, these were backwoods cherry bombs. Short, dense, buoyant. This was perfect. Until you caught a fish, that is, in which case the fly was hopelessly sodden and lost.

Gel floatants ruin CDC—too much of a good thing, I guess. The answer was amadou. We didn't think of this answer; we simply read about it. Suddenly, the dusty leather-backed patches of amadou that had been sitting on the shelf since I'd worked in the shop, priced unattractively at $25, began to disappear.

CDC and Amadou, a love story . . .

This isn't the story of invention—none of this news is new—but since that day the vests of Trico fans up here have changed dramatically. Where once we had simply Gink and #22s, we now have fungus, duck feathers, powder floatant, and #26 or smaller flies, tied on 2488 Tiemco hooks (2X short scud hooks). We now fish flies with bright white wings that we can see. We use 8X fluorocarbon because fluorocarbon doesn't stretch and then twist when we tighten the knots.

There's a method to this:

1. Rinse the slime of the previous fish from the fly by swirling the fly in the river.
2. Blow off the water.
3. Squeeze the fly in amadou.
4. Apply powder desiccant to the fly. This can either be brushed on, as with Frog's Fanny, or shaken in a container, as with the Loon and Dry Shake products.
5. Blow off the excess dust.
6. Cast to the next fish.

To the casual observer, it appears that the angler is casting a spell, complete with a detailed procedure and occluding white dust.

One can actually become addicted to the procedure and go "dust crazy," shaking his or her fly after every third cast, striving for the perfect high-floating dry fly. Like all ideals, one must learn to accept that reality is somewhat less than ideal. A fly—even a well-tied CDC fly treated properly—will not float forever, and must be retired. To this end, it should be placed on a foam or sheepskin patch and allowed to dry in the sun. After the entire rotation of CDC flies is exhausted, the first fly should be well-dried and ready to float, almost—but never quite—as good as new.

We now use this fly for nearly all our hatches of small flies. Only recently have we begun experimenting with the fur from rabbit's feet instead of CDC. This fur is coarse and seems more resilient to trout slime. It is a bit tiresome to use on small flies, but if it's treated as if one is posting Hi-Vis for a parachute—tying a strand in the middle, and then standing it up and posting it with thread—it is rather easy to work with. Only the soft fur should be used for this fly, as the coarse stuff near the toes of the foot is simply too coarse. I'd say we invented it, but I think the late Fran Betters would beg to differ—and rightly so. His fly, the Usual, is just about the same thing. Considering his river was the AuSable in New York, and ours is the Au Sable in Michigan, I think we can call it the Au Sable Trico.

Though the north and main branches of the Au Sable have the heaviest and most famous Trico hatches in the state, there are many other rivers that produce their own morning fishing. I have been surprised on the South Branch of the Au Sable, and on the Manistee, with excellent clouds of spinners and good fishing for several hours afterward. Probably every decent trout stream has these insects in some quantity, and this, as with all things Trico, is both a blessing and a curse.

Take, for instance, a trip I took to the Black River, a lovely, wild stream that is 99 percent brook trout and sits in the largest contiguous stretch of undeveloped land in the Lower Peninsula of Michigan. There are elk here. There may or may not be cougars. There is more than enough forest to get lost in: an endless forest of aspen, pine, and oak in the highlands, and classic northern bog in the lowlands, including large cedar swamps and miles and miles of tag alders. In the middle of some of these swamps are trout streams. One of these streams is the headwaters of the Black.

I traveled to this unseen stretch on a hot tip from a friend. My friend said that the stream there was knee-deep and full of dumb brook trout that would take just about any attractor on the planet. The quintessential small stream, he said.

What I found was water up to my neck. The creek was nothing more than a series of stair-stepping beaver ponds (and dams) that seemed endlessly escalating up through the tag alders. In areas the forest floor was floating. My feet actually seemed to push the earth down, like pushing on a lily pad with a finger. I assumed that the beavers had tunneled into the riverbank and now the earth sat like a skin above the hidden waters beneath me. Because the water was in the woods, the first several hundred yards were ruined by the wake I was forced to make in walking upstream. All the dams were fresh. My hot spot had been drowned, it seemed.

Finally I came to some high ground on the left. My spirits lifting, I hiked along a ridge and was able, below yet another dam, to find some fish eating Trico spinners at the spillway. The water here was far too deep to wade, and there was little casting room. The rises were very subtle, the size and shape of raindrops. I didn't want to fish a Trico on fine tippet. The tag alders were thick, and there was no good way to cast a small fly. Anyway, I wanted to fish a Royal Wulff on fat tippet. That's why I'd come to this spot.

So I tried the Wulff. They didn't want the Wulff, of course, nor did they want to continue rising after I'd made a few casts. I headed upriver and found another pod at the spillway of another dam. I tried an ant, on lighter tippet. No dice.

It went like this for the rest of the morning. Me bushwhacking to the creek, going one step closer to 7X and a Trico, failing, and heading upriver. Far from a blessing, the Tricos were ruining my fishing. There was no good way to fish the

This sign at Gates Au Sable Lodge means little to 99.9 percent of the population. But for that 0.1 percent in the know, it means it's small-fly time on the river! July and August offer excellent hatches of midges, several different olives, and the Tricos. It's technical fishing for small trout . . . and I love it.
JOSH GREENBERG

proper leader, or make a soft enough delivery. Much of this water was bow-and-arrow stuff. If I'd been able to get into the river, I might have been able to thread a cast between the lines of alders. As it was, the fish wanted one thing, and I couldn't provide it.

That's the rub with Tricos. When they arrive, there is little else for the fish to do but eat them. When fish eat Tricos, that's all they'll eat. Even on easy rivers, you must change your tippet and fly and match the hatch. In order for a trout to eat Tricos efficiently, it must hold high in the water column. This makes the fish very spooky. Suddenly your easy day on remote water has become a little more technical than you imagined.

The Tricos will last longer than we admit, but the excitement eventually wanes. The daily rise is too easily accepted. The *fact* of rising fish seems now a law. The fish will rise in the morning. The fish always rise in the morning. Then one morning, they will not. Perhaps, in January, we will think wistfully of those mornings during which we slept in, drank coffee, ignored this morning rise. The winter is a big white board, on which we write detailed plans for the following summer—plans requiring so much time and effort as to be impossible.

There will be days in September where, at noon, a sparse Trico spinner fall will surprise us. By then, our hearts are elsewhere. The flying ants and olives hatch in the afternoon, and the fish will chase small, gaudy streamers. The river is smaller, the leaves are changing, and so are the brook trout as they school up below gravel shoals, waiting to spawn. There is energy to these changes.

By the time October arrives, it's difficult to see Tricos as anything but a diminishing feature of summer. They are replaced—happily so—with an even smaller fly: the fall olive.

When it comes to tiny, nothing can quite compare to the tiny fall olives. They are a true #30, and though you can get by fishing a #26 tied short (by "tied short," I mean the body stops short of the bend of the hook), a #30 is best. We use 8X tippet if we can get away with, and 9X tippet if we can't. The fall olive begins hatching just as the last leaves have fallen—typically around October 15—and will continue long into November, eventually mixing with and being replaced by an even smaller midge, which is eventually replaced by snow.

Hatches of small bugs aren't just a summer and fall thing. Matt caught this fine trout on a #20 Blue Wing Olive in March. The early olives hatch in droves, and if the water temperature is right, the trout will rise to them, albeit reluctantly. Patience is a virtue on those first windblown dry-fly days of the year.
JOSH GREENBERG

The trout we catch during the fall olives are stunning. They are mostly brook trout, heavy with spawning color, the mouths of the males black, their bellies aflame. They rarely rise in the same sort of density as they do during Tricos. Instead, they are spread out along a pool or other quiet water. They feed slowly and deliberately and rarely do they eat every fly going over them.

The river is low and clear—it nearly always is on the upper North Branch—but the weeds of summer have either died off or are dying, and the bottom is a mixture of gravel and decomposing leaves. The light is low and the water appears to flow thicker, as if it's starting to freeze. I know this is an optical illusion, but that's what it looks like.

Fishing these small olives on a sunny day is so difficult that I honestly don't enjoy it. You must be able to cast sixty or more feet from an awkward position with a very long leader and *even then* you probably won't catch anything. The best days are the ones where the elements, and not the spookiness of the trout, are your adversary—when you could catch a pile of fish, if only you could feel the 8X between your fingers. Trying to tie a knot out of that fine gut in twenty-five-miles-per-hour winds reminds me of those movies where the battered hero attempts to disengage a bomb against a comically close countdown.

Though it wasn't my best day of fishing the fall olive, it was my coolest, and it happened on the South Branch. It was a pod of fish I found while taking a break along the river during an afternoon of hunting grouse. The fish were rising in a single deep, sandy backwater—a half-dozen or more of them. I returned the next day, sans dogs and gun, with my four-weight, a box of flies, and a winning attitude. The fish were back.

The day was right for it, if perhaps a touch too nice. There was a nice, level gray overcast, though it was warm—just over fifty degrees. I stood on the outside of the bend—a place I'd normally fish—and watched the trout rise. I had my leader ready to go, about twelve feet long and tapered to 7X. I fished a #24 because the South Branch fish simply aren't as picky about what they eat, or even how it drifts. The South Branch is a stream that *will* flood, that does have tannic water even when it's clear, and though it is rich, it doesn't seem to produce the same sort of selectivity in trout as does the main or north branches.

I did the right thing and studied the water and the rises. The olives were hardly hatching, but every single one that slipped into that backwater was eaten. One rise in particular caught my eye. At first I couldn't place what was so distinguishing about it. Then I could.

It was the first tail-head-tail rise I'd ever seen.

I had to stare at it for a long while to confirm what I was seeing. As a fly drifted down, a tail—small and faded white—would stick straight out of the water, followed by a head, and then a much larger, more trout-like tail.

I was able to catch the fish, though I had to wade halfway across the river to get a drift, and even then I had to feed line into it *forever*, watching with concern as the fly line bellied well below the fish and my little olive sort of hung there, looking guilty. The fish ate with a boil.

You'd have thought I had a trophy, as I swooped with my net.

It was a brook trout, about ten inches long, with the back end of the body of another brook trout protruding from its mouth. The dead trout was fading white. The live trout had been eating olives.

I wasn't sure whether I should remove the dead trout or not. So I didn't.

≈

There have been other days with the fall olives—especially on the North Branch—when it is snowing and windy and raining and sleeting and the bugs carpet the water and the fish pod up on the edges of the river. This is much like the caddis hatches of May, and I do best fishing two flies, one a #20 olive, the other much smaller. I'm not certain why the two-fly rig works so well during these small-fly hatches. I know that part of the success is obvious: You're fishing two flies. But it also seems that the bigger fly sort of holds the smaller fly in position, providing a buffer to the effect the current is having on your fly line and leader.

One day, in the good flat water downstream of Lovells, a beautiful mile of brook trout water, an east wind blew all the flies to the west bank, and the fish pushed up to the bank and began rising in untold numbers. Lots of fish. Some good ones. I parked the boat below the rises and my client and I walked up the gravel shoals. As we approached the fish, we silently dropped to our knees and began sneaking up on them.

It was really a perfect situation. The east wind blew his leader toward the fish while not affecting his fly line, creating a perfect curve cast. We fished two flies, and the second, smaller fly would actually hook all the way around the bigger fly, so that it came to the trout first. This is a neat trick, if you can do it on purpose. But a little wind certainly helped that day.

This guy creamed them. He was into fish on nearly every cast, and we caught some fine trout in the ten- to twelve-inch range, which are monster brook trout up here, especially on a fly that is about the size of a flea.

After we worked to the top of the run, he stopped and looked around. The river there is spread out and flat. In the summer it grows thick with algae. Now, it was just a single smooth gravel-run, nearly a hundred feet wide, flowing between stands of cattails and surrounded by a meadow interrupted by the occasional cottonwood tree. There were olives floating past us in sheets. Perfect little beings, with tiny wings and tails upright, and not a single one flying, it was that cold. Here and there, behind us, ahead of us, away from us, fish had begun rising again.

"It's like a mini Bighorn," he said.

"With smaller trout."

He waved my comment away.

"Context," he said.

Even in the best years, I don't fish the fall olive more than a half-dozen times. You become aware out there that you are standing at the eclipse of the dry-fly season, but that's not to say that you aren't wooed by other divulgences. Here there are olives, and streamers, and grouse, and deer. Elsewhere, across the state, the salmon have begun to ascend the rivers: pinks, cohos, rotting chinooks. Behind them will be the steelhead: bright, hard-headed fall fish. There will be days of streamer fishing for brown trout that are exceptional. And, as with all big-fish fishing, there will be days of nothing. Days where the wind is from the east, the day is high and sunny, and the cold rivers provide nothing but sore shoulders and long drives back home.

CHAPTER FIVE

In Dark Rivers

J. K. Rowling suggested that the novel will always be superior to the movie because, in a movie, everyone in the audience sees the same thing. In a novel, of course, we can see only what we imagine. That is, we each see it differently because we see nothing at all. Case in point: A half-dozen years ago, an angler walked into the fly shop with tales of a fish he hasn't been able to catch two nights running.

"He only comes out late. Way late. But once he's out, he's just sipping flies all night," he said. He imitated the noise, a sound like he was sucking a spaghetti noodle.

Day after day he came into the shop, bought different flies, considered different leaders. He may have even contemplated a new rod, as if *that* was the problem. We young, enthusiastic shop workers tied him a few custom flies: cripples, tipped-over spinners (with both wings on one side of the hook), low-riding spinners. Even the deadly Bottomed Out Hex.

His chronicle became something of shop legend. He spent his whole week to the exclusion of all other trout. He was locked in. Stuck. Forget all the other fish in the river. I want *this* one. Who knows what he imagined this fish to be? An epic fish—a trout of legend. A hook-jawed gasping brown trout that took four hands to hold.

Finally, near the end of the week, his persistence paid off, and he hooked and landed the fish: an enormous, twenty-plus-inch sucker.

≈

The *Hexagenia limbata* is either North America's largest mayfly or its second largest, depending on what expert you consult. The *Litobrancha recurvata* is probably the largest. Still, the Hex is huge. And the fact that it has the capability to hatch and spin in such profusion that it can show up on Doppler radar is a testament to the fact that the Hex hatch rather resembles a blight.

In fact, it is probably the most well-known mayfly in the United States, accumulating all over lakeside towns in the upper Midwest, and also in Texas and Louisiana. There, young lads who don't know a fly rod from a broom handle sweep dead Hex from the storefronts at which they're employed and complain about "the bugs." Or maybe some of the young lads *do* know a fly rod from a broom handle, in which case they complain about "work."

Locally the Hex are called caddis, or Michigan caddis. I don't know who was responsible for this misnomer, but there are still a few folks who call them caddis. Don't laugh too hard—even the most technical anglers still call brook trout, trout.

Hex imitations are plentiful, and range from beautiful to amusing. There is a fine line between imitation and attraction, and an even finer line between a great Hex fly and a practical joke. There are flies with four wings that look like helicopters. Flies with extended bodies. Flies of foam bodies. Flies with foam wings that spin through the air and twist tippets. Flies that are four inches long. Flies that are full of rubber legs. Flies that are all white. Flies that are all black. There are parachutes, emergers, cripples. There are flies that tip over on purpose, and flies that tip over by accident. And seemingly all of them have at least one person that claims it's the *one* fly that will catch them when others won't.

Usually this is the person that invented it.

Most flies imitate the Hex spinner, and most fishing is done during the Hex spinner fall.

I do carry a lot of Hex patterns—my Hex box is stuffed full—though this has more to do with the possibility of frustration than it does the possibility that I'm so in tune with what's happening on the river that I know when the fish have switched from spinners to emergers. The fact is, when a fish is rising and won't take your fly, having a box full of opportunity is better for the psyche than having a box that's not. At least for me.

The Hex is similar to the brown drake in that both are burrowing mayflies. The Hex burrows in the black muck that locals call "loon shit" or "mud patties."

Their breathing holes are visible as perforations in these banks. The nymph spends two years in the muck, making it a viable food source twelve months out of the year. On the Au Sable, they hatch in June. They emerge most often late at night—after the spinner fall—and will spend one full day and night in the trees before returning to the river. These are my observations, not necessarily those of scientists. Still, if you catch wind of a great Hex hatch in some spot on June 15, you can bet there'll be a good spinner fall there on June 17.

The Hex is a nocturnal mayfly. It typically spins after dusk on cool evenings, and much later on warm nights. The hatch usually occurs after the spinner fall, almost always around midnight. This means that a Hex angler fishes at night, usually casting at fish that are heard rather than seen. Even for an accomplished angler, it may take a few evenings to become acquainted with dry-fly fishing after dark. Hardly anyone steps into a river and *gets it* immediately. Even great casters might find themselves slapping the water on their backcast, or thinking their fly is right over the fish, only to discover they've hooked a tree across the river.

Nothing says *Hexagenia limbata* like a blooming iris. The irises grow from the firm edges of the Hex muck. If the irises are in bloom, the Hex are about to hatch.
ADOLPH M. GREENBERG

On the Au Sable, the Hex hatch typically begins around June 15. In a hot year, it may begin the first week of June. In a cold year, sometime around June 22. According to the old-timers, the Hex used to hatch in early July. A few years ago, they began on May 29. To some of us, this is foreboding. To others, especially the old guides, they simply plan on earlier Hex fishing.

The hatch follows the water temperature. The Au Sable warms more quickly both in its headwaters and down in its lower reaches. The water temperature of the middle section—from Burtons to Wakeley—is influenced by spring water and remains cool through most of the summer. The Hex hatches in this section come late and don't last very long. The last spot to get them is around Stephan Bridge, where they'll typically hatch once and spin once and be done with it. There are many reaches of the Au Sable that don't have good Hex habitat, and it has become an underground movement to fish these reaches during the Hex hatch because no one else is, and there are strong emergences of *Isonychia* as well as blanket spinner falls of sulphurs.

The Manistee River has a less predictable but very productive Hex hatch that begins about a week after the Au Sable and typically lasts through the July 4 weekend. By then, *everyone* seems to be fishing the Manistee and it can be crowded with wading anglers.

Many other rivers in the state have great Hex hatches, and finding your own less-crowded spot is a matter of keeping your ears open, your mouth shut, and doing some good old-fashioned boot work. I once heard of a place—a river between two lakes—that is far too warm for trout except right below a single cold-water tributary. There the fish from the lower lake will move up into the river to feed on Hex. These are big fish, the legend goes, up to and over ten pounds. I've seen the place, but only in the winter, and it looked as the legend foretold. But, well, it's over an hour from my house, and the Hex fishing is *really* good just down the road.

Compared to the whimsical, picky nature of most mayflies, the Hex is a strong bug that will try to spin on even the worst nights. Rob Thompson, Rusty, and I were once sitting at Rusty's old Hex camp on what we hoped would be a good night of fishing, when an uncommonly cold and severe storm blew in. It was almost cinematically violent. As the first wind swept down the river valley, Rusty said, "Here it comes." And almost immediately the wind hit and blew my full beer across the table like I'd slid it down a nice, polished bar. What followed was forty minutes of sideways rain and winds up to fifty miles per hour. Trees were falling. The river was white-capped and frothy. It was 9:30.

"You'll have fishing tonight," Rusty said before heading home.

We did.

By 10 p.m., the storm was done. It was cold and foggy. Rob and I went to the river, and in the gloaming I could see the first bugs flying upstream. And then more. It's an interesting multiplication, one that increases your heart rate in proportion, until, by darkness, I was turning on my light just to watch the bugs halt their linear flight upstream and create a swarming helical descent towards the light. There was no one around. The fog was thick, and the fish were stupid. We ripped them.

≈

I have two basic Hex fishing tricks. Perhaps they aren't tricks at all but common knowledge, but here they are anyway.

The first is simple: Don't thrash the water before prime time. Typically the best way to wade fish the Hex hatch is to hurry up and wait. When I was younger, we used to leave the shop at seven and sit on the bank for three hours waiting for bugs and usually drinking beer. By the time it was good fishing, our vests sounded like a recycling center, and we were too hosed to have the kind of fishing we thought our patience warranted. While claiming a pool is important, it's not that important, and now I'm more inclined to go home, do some chores, maybe ride the mountain bike or go for a run, and then, at dusk, just try to find a spot to fish. Once I do that, I wait on the bank until I hear a good fish feed. And then, and only then, do I get in the water. The object is to leave the river as undisturbed as possible until the fish get in a reliable rising rhythm.

Waiting for a big fish to rise is part of the Hex fishing tradition. The emphasis is on patience, restraint, and not shaking under pressure. The motive of this patience is not penance, but instead to leave the river undisturbed. If you catch that fifteen-inch fish at 11 p.m., that twenty-inch fish might not start rising at midnight. It's best to wait for the late risers, which are almost always larger trout. While there are holes in this theory, it does seem to work. Waiting for the rise also serves the purpose of lessening the chance of conflict on the river on a busy night. If half the people are waiting on the bank and the other half are wading in the river, there'll be, if not an argument, at least a few choice words. Around here, if you're sitting on a pool, it's *your* pool until you leave.

Of course, this tradition of bank-sitting etiquette gets abused at times. I once asked a guy where he planned on fishing that night, and he said, "Oh, just this run here, down through that bend . . . and up through that one, too," indicating at least two hundred yards of water which, on a night during prime Hex, is out of the question.

The second trick is to get directly downstream of a rising fish. In other words, do your casting with your legs. Because you can get so close to a Hex-eating trout, making a thirty-foot reach cast is either an exercise in self-gratification or the water is prohibitively deep and it's impossible to cross to get into proper position. Though it is common practice to sit on the inside of a bend and wait for the fish to rise on the outside of it, consider doing the opposite. Cross the river well away from your chosen pool, and sit back in the woods, far enough from the water so as to not spook the fish. By the time the Hex start dropping, the river will have relaxed, and you'll be right on top of the trout. Even the gnarliest outside bend tends to have a few spots to stand, and because your goal is a ten- to fifteen-foot upstream cast, there's little need for lots of backcast room.

This manner of fishing is far from elegant, and plenty of times I've had to cast with one hand while hanging onto a tree with the other. Trout rise in nasty places, especially big, wild Michigan trout. To get behind them will test your wading ability and overall fortitude. Hex water is typically slow, deep, and mucky. But if you can do it safely, do it. Last year, while sitting on the inside bank, a trout rose in a dead calm backwater across the river. There were few bugs, so I went for it. I spent over a half hour tracking that trout down, crossing the river, forging through tag alders, tromping through sucking muck, and then waiting and waiting for the fish to rise. Which it did, about ten feet away. The rings spread on the surface as a grin spread on my face. It was an easy cast. An easy fish. But one—situated as it was in a backwater—that would have been almost impossible from across the river.

In other words, getting downstream from the fish counteracts the disadvantage of fishing in the dark. Rather than blindly casting at a sound, you can use the grade of the river to increase the amount of glare on the surface. On even the darkest night, there is usually some light reflected on the river. You see far more light facing upstream than you do facing downstream. Try it on your local river. It's amazing the difference facing into the gradient has on your ability to see the surface of the water.

Making a short ten-foot cast to a fish you can see rising is far better than trying to make a twenty-foot cast to a fish that you can't. Working the glare also allows you to see the soft plop of your #6 Hex imitation hitting the water. And while you won't be able to see your fly on the river, you'll have a pretty good idea where it is, and if the rise of the fish was to your fly or not.

Because of this close-in fishing, my Hex rods aren't your modern-day, fast-action rods. A stiff rod is next to worthless for short casting, especially with a dry fly. A lot of the old-timers still use the fiberglass rods, and I think they're onto something.

Be sure that the rod you take Hex fishing is, first of all, able to cast a big fly. But it must also allow you to feel the distance of your cast. Some rods are simply better at this than others. I typically fish an eight-and-a-half-foot rod—the Winston IM6 five-weight. I've heard this rod described as the staff of Moses. It is a rod that has a powerful butt and a long middle section that seems to transmit directly to my hand the length of line I'm carrying on my backcast. It is too weak a rod for throwing long casts with a Hex, and if I knew I was putting myself in a long-casting situation—such as wade fishing bigger water—I'd probably go with a heavier, longer rod. I find that Winston makes the best Hex rods and, for that matter, dry-fly rods on the market. Scott also makes nice, soft rods that let you judge distance—that most critical requirement for dry-fly fishing after dark.

What is new to the Hex fishing tradition is, well, technology. As little as ten years ago, no one so much as shone a light during the Hex. This lights-spook-fish stigma is still ingrained in a number of anglers and it's probably a good thing, even if it's unnecessary. The worst thing a light does is blind you, not the fish. I use a red light for all my close-in work, and save the LEDs for getting in and out of the river. Still, I've seen little evidence that lights put down rising trout unless they are very bright, and are shined right on a feeding fish. Even then, most fish will return to feeding within minutes.

Some folks have begun using glow-in-the-dark flies, lines, and strike putty. There are laser pointers that can be used to check your distance from the bank (or scare the shit out of an encroaching angler). All in all, this twenty-first-century night is a much brighter place. I have used some of these luminescent aids and, for the most part, I've found them very effective. The exception being the glow-in-the-dark Hex, which, unless the glowing portion is the faintly lit parachute post, seem less effective than normal patterns. But the other luminescent tools are just that, tools, and if you're not adverse to tipping the scales in your favor, they do help.

The glow-in-the-dark line, manufactured by Rio, is especially useful. It's best charged by UV light, which won't kill your night vision. Some people consider a glow line cheating. It's personal, I guess. But a typical conversation in a guide boat goes like this:

Guide: "You're welcome to use my rod. It has the glow line on it."
Client: "Well, let me get a few more casts in with this."
Guide: [Silence.]
Client: "Am I getting close?"
Guide: "I think so. I can't really see . . ."
Client: "Maybe we'll try yours."
Guide: "Sure thing. I mean, I think you were putting it over him, but . . ."
Client: "Got him!"

Okay, it's not always like that, but close. A glow line not only lets you gauge distance, but also allows you to actively mend and otherwise control your drift, which is probably more important. An added bonus is the joy of watching a glow line, freshly charged, being cast on a dark night, even when the fishing sucks.

Several people have hit the river with night-vision goggles. I haven't, but I would. Not for the fishing—to me, that would be cheating (though it's probably hard to cast with those things on). But I sure would like to watch the fish rise on a good Hex night—or, better yet, watch people try to catch them.

≈

My best memories of the river seem to always involve a boat, and my favorite experience in fly fishing—without exception—is to be working a big rising trout from a riverboat, whether I'm the guide or the angler. This past summer one of our shop staff, a geology student named Jon Haynes, and I went to the lower Au

The camera captures the rare sight of a guide at work at night. With paddle in hand, the Au Sable riverboat becomes a silent vessel on a river where, to the angler, the ability to hear soft rises is the key. More time is spent floating than casting.
JOHN SYVERSON

Sable during the tail end of the Hex. It was a half-moon and the river was almost empty. We saw two boats, though one of them may have been fishing for walleye.

It was a beautiful night, but it was very late in the hatch, and we were uncertain whether we'd even see a bug, let alone enough to make the fish rise. Most of the guides were either fishing the Manistee, where the hatches are typically a week behind the Au Sable's, or had given up on the Hex completely. Which is why we'd come here. I will guide in a crowd, but I won't fish in one.

We were fishing just upstream of Mio Pond, where the river and pond begin to merge, and big jams of driftwood have created bends in the river. It's big, slow, haunting water, and very busy during the peak of Hex season. It is a stump-filled mess with cuts sawed through the jams that the canoe racers use in the Au Sable River Canoe Marathon, an overnight dash from Grayling to Lake Huron. In other words, they are shortcuts. We call these cuts the "racer cuts" and reference them in our stories, as in, "It was rising by the first racer's cut, next to that stump . . ."

We stopped just downstream of one of the jams and sat on the bank and talked. I had a cigar. Jon had some breath mints. Two small raccoons were in the tree above us and we watched them and talked about fishing. We talked about the things we wanted to try. Because, even in your home river, there is more. End-lessly more. The truth is, the techniques of fly fishing will never be exhausted, new theories never nonexistent. As much as we know now, we'll know more later, even if we forget half of what we should have remembered about what we used to know. If that makes sense.

The bugs flew that night. Far more than we expected. Thousands of Hex spin-ners flying upstream make a hum. It sounds like nothing more than wind in the treetops. Later, when the spinners are lower, they sound like electrical wires. Even our relationship to the Hex mayflies themselves is audible.

They began to hit the water, their quivering bodies existing within the water rings of their struggle.

"Dude, we've got bugs," I said.

Deb with a handful of Hex. During a heavy spinner fall, many experienced Hex anglers choose to sit back and wait for the bugs to thin out before starting fishing. It's not uncommon for the spinners to still be on the water as the sun rises.
DEB FREELE

And then, well before I expected it, there was a great rise near the tail end of the jam, out about ten feet, in the middle of the bubble line.

We nearly tipped the boat in our rush to get at the fish.

Our first position was directly behind the fish. We faced upstream, with the bow resting on a log in the water, the boat held stationary because of it. The trout was about twenty feet in front of us. The moon was too bright to risk getting close to this fish, and Jon had to stand to get his backcast over a small bush. The trout was moving all over the river, covering at least a hundred square feet. I pushed the bow off the log and paddled upstream and held us there, paddling lightly while Jon, standing, attempted to predict where the next rise would be.

The fish fed left, and then dropped back. It then fed up the bubble line, worked left, and dropped back. Once the fish dropped back and rose, Jon put his fly above it, and it was one of those casts that you knew was the cast, except it wasn't, and so on, with me creeping the boat up and then sliding to the right to keep his slack line in the slower water, hopefully allowing an angle so that the fly would go over the fish before the leader.

"Sorry," he said, breathlessly.

"I love this," I said, and I meant it. "You couldn't be doing it better. No one I know could be doing it better than you are," I said, and I meant that, too.

Finally it came together and the fish moved to the fly, but refused it.

I backed the boat out and we waited there, with Jon holding to the bank.

"Should we find another fish?" he asked.

"I'm not sure if there'll be another," I said. "There aren't many fish down here, and a lot of them are in live wells or sick of Hex. Matt was down here yesterday, and they only found one rising fish."

"Maybe it was this one," Jon said.

I later found out that it was.

After a long time—I mean, a really long time—the fish started rising again, this time ten yards up. It was the same moonlit rise form as before. The same sound. We decided to try another tactic, and I paddled to the middle of the river and swung the boat so Jon was to the side of the fish and facing downstream. I held the boat with the pole. This trout was now on the move, working up and down the bubble line, sometimes dropping all the way back to his original spot, other times rising twenty yards up the river. We had several times we thought the fish had taken, maybe a refusal—it's always hard to tell at night, even when the moon is out—and then it settled back to its original spot, where it had begun the night, and started rising again.

We drifted down and I spun the boat and paddled up behind the fish *again,* this time past the submerged log, and tried to get along the bank, in the three feet of quiet water inside the bubble line. We were less than fifteen feet away from where it had last risen.

"Should I try a new fly?" Jon asked.

"The fish is just moving around too much," I said. "It's not the fly." Then I said, "Yeah, try a new fly."

We watched the fish complete a new cycle, which was to rise up in the bubble line, three feet separating rises, for ten or fifteen yards, and then drift back to the original point, before starting again. There's no way to be certain, but I figured that it was the boat, and the slight wakes we were making, that was causing the fish to change rhythms and feeding patterns. Because once it got onto a pattern, it seemed to stick with it for a long time until, suddenly, it would quit rising for a minute or two, and then start a whole different pattern.

We waited until the fish rose near us. Then, as it began working its way upriver, we followed it with slow paddle strokes and held our breath. When it stopped rising, I lifted the paddle and we drifted backward until the fish began rising again. Jon directed me. The moon also made it easy for me to know where the boat was in relationship to the fish. A dark night, and it would take a more skilled guide. But the moon offered me a handicap, even if the moonlight was also making the fish that much harder to fool.

It was the most fun I've had with a Hex fish. By then, we'd been with the fish for a long time. Like some bar girl. You don't know her yet. But you love her.

Jon hooked the fish as we were drifting backward behind it, at its original position, seconds after it rose before starting its new cycle, probably in the exact same spot we'd seen it rise two hours earlier. The rise to the fly was vicious—far different than the rises to the naturals. This is a common phenomenon and one for which I have no explanation, other than our flies aren't as good imitations as we might wish.

By the time he hooked the fish, the boat had been everywhere but directly upstream of it. I was pleasantly exhausted, like I'd stayed up all night reading a book simply to get to this point, those last few savory paragraphs, where . . .

The fish shook its head. The hook came free.

≈

Losing a fish at night hurts more than it does during the day, especially if you never even catch a glimpse of it. A rise in the dark is a footprint in the mind, and the bigger the footprint, the more you want to see what made it. When you're locked in on a fish, as Jon and I were, the possibility that you might *lose* the fish without ever seeing it rarely crosses your mind. It is much like surviving the climb of a mountain, only to be lost in a blizzard on the descent.

For those who haven't Hex fished, the sound of any big trout rising is a terrific thing in and of itself. Some fish throw spray two feet in the air, that sudden burst of whitewater visible on even the darkest nights. Or they may sip in the backwater, a soft pop, and the click of jaws shutting. It may be a characteristic of anglers to claim that all fish lost are far larger than those landed. At night, there is no way to judge the size of a fish, other than by the sound it is making. As most people—myself included—are unable to reliably differentiate between the sound of a eighteen-inch fish and a twenty-four-inch fish, the uncaught fish are almost always of the twenty-four-inch variety, and the caught ones are almost always smaller.

The oft-quoted rule is that a large trout makes a deep rise: *blahp!* This is true. But some make a very soft rise, more of a popping noise. Others crash the flies, leaving no doubt as to their size. Then there are the splashy rises, which are by all accounts small fish.

Sometimes, though, these splashy rises are big fish. One great trout Joe Guild caught years ago during a guides-night-off float was making a splish-splashy rise next to a log. If it hadn't been after midnight, when the big ones traditionally are the only trout still feeding, we might have skipped it. It was an enormous fish—I still remember when the flashlight beam first showed it to us.

You get fooled at night. Often.

Last year I worked a trout for nearly a half hour. It was tucked away in a backwater, making a nice little popping noise, the same noise a person can make by opening their lips against their own suction. It was a hard cast, on a dark night, early in the hatch. I'd had at least a half-dozen rises that I thought were to my fly. I figured they were refusals. Finally I hooked the fish—"Got the bastard!" I yelled to

One uncommon obstacle is the effect that light has during a full-blown hatch of Hex. They swarm the light and everyone around it, creating something that, to the general population, would be Hitchcockian. To fly anglers, though, this is ecstasy.
JOHN SYVERSON

nearby friends—and it came rocketing at me, less than ten inches long, its refusal rises nothing more than its vain attempts to fit a #6 fly into its mouth.

Some great big fish really do crash the naturals, especially during the first few nights of the spinner fall. In the great flats below the North Branch confluence, Willy and Jack Franzen and I were two giant bends upstream of a fish when we first heard it. That's a long distance to hear a fish, and I wouldn't believe the story if it weren't mine.

"Don't get your hopes up," I said. I figured any rise that loud would attract boats like Hex to a streetlight.

But the pool was empty of boats and everything else except the great rising trout in the middle of it. The water was ten feet deep and fast, and I had to hold the boat pole with both hands, and hook myself to the boat by locking my legs under the seat, just to keep us still. It was hard work. The fish must have been eating every bug, and doing so with anger. These were terrific, explosive rises. It was undoubtedly a big fish. The physics would not allow it to be anything but enormous. The grunt work of holding the boat rendered me speechless. But this father-and-son team knows their Hex fishing, and Willy can cast a hundred feet, so thirty-five wasn't bad. He had a luminescent line, so the three of us could follow his drift.

"I think you're too far," Jack said.

"I'm not too far, Dad," Willy replied. "I'm right over the fish."

With each rise the boat shook. Not from the wake, but from our scared wits.

"Willy, you're too far."

"I'm *not* too far."

"I think I'm losing my grip," I said. And I did.

We floated past the fish and I went to the inside of the bend and pushed us back upriver. I wanted to spin around on the fish, but a huge whirlpool on the far side of the river would have made holding the boat impossible. And the fast, deep water made dropping the anchor risky. If it didn't hold immediately, we'd slide just downstream of the fish, and casting back upstream with all that fast water would lead to instant fly drag. So I planted the pole, hooked my legs under the seat, and hoped for a quick resolution.

"Now you're short," Jack said.

"I'm right on him. Right on him."

"Strike!" I yelled

"It wasn't me," Willy said. "I struck."

The intensity of Hex fishing is second to none in angling. All senses focused not on but *toward* the possibility that a fish has eaten your fly. This not a perfect science, and savvy anglers know to set the hook when a fish *might* have eaten their fly. There is no other way to know.

We weren't parked next to that fish for long—ten minutes at the most—but the sheer, broad physicality of the river and the giant rises of the fish were wearing and exhilarating. We'd signed on for a pleasant float on the gentle Au Sable, but this was anything but. When the fish finally ate, it was far from subtle, and the fight was unbelievable. It made me doubt Marinaro's assertion that the rise itself was the climax.

Almost immediately the fish leapt, and then ran strongly upstream, taking drag. Yes, yes, we were using heavy tippet. And yes, we had stout rods. Willy has landed billfish on a fly rod. He knows what to do. But the trout blitzed us with sheer aggression. The line buzzed over my head, and I spun the boat so Willy, in the front seat, could fight the fish facing in the direction it was running. The trout then ran around the boat and I spun with it and began pulling hard for the far bank, thinking we could land it there.

I grabbed my net—Willy and Jack now had their lights on—and hurdled over the side of the boat. I went immediately over my head (one reason not to wear waders on a Hex float). I lost contact with the unanchored boat for a heart-racing moment. Real dark. Big river. Runaway boat filled with clients.

When I surfaced, the boat was drifting upstream in the whirlpool. I grabbed the side near Jack and swam forward, one hand on the gunnel, to Willy, who had played the fish into short, hard circles. I netted the trout without stepping foot on the bottom. I then pushed the boat into the weeds and hauled myself through a waist-deep muck bank, the smell of methane dizzying. And none of this is the point of the story.

It was a grand fish, and we immediately proclaimed it well over twenty-five inches, perhaps thirty. We huddled over it in the net and Willy produced a tape measure, and we watched the ruler stretch and stop at twenty-four. It was a female. Small faced. Huge, sleek body. It would turn out to be my largest trout of the year with or without a client. *But* it somehow stopped short of what we'd thought it was. Perhaps well short of what we wanted it to be. And definitely much smaller than it would have measured in our minds had we lost it.

All this talk of rising fish, the endless varieties of gurgles, burping sounds, splashes, sips . . . these are all trout noises. But there are a variety of other noises that are mistaken for trout noises. Some are easy to recognize as non-trout noises. Others are not and must be investigated.

The first noise to ignore is perhaps the one that fools most folks. It is the noise that fooled the gentleman in the beginning of this chapter: the rise of the sucker. A sucker rise sounds great when it rises once, and this most often occurs on nights when the spinner fall is sparse and the bugs don't accumulate in the jams as they normally do. But even on sparse nights, if you wait long enough, you'll hear the *sip-sip-sip* and know it's a sucker. It's identical to the sound of a person making repeated, soft, kissing noises. It is not a trout. Most suckers rise within logjams, making their existence even more frustrating to an angler intent on believing it's a trout.

Sometimes it gets more complicated. Often a sucker will be rising within a logjam, and a trout will be rising just outside of the jam, eating the bugs getting swept against the leading log. Typically the sucker rise is far more consistent. And, to make it worse, occasionally a sucker will make a sound exactly like the sound of a trout within its feeding pattern. Or perhaps that *was* the trout?

Invariably someone you know will float by you as you're casting at the trout, will hear the sucker rise, and assume you're an ignoramus.

The only sucker I've ever caught jumped into the boat the second I turned on a flashlight. When it comes to difficulty, catching a sucker on a Hex is far more difficult than catching a trout, which makes them somewhat higher game than trout. Though this probably is a weak consolation prize for the unfortunate angler who manages to do so.

I'm told that our bottom-dwelling whitefish also rise to Hex. But if I've heard them rise, I didn't recognize it as such.

Another common faux rise is that of the frog. Not the sound of it eating Hex, but the sound of it leaping into the water. The soft, deep splash followed by the gentle rings by the bank do seem right. But the sound of an object entering the water is different from the sound of one leaving the water, as a trout's head initially does during the rise. The beginning of the noise will be far sharper than the end. A rise is loudest in the middle. If you hear a plop, it's probably not a trout, though you might want to check it out just to be sure.

Muskrat are commonly mistaken for trout as they work around the banks and in the weeds. They can make a series of noises that almost sound right. As do ducks, mergansers, and geese. Geese will eat Hex, though it's typically the sound of geese repeatedly ducking their heads to eat water weeds that fools anglers. Even deer crossing the river can momentarily beguile anglers, though I've never heard of anyone actually casting at a rise that turned out to be a deer.

The splash of a beaver's tail is far too loud to be a trout eating a Hex. And wading or floating over to the spot just to check it out could result in you getting a serious case of the night shits should the beaver repeat the performance beside you.

This fish was rising consistently when it was caught along a weed edge, though the light in the picture reveals not a bug on the surface. We figured that the presence of our boat in the weeds was actually pushing the collected spinners into the current where this trout unexpectedly took up position and made our night.
JOSH GREENBERG

Then there is the sound of the river itself. The river has a multitude of gurgles and bloops caused by nothing more than the current itself. It could be boiling over a submerged log, or lapping against a cut bank. These are the hardest sounds to recognize, especially if you're wading in fast water, where the noise of the water around your legs competes with the noises beyond you. If you spend all night casting at what turns out to be a stick bouncing in the water, rest assured that I have, too, and so has everyone that has ever Hex fished.

Which is what happened to Joe Bartha on a night last June. The same night that I accidentally lucked into a guide trip. It was a surprise fill-in float due to an unexpected guide shortage (I'd long since hung up my boat pole and taken over shop duty). My client that night was actually one of my old clients, Brennan, a young—in fly-fishing circles anyway—fellow from Colorado who is an excellent angler. He also tends to show up the week after the Hex hatch has ended. This year, the spring was cold and the Hex came late in the season, and Brennan came early.

"We'll hit them tonight," I promised.

We did. It was a cold night, and the mist came heavily after dark, as we expected. The spinners were moderate but ample. The fish weren't on them very well at first, and as the mist rolled in, I was worried that we wouldn't have much of a night. Sure, there were a few trout to cast to. And I think we caught a couple teeners that fought plenty hard. But it wasn't the night, I thought. It was just *a* night.

But at midnight, with the bugs draining quickly from the river, we found a fish rising in a logjam. Farther down, a good trout was rising near the clay bank. And so on, one or two fish per bend, all rising consistently and harder than hell to fool. This is the phenomenon of washed-out spinners.

A "washed-out spinner" is what we call a bug that has long since fallen and died, and is floating half-drowned down the river, getting hung up in jams, in weeds, in back eddies, and then finding the current. This trickle of bugs is far more numerous than your flashlight will reveal. And it's possible to find a trout rising every ten seconds despite the fact that your flashlight shows little in the way of whole bugs. Sure, you might see a wing there, an abdomen here . . . but the food supply seems hardly enough to sustain the feeding activity you're hearing.

For most of us, the true Hex fishing occurs much later in the night than does the actual spinner fall. When the Hex first hit the water, small trout respond immediately. Then a few medium fish. And finally the large fish. After an hour or so, the rises will begin to diminish, and the first wave of anglers leaves. But the rises never stop completely. The slurper under the bushes is still slurping. The chomper on the inside bank is still chomping, and so on. The targets, only an hour earlier too numerous to focus on, are now individual, unique, and challengeable.

For years it seemed that 90 percent of anglers left too early. Now that number is more like 10 percent. In general, the angling populace of the Au Sable is far better than it used to be, and staying late is no longer an easy road to big, dumb fish. These fish are educated. Brennan and I worked four good, steadily rising trout before catching one.

The fish was rising against a rocky bank, about a foot off of it. We changed flies a half-dozen times, and changed boat positions more than that, before we got it right. I'm not sure what it was: There weren't many bugs on the water, and there weren't many currents to contend with. The fly we caught it on was the same fly we'd started with. Most of the time, I think a fish is fooled not because of a fly change, but simply because your fly was in the right place at the right time. The fish was rising downstream of a long backwater full of logjams, and my guess was that there were plenty of soggy Hex spinners washing over that fish. It wasn't until the natural flies thinned out that our fly registered on the trout's radar.

"That's over twenty," Brennan said as he held the fish. "That's a *nice* fish."

We painstakingly worked four more good trout that night without catching one. We changed tippet. We changed flies. We tried reach casts, pile casts. We really tried everything that we knew, and a couple of things we didn't know. At some point some Hex had begun hatching as well, and we even tried a two-fly rig with a floating nymph—which is borderline desperation for me. It didn't work. Nothing worked. The fish would rise three times in a row, we'd cast, the fish would quit rising for five minutes before beginning again.

We hit the landing at 3:30 in the morning, and we were freezing. There was no truck at the landing—not mine, not anyone's. The guys at the shop had forgotten to call my spot in to the car spotter. We had no truck, no trailer, and no way home.

"I'll call Joe Bartha," I said. "He's probably on his way back right now and can swing by and pick us up."

As we stood by the boat, a trout began rising just upstream, and Brennan waded out to throw a few casts. I called Joe.

"You still fishing?" I said.

"Just loading the boat," he replied.

"No one spotted my truck, so we're stuck. Can you give us a ride?"

"It'll be a half hour. Maybe less if we hustle."

"Hustle. We're freezing. How'd you do?"

"Got a twenty—"

"Nice," I said. "Sweet. Well . . . I'll call Katy and see if she can pick us up instead. If she can't, I'll call you."

Katy came with our newborn in tow and picked us up.

Joe met us at the lodge, where my truck was still parked. Brennan headed home, as did Katy. Joe hopped in with me. I was trying my best not to be pissed off about the missed car spot, or having to open the lodge in a few hours and work without sleep during a busy Hex day.

"So you got a nice fish?" I asked.

Joe laughed in a you-can-say-that-again manner.

"Twenty-eight-incher," he said.

"Oh, I thought you said twenty."

"My phone cut out."

And that's when I got the story.

Joe and his friend Casey had decided to hold up high that night. This meant, on a four-hour float, they stopped an hour downstream of the launch. The spot they dropped anchor in is a big wide flat, right next to a house with an ancient mounted bobcat that sits in the window and has been bleached white by the sun. They were entertained by the sounds of an enthusiastic courtship resonating from the house during the lackluster spinner fall. They pricked a few fish, but nothing of consequence.

"They were really going at," said Joe, of the courtship.

Joe and Casey pulled anchor and floated for over a mile. A long, silent mile. The bugs were fading fast from the main flow, though there were plenty in the backwaters. The cold was pushing down into the river valley. The same fog that Brennan and I faced was even heavier in the bigger water. Like us, they'd struggled for a time to find a feeding fish.

In a sharp S-bend, with a gigantic whirlpool on the north bank, they finally heard a rise, thirty or more yards downstream of the sound of a stick bouncing in the riffle that fed the pool. Casey hit the oars and slid the boat into the whirlpool *above* the fish, figuring the fish would be facing downstream and into the inverse current of the whirlpool. They dropped anchor and waited for the fish to rise below them.

The stick above bounced—*pish pish pish BLOOP! Pish pish pish.*

They strained to hear the trout below them. The stick above bounced— *BLOOP! Pish pish pish BLOOP BLOOP pish pish pish.*

"I think that's a fish," Joe said.

"What's a fish?" Casey asked.

"The bouncing stick."

"The bouncing stick is a fish? Or that's a fish by the bouncing stick?"

"I think the bouncing stick is a fish."

This is not your typical big-fish-caught-by-a-guide story, even if Joe is a guide. He didn't sneak up on the fish. His heart didn't race. No, this is more like the story of the eight-year-old who catches a state-record brown on a foil gum wrapper attached to a bait hook.

Joe had broken off the previous night and had only a four-foot leader tapering to fifteen-pound Maxima Chameleon. He simply tied a Hex spinner to that and threw a blind cast far upstream behind the boat, across about ten currents, some of which were going backward, and hooked the bouncing stick cum fish.

And you think of all the times you tried so hard.

The fish fought heavy and strong, and they knew it was enormous. The light shone on only parts of the trout as Joe wrestled it to the surface. They taped it and took photos ("perhaps a few too many," says Joe). Its hooked jaw and humped shoulders, the long lean body and great propulsive tail of a hunter. They released the trout gingerly, though hardly a person would have howled had they kept it. It revived, and swam slowly away. (A few days later, it was caught and kept by a person who keeps them all.)

I guess the really big fish sound like bouncing sticks.

I stopped the truck and returned to my house for a bottle of whiskey I keep in the barn for such moments, and we greeted the dawn with tumblers in hand, just talking Hex. The dark nights the two of us had shared—and the great nights that we hadn't. Stories of other guides, the way Nethers tells a Hex story, or the more secretive guides do not. Theories on why that night, with its middling spinner fall, became, at midnight, the night. I made him tell the story of the fish three or four times. We pondered it. We stopped to swirl our drinks. I told the story of Brennan working those trout. The many different angles. The way the fish worked around our flies, pausing in their rise pattern only to let our imitations go.

And then it was day, and that world of the Hex—the one of the fireflies in the weeds and the slow dark rivers and the corridor of stars between the trees and the smell of DEET and muck and the sting of the cuts of trout teeth on your thumb and the bobbling flashlights and lost nets and the great big wide stories of adventure—was lost to the world that was.

I made it to work and switched to coffee. Did the checkouts, shook hands with the early risers. The heat burned out the cold on the ground. Breakfast smells blew through the door that separates the fly shop from the restaurant kitchen. Photos drifted into my inbox: of anglers who looked as if a trout had fallen into their arms in the middle of the night. I shook hands and smiled. I listened to stories. It was wonderful.

CHAPTER SIX
Mousin'

The man who taught many of us young 'uns how to night fish, or mousing, as we call it, is a man that was long ago nicknamed Picket Pin, after the night fly he used to fish almost exclusively. Thin, active, with deep-set eyes, a snow white beard, and a floppy fishing hat that could double as a wizard's cap, Pin is a retired biology teacher with a passion for wild spaces. The two don't always go hand in hand. One may love great art and not be an artist. To hear him hoot in an owl, or several, and then fish happily up through their calls *for him* is to witness an angler immersed in something that he not only loves, but understands. It's beautiful.

He's one of the few that came to night fishing because he loved the night. When Rusty showed him mousing, well, Pin liked that as well. And when a mind like Pin's—an incessant diary-keeper and tinkerer—starts into a facet of an activity, his continuing invention soon strains the rules and bounds of that activity. In other words, the mousing that we now do on the Au Sable is how Pin does it, and not how it was done before Pin did it, if that makes sense.

For years he slept in the back of his pickup truck, parked wherever he'd decided to fish that night. For a period he fished some of the more remote water out of a float tube, but quit doing that when the float-bladder popped and he was forced to bushwhack through a mile of swamp at one in the morning, the deflated tube wet and heavy on his back and water sloshing in his wading boots.

He used to tie flies in the Board Room at Gates Au Sable Lodge. For a while he tied all the night flies for the lodge: the HLS, the HLS Blaster, the Picket Pin, the regular Blaster. Many of these flies featured the same basic components: a red yarn tail, a black body with silver tinsel, a wing of white and brown bucktail, and either a hackled head (the standard HLS and the Picket Pin) or a deer-hair head (the various Blasters).

But Pin is a tinkerer, and quite soon new flies began to appear in his box, beginning with the Zoo Cougar—a streamer developed and popularized by Kelly Galloup—and quickly morphing into a series of sculpin-style flies, quickly replaced by a pile of foam flies. Pin is not a quick tyer. He's meticulous. He invents—absolutely. But he's quick to point out past flies that inspired his own—a trait lacking in many fly tyers nowadays. What I think makes Pin a great fly tyer, though, isn't innovation. Instead, it's his ability to adapt flies from other parts of the world designed for other applications, and to bring them to the styles of fishing that he enjoys. He then *takes the time* to test, alter, and otherwise tailor the flies and the methods he uses to fish them to the specific criteria of his fishing situation, be it at night or during the day. (Pin routinely catches big browns in the middle of sunny days on streamers, though how he does this is a secret that he wouldn't like me to share!)

He is, in the Information Age, the ultimate fly tyer and angler. And I don't mean this based necessarily on his success ratio, his trophy-board fish, or any sort of fame his flies and personality have generated. No, what I mean is that Pin doesn't have his own line of YouTube tying videos (this is not to knock those that do). He doesn't claim himself a visionary, or even an expert. He does one thing better than anyone else I know: He invents whole methods of fishing and then refines them more quickly than those of us who follow in his footsteps. So that by the time we catch up to where he was, he's well onto something else.

Perhaps Pin's greatest contribution to night fishing was his introducing the rest of us to the Gartside Gurgler, invented by Jack Gartside. It is a segmented foam fly, featuring rubber legs fore and aft, and no shortage of marabou. With its body of foam, it lands with a soft plop on the water—a sound unlike any other night fly. And the propensity of trout to quickly hit this fly indicates that the sound of its landing is as important to this fly, and maybe all other night flies, as any other attribute.

Pin's tinkering nature wouldn't stop there, and the last time we fished he'd taken to fishing a number of Gurgler mutations while I continued to happily fish the same old Gurglers to the same old spots. But it was the introduction of the Gurgler that was a watershed moment on our local night-fishing culture which, like so much of fly fishing—particularly streamer fishing—was undergoing

The proof of a good night is written in foam. The Gurgler has changed not only the flies we fish at night, but also the way we fish them. Instead of the old heave and hope, anglers now fish the river from a variety of angles and make targeted casts in and around cover, working the river as they would during the day.
JOSH GREENBERG

an unprecedented specificity to its practice, the patterns of yore quickly being replaced or altered by not only new schools of thought, but also the introduction of the infinite variety of synthetic materials. There was the Gurgler, and then the Morrish Mouse, which features the head of a Gurgler and the rough-hewn deer-hair body of a standard mouse. There were articulated flies galore, and even triple articulated flies! But to my knowledge, Picket Pin was among the first to bring the Gurgler to the world of Michigan night fishing.

It was, in fact, the last time we fished that Pin introduced yet another new fly—a wet fly. After a good fish exploded on my Gurgler, Pin hurriedly said, "Try this, try this," and handed me a fly I won't name. He instructed me to cross the river, and to cast it up and across and "make it slither with the rod tip."

"You'll feel a tap-tap," he said, and I heard a smile in his voice. "They like that fly."
I felt a tap-tap . . .

≈

Mousing is as rife with mythology as is Hex fishing. Here are some of the absolutes I've heard through the years:

1. It's never good in the full moon.
2. It's never good in the mist.
3. It's never good when the air temperature is under sixty degrees.
4. It's never good in high water.
5. It's never good before the Hex.

Sure, it's easy to design the perfect night-fishing evening. It should be August, with a daytime high in the mid-eighties and a forecasted low of sixty degrees. There should be a light west wind (because we all know that "when the wind is from the east, the fish bite the least"), a thunderstorm safely in the distance. It should be the dark of the moon. The stars should be out. According to author Jim Bashline—who wrote the only tome on night fishing that I know of—one hopes there was a colorful, vibrant sunset. According to Picket Pin, you'll want this to be on a Saturday—a fine, hot Saturday—when all the canoeists have been down the river, partying, taking Jell-O shots, and otherwise making it impossible for a big brown trout to do anything but sit under a logjam, sulking, and wait for nightfall. These are the elements of success, and they converge only a half-dozen days a year—and that's just not enough.

Unless they deal with birth and death, absolutes are merely guidelines. The biggest fish I've caught on the South Branch of the Au Sable was in the full moon on a clear, warm night. The fish ate the #2 Gurgler like it was a beetle, its head a sudden dark triangle in the silver water. It was the prettiest fish I've seen anywhere. I had no camera, I thought, in my pack . . . only to find it later, in the pack.

Yes, sometimes they bite in the moon.

Last year, at our own tongue-in-cheek one-fly competition, the Midnight Derby, the nighttime low dropped to below freezing, a heavy mist covered the water, and the four biggest fish of the night were taken after 1 a.m., when most contestants were back scooping up the remains of the barbecued pork, drinking beer, and standing backward by the campfire.

Yes, sometimes the fish will feed when there's ice in your rod guides and there's mist on the water.

It was a drab September evening with a strong east wind, spitting rain, and a half-moon when I caught one of my largest trout to date. It took a wet fly off a current seam as I contemplated quitting. It was a mean old male fish, with a kype that could swallow my hand and a stomach already darkening with spawning colors. I briefly considered tying it to a logjam and running home for a camera, until I came to my senses.

Even the east wind won't stop 'em.

And it was May 9—my birthday—when my client and I were faced with the aftermath of an early hendrickson spinner fall. It was dusk and the river was dead. I would have soon quit—we'd been on the water for nearly nine hours and caught so many trout, it seemed silly to try for another—but there was water left between us and the bridge. We tied on a Picket Pin and began swinging through the deep holes, and in the corner of a rather nondescript pool, beneath an overhanging cedar, a fish took solidly and thrashed hard into my net—by far the best of the day.

Who knows how early is too early when it comes to night fishing?

Night fishing is about big fish—that is what drives a normal angler to go to the dark side. If you want to see one of these fish, there is often only one way, and that is after dark. A big Midwestern brown, at least in the warmer months, is a nocturnal creature. There's a lot of sappiness about how, by catching a fish, we connect to it. And I believe that sap, I really do. I won't go so far as to say that we honor the fish by capturing it. We don't. But we certainly honor it in all the shit we go through at night trying to.

If you fish at night long enough, you will get scared to death by a beaver. In fact, you may hook a beaver, as my friend Michael did, and have it run strong across the river ("big damn fish!") and then scurry up the far bank ("ummm") and up the hill before the hook returns with a patch of hide. You may also hook a muskrat, as my friend Joe did ("big damn fish!"), and drag it ass-backward by the tail. I know a guy who had an unseen heron snag his mouse fly at twilight and take off with all the commotion of one of those old-timey, doomed flying machines. I've seen bats hooked. I've seen friends snagged. I once caught a walleye. These things happen.

You will get lost in the woods. If you don't have a compass, you'll have to either try to retrace your steps or align yourself with a star and walk in as straight a line as possible while avoiding the nagging feeling that you are paralleling the road rather than walking toward it. The northern Michigan woods are unforgiving, but they used to be a lot worse. Now they are positively riddled with two-tracks, though finding a small two-track without the benefit of direction can make for a long night in and of itself.

You'll get scared at night. Or if not scared, at least spooked. Matt and I once left a remote stretch of a remote river because something just didn't feel right. There were coyotes howling all around us, and one of them, I swear, kept saying "Help!" It was convincing enough that I checked the Internet news for a few days afterward to see if anyone had gone missing.

Matt and I had another eerie experience on the South Branch, at Smith Bridge. We were settling in for a very late-night fish because the daytime temperature had nearly reached triple digits, and we figured that, although the river temperatures weren't lethal, the fish wouldn't become active until well after midnight. As we were getting ready, we heard a vehicle go speeding over the high bridge behind us. There was then the unmistakable sound of screeching tires, followed by the crash of metal and glass.

We quickly hopped in my truck and drove up the road, and found an old blue van rolled over on its side. It was clear, from the marks in the road and the soft shoulder, that the van had done more than one flip before it finally found its resting place. We got out and checked the van, but it was empty. Both the driver's side and passenger windows were broken. We called plaintively into the woods. And then, up the hill to my left, I heard the crack of a stick.

"Hey, man," Matt whispered to me. "Whoever it is doesn't want us here."

It was after one in the morning.

"Let's go," I said.

We fished for a few hours and caught them on wet flies. It was after three in the morning when we drove up the road to check on the van. It was gone.

I like a nine-foot six-weight rod for night fishing, with flex down into the hand but not a weak tip. A good night-fishing rod will be a great roll-casting rod, and if you're shopping for a night-fishing rod, or simply pulling one out of your quiver, simply try roll-casting the thing. Whichever one roll-casts the best will perform the best at night, whether you're roll-casting or not. Some very good night fishers will use a seven- or even an eight-weight rod for night fishing. If you're going to err, err on the big side.

The perfect rod, I think, would be a nine-footer with a switch-style handle, allowing for two-handed roll-casting or even some basic Spey techniques. A longer rod would be endlessly ensnared in overhanging branches. But a shorter switch-style rod would work wonders. I don't see this rod being available on the market anytime soon, so I'm thinking about commissioning a rod builder this winter to build one.

Because the flies we're using are big and heavy (even if most of them float), the line choice for night fishing is even more important than the rod. The introduction of several single-hand Spey lines—Rio's Outbound, Scientific Anglers' Titan Taper, and Joan Wulff's Ambush, to name a few—has made casting big flies much easier. These lines feature a twenty- to forty-foot head that quickly tapers to running line. The extra weight of the line not only helps anglers turn the fly over, but also allows the line to control the fly, giving you more accurate casts. They also roll-cast far better than traditional lines, which is important when fishing a narrow, forested stream.

Fly choice is not as critical to mousing as it is to, say, the hendrickson hatch. But it does matter. I've had nights where the fish all wanted the wet fly. Other nights where the Gurgler outperformed everything. There are nights where a giant fly, such as the Morrish Mouse, will work better than a small fly. There are a few basic edicts. The darker the night, the bigger the fly and the slower the presentation. On extremely dark nights, multiple slow swings across the pool with a fly in the three- to five-inch range seem to do best. And you'll want this fly to move some water, or "make a wake," as night fishers say. On moonlit nights, a small black or yellow Gurgler is tough to beat, and fishing it more in the style of a dry fly, with a few twitches thrown in, seems to work better than methodically beating the water.

This summer my friend Matt Haley—our chef at the lodge—and I went night fishing on the South Branch. The moon was three-quarters full and high in the sky. He was using a tiny Gurgler—no longer than two inches—and he was blowing up lots of fish but not getting many hookups. Instead of switching flies, he began twitching the fly instead of letting it swing. It worked. My best guess is that on a bright night the fish can see the fly *too* well and they short-strike it. Giving the fly some animation not only makes it look alive but also, more importantly, makes it appear as though it's trying to get away.

On cold nights, very hot nights, or early or late in the season, I've done better swinging wet flies. The Picket Pin as well as a number of Spey-style flies (tied drab: flat olives, browns, and blacks) have been best. The night Matt and I saw the flipped-over van, it was very hot and we found that a wet fly was more effective than the Gurglers that we intended to fish. A wet-fly imitation seems to work best on nights when you'd expect the fish to be lethargic—when it is very cold, or very hot.

What exactly are we imitating? Well, we call it mousing, and I'm sure that fish do eat mice at night. I've seen mice on the water at night, but I've seen a lot more frogs. So it's here that I have to confess that I kept a fish on the South Branch a few winters ago. I was running a small trap line with one of our guides there in the depths of winter. The trap was set far up in a muck flat next to an undercut bank beside a muskrat den, and it was so cold that we had to bring axes to cut a hole in the shelf ice along the river to set our traps. I was excited upon returning the next day to find the trap sprung. I was less excited to see that I'd caught a nice, nineteen-inch brown trout, which the trap had quickly dispatched. I took the fish home—it was out of season, but I don't think anyone would blame me—and cut it open.

It was full of frogs. There were at least a half-dozen in there, some looking relatively new.

This was in early January, and considering the giant muck flat I'd caught the fish from, I could only fathom that the fish was rooting the sleeping frogs from the muck and eating them. I don't know. But as I don't keep trout, I have little proof that this wasn't an anomaly. I do know that walking a riverbank in the summer, you kick a lot more frogs in the water than you do mice. And I also know that many of the fish that we catch are along those soft mucky, weedy banks. While I've rarely gone to an outright frog imitation, I don't think it would be foolish to do so. But it seems that in night fishing attraction trumps imitation, and a Gurgler suggests a frog more than it suggests anything else.

More frog evidence.
JON RAY

The most common method of night fishing is to wade down the river, letting your fly swing across and below you. One of the tenets of night fishing Pin preaches is to present your fly *broadside* to the fish, or, in other words, perpendicular to the current. This, he says, will result not only in more takes, but in more hookups as well. This seems to be true, for the most part, though my adventures in swinging flies for steelhead suggest that perhaps the problem is that most folks set the hook upon feeling a take instead of letting the fish take it themselves. Either way, I'll stick with Pin's dictum. To present the fly in this manner, you can't just wade down the river casting. Instead, you have to think your way down the river. Because of this—and for safety reasons—it's best to have a pretty fair sense of what the river looks like in the daytime before you go there at night.

How you position yourself in a run is critical to how many trout you'll take out of it. On many stretches of our river, a fast deep bend will be shallow and bumpy on the far *outside* of the bend, while the inside will be deep, sandy, and strewn with logs. This is important. In this sample pool, any decent brown will be on the inside bank, not the outside, and so you have to either wade to the far side of the pool and cast back to the inside, or stand way to the inside and lead your fly from the middle of the pool toward your side of the river with your rod tip. You can also exert a lot of control on your swing by throwing downstream mends to carry the fly at a proper right-angle to the current. In a strong bend pool, this may require an exaggerated downstream mend that nearly puts the line onto the bank. The fly will follow the line, and the extra two feet of swing might make the difference in your night.

Another situation that warrants special mention is the water behind a logjam, especially a big logjam with good depth nearby. Trout love these spots at night, but approaching them from upstream is impossible (unless you can throw a good thirty-foot curve cast in the dark—I can't). Instead, wade down past the jam and throw the cast up behind it. By lifting the rod tip while simultaneously pulling line with your line hand, you'll create a slow wake on the water as the fly swims back toward you, head first. This technique is great for bright nights, when the fish sometimes prefer a fly fished with something resembling a dead drift . . . and are also sitting in spots where they feel comfortable, and offer a bit of shade.

≈

Finding your own beat for night fishing is an adventure in and of itself. Most people go to the deepest hole they can think of. That's not a bad option, but there are better characteristics than depth alone. Our trout move at night—sometimes up to a mile. One South Branch fish, currently tagged as part of an ongoing telemetry study, left its logjam every night at 10 p.m. this summer, went upstream two hundred yards, sat in thigh-deep water, presumably fed, and then, by morning, was back under the same logjam. Another fish, on the Main Branch, dropped back an even longer distance at dusk, sat under an old bridge, and returned to its upstream lair by dawn. Fish move into feeding spots, so finding a feeding spot, rather than a holding spot, is essential. In other words, think not of a good deep pool, but a series of them.

Consider a stretch of water that has several big logjams and a couple hundred yards of slow, thigh- to chest-deep water, with decent cover nearby. Look for where the springs and feeder streams enter the main river. In other words, don't get sucked into the trap of only fishing one or two big pools.

There's one particular spot that I'm thinking of on the South Branch that looks about as productive as a swimming pool. It's also one of the most reliable night spots on the river. Here the river tails out after a mile of slow, loggy flow into a wide sand flat. River right is a weed bed/muck bank. River left is another weed bed and a single small logjam. Below this spot, the river bends and enters several miles of fast water. It's a transition point between two very different types of river. And for some reason, the fish move in there. They aren't there during the day—in fact, I've seen this area surveyed with electroshocking equipment—but they are in there at night. When I fished it with Picket Pin a few years ago, he wouldn't leave until he'd caught a fish there. And after dozens of casts, he did. And after that, he caught another. It was almost as if they were moving into the spot as he was casting to it. And, perhaps they were.

You can literally beat a spot to death night fishing and then, suddenly, catch a fish. I'm not sure what triggers a trout to suddenly eat a fly after ten minutes of not doing so. I'm beginning to wonder if this has more to do with the transient nature of night trout than quirks in their feeding habits.

On the main stream of the Au Sable, between the lodge and Wakeley Bridge, there's an old earthen dock that is one of our must-hit spots on a night-fishing float. It's not deep, but it has a good slow flow and nice cover, as well as a few springs that enter the river upstream of it. I was disappointed to learn that a recent electroshocking survey there only uncovered a single seventeen-inch fish under the dock. This past summer, when the survey was conducted, we had clients catch two fish over twenty inches right at the dock. Clearly, this is a spot the fish move into.

A few years back, I had the pleasure of floating Geoff and his son Robert. This was a makeup float. I'd taken them once the summer before, and it had been very cold (it was late September, which is a bit late for consistent mousing). While we'd caught a few small fish after dark, it fell short of expectations (more mine than theirs, I think). The night of the redemptive float was much different. It was August. The moon was dark. The daytime highs had reached nearly ninety degrees, and the water temperature was sixty-five when we started. Perfect.

"This will make up for the last one," I promised.

It didn't. We went almost fishless for the entire stretch of water I consider the Au Sable's Miracle Mile—a conglomerate of solid water with great depth and lots of consistent feeding spots. I only had a few cards left in the deck—it was after midnight and we were running out of water—and the strongest one was the earthen dock. We pulled up alongside it in the riverboat and I decided to drop anchor and walk the boat through the short run, with Robert in the front, casting at the dock.

"Cast at the dock and let it swing through," I said. I flickered my soft light so he could see the distance. The cheap $5 lights *without* the LED, held close to the water and flashed quickly, seem to have no effect on a fish.

Robert began casting, and I began pushing the boat closer and closer to the dock until his fly touched the grass. Perfect. Sometimes it's easier to gauge distance by moving yourself rather than letting out line. We worked that run, which is no more than fifteen feet, for as long as I hope to ever work another run. It was boring. I think even Robert thought it was boring. I'll bet we made twenty casts before I moved the boat down a foot—which means we made about a hundred casts into that spot before a nineteen-inch fish clobbered his fly and made not only that trip, but the previous trip as well.

I think a lot about that night, not only because of our success, but also because we'd cast the same fly in the same spot for so long. Did my flashlight spook the fish and did it take that long for the fish to recover? Did the fish get sick of the intruding fly and finally decide to smash it? Did the fish get drawn

Keeping a trout in or near the water for the camera makes for a great picture and a healthier fish.
JON RAY

out from the cover by the repeated splashing of the fly? Or did the fish just happen to move into that spot at just the right time?

I once stood atop a bridge with a 150-lumen flashlight and shone it on a brown trout between a friend's casts. The fish took within seconds of me turning off the light. It *might* have been the flashlight. But probably not.

The fish might have gotten sick of the fly and killed it.

Or, relatedly, the fish could have been under the dock, growing more and more curious as to what kept falling off the dock and swimming across the river.

But I think that on that perfect night, the trout were just late in leaving their cover. All those great spots we'd fished with hardly a swirl. All those spots that year after year had a trout that would take a big fly. It seems to me that it's not only that the fish weren't on the feed, they might not have even left their hiding spots.

A few weeks after my float with Robert and Geoff, another guide and I were out on a night float with our clients. It was a perfect night again except for a full moon, and aside from a brief flurry of activity just after sunset with smaller fish, the mousing was dead for hours. And hours. And then, at about 2 a.m., the river lit up. The moon had not set. The wind had not shifted. It was, in fact, windless. Aside from the temperature's slow, steady drop, nothing had changed. But between two boats, separated by several hundred yards, we reported the exact same experience. At 2 a.m., the fish were feeding. And it was great.

Which brings me back to the Midnight Derby . . . or really the night before the derby. I'd auctioned off a trip that night for a fund-raising event, and I was considering canceling the trip and rescheduling it. The overnight low was to be below forty, and perhaps below freezing in the river valley. People were covering their gardens as I drove to the lodge to meet my clients, Rob and Sam. We were going to float a remote stretch of river, the kind of tight, nasty, gnarled water that makes guides thankful for the off-season. This was a night-fishing trip and a night-fishing trip only. I knew the mist would be on the water just after dark, and I'd always been taught that the fishing sucks in the mist. My own experience had proven this to myself. In fact, after a slow stretch of night fishing, it's common for us to turn on our lights, see mist, and say, "Well, no wonder it started sucking. There's mist."

But when I arrived at the lodge, I saw Rob and Sam dressed to the hilt, smiling and innocent—well, there was no way to cancel the trip. They were going to Disney World. I was driving.

"Bring your winter hat and gloves?" I said.

"Yep!"

On the way to the river, I hatched our plan.

"Our best fishing is going to be just after dark," I said. "So we're going to fish the daylight for a bit and then paddle all the way down to the best hole I know of down there. I want to be ready to go the second it's dark. And then we'll just fish until the fish quit."

It went according to plan for a few hours. And then, as I paddled through sunset, Sam got sick. Real sick. He started puking. In the boat. Out of the boat. By the time it was dark, he was huddled in the middle seat, shivering. They were young guys, in their thirties.

"You all right?" I asked.

"Great."

"You awake?" I asked later.

"Barely."

"Well, don't fall out of the boat," I said.

I considered quitting, but I wasn't sure how. There were a few homes we could pull over at and I could call someone to pick us up. But describing how to get somewhere in northern Michigan can be like teaching someone how to tie a clinch knot over the phone. It would be just as quick to paddle down to the truck. Rob seemed, if not unconcerned for his friend, at least unfazed. As if sudden bouts of upchucking were all a part of a day on the water with Sam.

They didn't say quit. So I didn't say quit either.

We stopped at the head of a large S-bend. A bend left, then a bend right. This was a pool with everything: nice, easy current, huge depth, many different soft-water feeding spots, a tail-out, a dramatic inside bend with plenty of cover. Years ago in this pool, one of our guides had a client hook and lose an enormous fish on an orange sedge (a sporadic, nocturnal caddis that smells of old wood and turpentine between your fingers) after dark, in August. I was behind them, and when I floated by, our guide was saying, as gently as possible, *Next time let him run* to his client, who'd bowed her head in anguish.

If we only had an hour of good fishing, I wanted to have that hour in here.

With Sam now huddled into a black heap that occasionally bobbed with dry heaves, I tied Rob on a Gurgler and we began throwing short casts into the main current, which, in this slow pool, was the best place to fish. If the water is slow, I find fishing the fastest water is best. The inverse holds true for a stretch of fast water. Both these guys were good anglers who I'd floated before, and Rob was doing a good job of keeping the fly on the water through the whole swing. Even letting the fly sit and wave below the boat for an extra second is worth the time it takes.

It was already cold when he caught a trout. It was a big one, and when I turned my light on to net it, I saw there was mist on the water, and I knew our night—which seemingly had just begun—was nearly over.

Except it wasn't.

We kept fishing. By midnight, and with only a few half-hearted splashes at our fly, the temperature was in the mid-thirties, the mist was thick, and it was *dark*. It was so dark, I could hardly see through the fog to the tree line. We were bumping logs, the boat was sliding all over the river ("stitching the river together" is guide-speak for bad boatmanship around here), and even our flashlight beams were dispersed by the mist. Sam's illness had lessened, and he'd taken the front seat.

"All I'm saying is, it's a good thing I'm wearing waders," Rob said from the middle seat where Sam had been sitting, and vomiting.

"Sorry," Sam said.

"You should take Josh's boat to the car wash tonight," Rob said.

And then—in the cold, in the mist—the fish began feeding. Or they moved into their feeding spots. Or those two things are one in the same. The best was a twenty-two-inch fish that destroyed Sam's fly. In close quarters. With air temps in the mid-thirties. On a quiet night. It's that kind of jack-in-the-box experience that you love to dread.

We talked about it on the drive home, and we came to a conclusion that was strengthened the next night at the Midnight Derby: that temperature—even in degrees—is a big part of why fish do what they do. We hypothesized. We rationalized. We figured that on the cold nights, it's not the cold that keeps the fish subdued, but the dropping temperature. On a hot day, it's when the temperature of the

A large brown trout is a lazy trout. This great fish ate on the inside of a bend on the obvious seam between current and dead water. The "rise" was subtle. Though large, this trout was landed in seconds and quickly revived. Overplaying a fish at night not only is bad for the trout, it also decreases the chances of landing it. Use stout tippet and a strong fly rod.
JOSH GREENBERG

water slides into the comfort zone that the fish are ready to feed. On cold nights, it's when the temperature quits sliding—when it bottoms out completely—that the fish are willing to feed. Could it be that on the very coldest nights, the best fishing is after midnight? We wondered. We slept.

The next night, about seventy-five people gathered for the Midnight Derby. They would compete as teams of two. Before dinner, participants took turns casting flies at a distance of sixty feet toward an open mailbox filled with rabbit strips. Hook the rabbit strips, win the rod you're casting. $5 a shot. All proceeds, from the entry fee to the casting contest, benefitted the Pigeon River, a river that had its trout fishery destroyed by a mismanaged private dam. We had some close calls, but no one won the rod.

At 8 p.m. I rang the starting bell, and the people were off. The return time was three in the morning. Participants could fish anywhere in the state provided they returned by the cutoff time. We had awards for the first fish picture, the biggest fish picture, the best picture, and the best fly. Jordan—who works in the shop—caught a nineteen-inch fish just after dark and returned with the picture, taking home a net for first fish. A few fish fed early, just as happened the night before. By midnight, most folks had returned. It was *too cold*. But some were still out there, and by 1 a.m. I began getting text messages from folks still on the river, wondering what the biggest fish reported was, because now—*now*, with their guides freezing and their breath condensing, with mist all over the water, with winter gloves and balaclavas and winter hats and down and fleece—the fish were on the bite.

The winning fish was twenty-two inches, an inch bigger than Picket Pin's team managed. The same size as Sam had caught the night before, and it was caught at 1 a.m. It was when the temperature stopped dropping and held steady at thirty-one degrees.

Could it be that the fishing is better *later* on cold nights? Could it be that hot nights are overrated? What is it about those colorful sunsets anyway? And should we even curse the moon?

Unlike most fishing, the mystery itself is mousing's only rule, and we—lowly, flash-lit subordinates—will be out there because of it. Because at night there's less separating us from what we know and what we imagine. And it's knowing that we don't know what's out there that keeps us trying to find out.

CHAPTER SEVEN

The Chase

I'm camped out in the basement. The door to the tying room is shut. I've got my first beer opened. There are two vises set up at the bench. The first is for commercial flies. The other is for something else entirely. It is surrounded by neatly stacked piles of bucktail and schlappen and various tinsels, mounds of deer hair and ram's wool, boxes of wide-gapped hooks, packages of eyes and cones, spools of lead-free wire. There are two reels out, both with full-sinking lines. A briefcase-size fly box is open in front of me.

In less than an hour, the whole room will be a mess, the orderliness of preparation having been tossed to the winds of late-night creativity. I will call and text friends. I will pause to shoot out random, excited e-mails—a scattershot of bad casts across the virtual interface. I'm on the verge of a veritable streamer-tying extravaganza.

On April 1, 2011, many miles of river opened up to year-round fishing that had never been opened to year-round fishing before. It was a change in regulations that resulted in some of the finest streamer water in the Midwest being opened during some of the finest streamer months of the year: March and April, and October and November.

Like all changes to fishing regulations, it didn't happen overnight. In fact, the new regulations—including the extension of gear restrictions to some seventy miles of trout water in Michigan—were born nearly a decade ago, where, in exchange for letting kids under twelve keep a trout on catch-and-release water, the miles of river receiving special, restrictive regulations could be extended to 212 miles. *Could be.*

For me, the culmination of the ensuing, decade-long argument occurred at one of the series of town-hall meetings that the DNR held across the state in 2010. An older gentleman stood up and lambasted the idea of gear restrictions, somehow blaming the restrictions on both gear and creel limits for what he considered the rotten fishing on the river. Glen Eberly, a well-known historian and conservationist in the area, retaliated succinctly, saying that "if it weren't for that kind of talk, we might still be fishing for grayling" (catches of the once-native grayling were measured in the *hundreds* of pounds).

After intense negotiations and closed-door meetings, and countless trips down to the state capital of Lansing, a set of regulations was agreed upon in December of 2010. In total, there would be 147 miles of gear-restricted water—a far cry from the 212 miles we wanted—and the regulations on the rest of the water would be condensed slightly in the interest of simplification. Somewhat bloodied, jaded, but more or less happy, we took off our nice clothes and began to eye our waders. In only a few short months—April 1 being the start date for the new regulations—there would be new water open to year-round angling (year-round angling being one of the perks of a stretch of river being declared gear-restricted).

Imaginations ran wild on March 31. Here were waters that had not been fished before opening day in decades. Here were fish that had never seen a streamer this early. Here were hungry fish, big fish, that would have the type of innocence one travels across oceans for. Suddenly there was new water, even if it was just the same old water fished during a different time of year. But a good trout river is like that, changing its character with each season, altering the contexts in which we fish. Around here, a twelve-inch brown caught on a Trico in August is a big fish, while that same fish, caught on a streamer in March, is considered a little fish.

Identifying, understanding, and enjoying contexts must be somewhere near the heart of why fly fishers fly fish in the first place. Which is what makes streamer fishing so different. It's that one rare opportunity for us to shed the contexts almost completely, and to cast with the hope of catching the very biggest trout in the river on whatever fly we think will catch it. It's as close as a fly fisher will come to violating his or her own, pleasurable, purgatory.

≈

My first day in the new water was to occur below Mio Dam with my friends Kevin and Matt. But I woke to lightning, and after a few early phone calls, we postponed our trip until noon. The river below Mio was nicely colored at the put-in—the clouds were low. I chose yellow; Matt, olive and white. Kevin reared on the oars and we began firing casts at the very first shelf—that color change where the river faded from gravel into mysteriousness. We flung our flies up into the shallow stuff and stripped them across the drop-off, using our rod trips to impart action and our left hand to collect the line. It is work. If it weren't for the chance of a fish, you'd have to put an ad in the paper to get anyone to do it.

Just downstream, on the south bank, the first tributary dumped in opaque, muddy water. A sign, I suggested dismally, of things to come. But not a minute later, my six-inch yellow fly disappeared, and I set the hook—felt resistance—and then nothing. Matt's fly happened to be swimming along the same path as mine, and the fish exploded on it, flashed, but didn't take. We'd had two strikes from the same fish within seconds. Excited, we frothed the water while Kevin tried to hold us in place. Early-spring fish will return to hit a fly, sometimes. Not that one.

What followed was a nice float down the river. The clouds broke. Fog poured from the shadows, from the melting snow beneath the cedars. The Au Sable below Mio Dam is big and beautiful, a sweeping river of round rocks, some golden or rusty red, and greenish water and cedars and hemlocks. There are few houses, and much of the land is Forest Service. It's a tailwater, but the dam is not a bottom draw, which means the water coming through the dam is hot in the summer and cold in the winter. Trout do not survive well. Those that do grow bigger faster than any river in Michigan. Mio is a paradox. It is generously stocked before the official trout opener (the last Saturday in April), and the stockers provide consistent sport throughout the spring, summer, and fall. It is a great place for beginners.

Yet, it is a river for the trophy hunter. There are probably just as many sixteen-inch fish in this river as there are twenty-inch fish, and just as many twenty-inch fish as twenty-four-inch fish. And they get bigger. If you believe the stories, much bigger. I once sat on a good bend with famed big-fish hunter John Elkins, and he told a story about a fish he named Leroy, which he figured was over thirty inches long. As we sat there, John looked at his watch and said that it was about time old Leroy showed up.

Old Leroy showed up.

Across the wide riffle in front of us, the water exploded with the force of an underwater detonation. From the froth a twelve-inch trout went skipping across the top of the water, more airborne than waterborne, and behind it a wake accelerated, rose into a wave, and broke over the flying trout.

"That's Leroy," John said, as if I couldn't figure that out.

There are big fish down below Mio, and that's why we fish it, to chase what Matt and I that day began to refer to as *The Mio Dream*. And despite the sun, and the first good, hard sweat of the year, and the increasingly dirty water, we were optimistic. Not only had I stayed up all night tying, but Matt came over in the morning and we'd sat out the lightning and tied even more flies. We were, for once, prepared for everything. It seemed that yellow or white would be best in the dirty water, but I switched to black—for wont of not knowing what else to do—and coming off a long, sweeping, fog-filled bend to the left, my rod was pulled sharply. I strip-set, but touched nothing.

"Fish?" Kevin asked.

"Had to be," I said. "Had to be."

Then, three bends in a row, I struck against the taps of rocks. I became less certain if the first was a fish or not. The sun was high and the sky was clear now.

Big-water floats in Michigan offer stunning scenery and the chance at very large trout . . . and the chance of getting skunked. Such trophy hunting requires hundreds of casts with big flies and sinking lines. Rowing acumen and river knowledge is at a premium. It's the difference between floating over that secret midstream trench and fishing it.
GREG BEUERLE

We were casting into the shadows on the right bank for so long that my neck hurt, and I suggested we fish the exposed left bank just to ease the muscles of my contorted body. The river was big enough, and had enough cover, that there could be fish against either bank, we decided. The obvious spots were obvious, but good streamer anglers know that as good as the shadows and outside bends look, it's the inside bends, the submerged cover, the innocuous shallow backwaters and sand bars, that often produce big fish. A big trout is usually a resting trout. Lions spend most of their time *not* hunting. But if you dangle a wounded gazelle in front of them, *any* lion will attack.

I don't know how many times I've seen big fish chase streamers from what seemed to be the wrong spots. To a dry-fly angler, you fish bubble lines, seams, drop-offs, and tail-outs. You stand on the inside of the bend and cast to the outside of the bend. You know, where all the good water is. A streamer angler, though, reads water differently. He sees the river in terms of cover, and velocity, and depth. He casts at the cedar sweeper arching over the deep hole, but he also casts at the loose jumble of logs up in the deep sandy inside of the bend. And he makes both casts with the same sort of optimism.

It's from one of these inside bends that I finally hooked a trout. It took on the second strip. A solid weight. Unmoving. A cold, humongous, lumbering brown trout. The fish levitated, rolled slowly over on the surface, over and over again, toward the middle of the river. I knew fish don't consciously make tactical decisions while hooked, but I also knew that this big trout, like almost all big trout, had done the one thing that might break my heart.

I stood in the bow with my rod high, shocked. They call it buck fever, we'd later joke. The fish rolled. Kevin rowed. The hook pulled out. The cold, humongous brown lumbered downward and disappeared. I squelched the notion to throw my rod javelin-style at it. It was the last trout we moved that day, and as we headed home at dusk, I thought that perhaps I could return the next day, just for an hour, and work that inside bend. I might have a shot. Golfers call this the old birdie on the eighteenth hole. You know, the one that makes you think that everything would be different, if you could just go back and do it again.

There are two basic streamer seasons in Michigan. The first is the spring season, which, depending on who you talk to, extends from January through June, though the best months are usually March, April, and May. Many of the biggest fish of the year are caught during this time, though each fish represents quite a few hours of hard work. Streamer fishing isn't easy.

Spring streamer fishing attracts a different breed of angler. (I almost said "younger," but that wouldn't be entirely true. Let's just say they aren't traditionalists.) Some of these folks *are* big-fish fanatics, meaning their yearlong fishing season is spent chasing big fish across the state: streamers and Hex for the trout, then smallmouth, then salmon, then steelhead, and so on. It's possible to chase hard-pulling fish twelve months a year in Michigan, on big rivers, at river mouths, and on the lakes themselves. It becomes a bit of a drug, this big water/big fly thing. The box of a die-hard Michigan streamer fisher would be at home on a striper beach, or even in the blue water, chasing tuna. The thrill—the chase and attack—are the same.

The fishing itself is very clean. You fish large, well-tied flies on long casts with thin, sinking lines and high-end graphite rods, with reels with good drag systems that you don't need. You stand in the front of a drift boat with polarized shades and $400 rain jackets, and your lips get chapped and your cheeks are burned by a combination of sun and rain. The best streamer anglers are systematic anglers. My buddy Greg is extremely systematic. He thinks his way through every fly purchase, knot (or in his case, swivel), and cast, and this attention to detail results in just a few more fish than the rest of us.

In the spring, the river is usually high and cold and off-color. Our runoff isn't like the runoff of the mountainous states, which can last upward of a month and makes the rivers unfishable. Here, some of the very best streamer fishing is *during* the runoff, and while the majority of fly fishers are bemoaning the high water, streamer anglers are rejoicing. Nothing kills spring streamer fishing like clear water and high skies. It's dark water and cloudy, rainy days that stir the streamer angler.

And the flies! The list, once so simple, has grown exhaustive. The names of these flies are ridiculous, or even profane. Sex Dungeon, Peanut Envy, Butt Monkey, Goat Bunker, Ditch Pig. They are transported in hard plastic waterproof briefcases from drift boat to drift boat. Some folks even keep them sealed in single-serving ziplock bags, like contraband. It's unlikely there's anyone as crazy about their flies as is the hard-core streamer angler. A streamer, unlike a dry, is admired for its look *in* the water, and testing a new streamer offers the same anticipation as does any premiere event. Some—most—are duds. They'll swim on their side or twist, or they won't move correctly, or at all. But a few will pass the test, and either be squirreled away in one person's streamer box, or passed among friends, or tied for production, or farmed out to fly catalogs to be assembled across the ocean.

I break all streamers down into two categories: jigging type and swimming type. The jigging flies are heavily weighted, especially in their front end, either by a cone, weighted eyes, or just wrapped weight. These flies are best fished with

It's not uncommon to have a trout regurgitate the remains of its last meal when hooked. The decomposing head of the consumed brook trout was hooked to the fly as Greg fought this fish, giving us a "what the . . .?" moment. Trout in the spring will take on big meals, and anglers shouldn't be surprised to find that a big fly often gets more looks from trout of all sizes.
GREG BEUERLE

The modern streamer box will have flies of all sizes, colors, weights, and silhouettes.
JOSH GREENBERG

an up-and-down movement of the rod tip, accompanied by a strip. The idea is to create as much vertical movement as possible while holding the fly near a logjam, or shelf, or depression. Jigging-type flies work best in cold water, or clear water.

Swimming-type flies are meant to *move*. They streak through the water, and most often have bullet-heads of bucktail and large glue-on eyes. They are great fun to fish, if only because they look like fish trying to get away. The suspense can cause heart palpitations. You turn the crank, and the huge brown attacks.

You miss a lot of fish while streamer fishing. The most common miss is the old you-can't-have-that routine, in which a sighted fish opens his mouth to bite the fly, and the angler snatches the fly away in an enormous, premature hook-set that is slightly embarrassing. The other miss is the old lost-a-hold-of-my-line, in which the line is dropped at the sight of a big fish—kind of like dropping your pistol in a gunfight—and when you set the hook, the only thing that happens is the line slides through the guides and the fish spits out the fly.

Another problem is that some of the bigger trout can close their mouths so tightly on a fly that you can't pull it through their teeth with the hook-set. The hook never reaches the mouth. Again, the fish spits out the fly. Picket Pin thinks this is the explanation behind why hard strikes don't always result in good hook-ups. I remember one great day in late April—an evening, actually—in which, on my first cast, I caught a beautiful sixteen-inch brown, and then, over the next hour, I moved nearly twenty more. All swirled. All pulled. All escaped. How could this be? I changed flies. I paused on the hook-set. I struck harder. Lighter. I sharpened hooks. Nothing.

The very best streamer anglers are mad about their hooks. One of the very best streamer anglers I know rants and raves about this-or-that hook he's found, or has just come out, and describes them in numbers as if all the numbers of all the hooks are common knowledge. He uses such sharp, big hooks that once, while fishing, he buried a huge Gamakatsu hook in his neck and had to have it surgically removed by a doctor-friend. Some streamer anglers stay up late sharpening their hooks, which makes sense on a hunter-gatherer level. We are hunters after all. Hooks are like arrows. Sharp ones work better.

Sometimes it's not the hooks. With the advent of newer, bigger flies tied on larger, thicker gauge hooks, a stouter rod is required. The case in point troubles me, as it took place on a great fall-streamer year. I hooked multiple trout in the mid-twenty-inch range on big flies in big water. And I lost all of them. There was the monster on the lower Au Sable that came off right at the net. The other, on the lower Manistee, that leapt, and leapt, and dug deep, and shook free.

"I can't figure it out," I told Greg. "I do fine on the small rivers and then I get out here," I said, sweeping my arm to indicate the big river around us, "and I can't hook a thing."

I took immediate action. I bought new hooks. Sharpened them. I made sure the gap was exposed when I tied my flies. I used stiffer tippet. (Was the tippet stretching?) And then I went out and promptly lost two great big fish on the new, sharpened hooks.

Finally I turned my attention to my fly rod. It was a ten-foot seven-weight that I'd bought to alternatively catch steelhead, which it did just fine, and throw streamers. It threw streamers fine, but, I theorized, the tip was too soft to drive home these bigger flies that we used on bigger rivers. Sure, it might hook a few of the smaller fish. But a big trout has a hard, bony mouth. So I went shopping, and ended up with a very stiff nine-foot seven-weight. I won't say that I started landing a lot more fish. I didn't. But I landed just a few more than I had been, and in the streamer game, those few extra fish are what make the memories.

≈

There are so many miles of good streamer water in Michigan that it was natural that the sport would boom here eventually. I think it's fair to say that modern streamer theory was most developed, on a national scale, by Bob Linsenman and Kelly Galloup's book *Modern Streamers for Trophy Trout*—a book in which the Au Sable features prominently. It details a trigger-happy, aggressive approach to fishing streamers. Full-sinking lines. Big, stout rods. And larger flies. The flies are fished on a jerk-strip retrieve. Not only does this cause the fly to accelerate suddenly, but also to pause—or even stop—in the water between strips. With the jerk-strip retrieve, the rod tip imparts the action to the fly, and the line hand merely collects the slack between jerks.

One year hardly anyone fished streamers. The next year . . . everyone did. At first they used the flies described by the authors: Zoo Cougars, Butt Monkeys, Stacked Blonds. But quickly, exponentially, there were new patterns. There were articulated flies by the hundredfold, some of which, like the Circus Peanut and Kraken (both originated by Russ Madden), have become staples. There were flies with lead heads that jigged. Flies tied on jig hooks that jigged better. There were enormous bucktails that kicked and fluttered across the river. There were chartreuse flies. Red flies. Fire Tiger flies. Nothing was off the table. Nothing, it seemed, was too gaudy, too big, too extravagant. We went from flies with two hooks to flies with three hooks. Out west—across the country, in fact—anglers began fishing large streamers for trophy trout. And the flies kept growing with the rapidity of a toddler. Within only a couple of years of the book's publication, there were anglers floating down the Au Sable fishing flies that were eight inches long. Or longer.

I lived on the periphery of this phenomenon, and I was a friend of some of the folks that drove this development. It was a wide-eyed time in fly fishing, perhaps the widest-eyed time in my life. Many of these folks had come to fly fishing because of *the movie*. And now came *the book*, pointing toward newly unlocked doors that led to a fly-fishing experience far different than casting at rising trout at dusk. Drift boats. Back rowing. Giant trout. It was an exciting moment in

High-water streamer fishing is a cult with a legion of bad-weather-loving devotees who don waterproof outfits and chuck big flies toward the banks. It's not pretty, but it's fun.
JOSH GREENBERG

Michigan, a sea-change in perception. Now you had Hydes and ClackaCrafts floating down the Holy Waters, the Mason Tract, and other narrow rivers where, for years, there existed only the skinny Au Sable riverboats. People balked. I balked—and I was one of the young guys!

I wouldn't say it got out of control, but there was some real grumbling. The Au Sable is a fine dry-fly river. In May and June, the trout rise to a plethora of hatches and people patiently stalk very wary, very educated, rising trout. The conflict was obvious. What do you do when you're standing in the middle of the river casting at a rising trout, and a drift boat comes around the bend? The answer is unfortunate: You get out of the way and let the boat stay as far away from the trout as possible. Which led to another sour question: How good is your dry-fly fishing going to be when you're wading downstream, throwing dry flies, and a drift boat floats by you and they're throwing huge streamers?

Not very. Not for the bigger fish anyway.

One fellow came into the shop and cornered me, wondering why he was being hassled on his float down the river (the lodge is a halfway point in the Holy Waters). He was red-faced and urgently angry. It was early June, and the shop was packed. He cast a glance across the shop, and then put his hands on the counter: "Are you guys anti–drift boat?"

I gave him a noncommittal I'm-at-work-right-now answer.

"Because," he said, rearing back, "some of the guys staying here were yelling at me about my boat. Look, I can put my boat in just as tight of space as any of your guides can put their riverboat."

"I doubt that," I said. Not to be pissy, but because a riverboat is three feet wide between its gunnels and a drift boat isn't.

There was a time when it seemed there'd be a defining conflict. And I know that there were some friendships lost over it. How we recreationally use water is a big deal to trout bums. But like most apocalyptical scenarios, the great conflict never came to be. For one, the streamer thing kept evolving, and it evolved away from the smaller water and toward the bigger water. The anglers kept evolving as well, and many of the streamer guys loosened up and brought a dry-fly rod with them and enjoyed that, too. Just as many of the dry-fly guys, like myself, bought a drift boat and started throwing some of these big streamers around.

Modern streamer fishing is about the chase, and perhaps the chase of one fish is just about as exciting as the chase of another. For me, trout are king, and so I remember their chases the best. The chase, and not the hookup, is the climax. It's what haunts the streamer angler before bed. It's what has them at the vise. It's what drives him to row into the wind on a terrible afternoon in February amidst shelf-ice and icebergs and wear out his arm for the only affirmation that matters: the nerve-rattling sight of a big fish in hot pursuit.

≈

A warm day in winter with Greg. This was on the Holy Waters on a January day near forty with crystal clear water and snow on the banks. A midwinter thaw can be the best streamer fishing of the season. The trout moved slowly, so we stripped the fly slowly. But the trout, while lacking the rocket-like aggression of May or October, more than compensated with their sheer determination to kill the fly. Mist over the snow. Mist in the dark corners of the river. Fish in the slack water behind the human-made islands, in the tails of the pools, off the little slack-water jams. They came singly, appearing from nowhere, lazy behind the fly until the line caught the current and the fly with it, and together they accelerated. The first fish we landed was twenty inches. The second was much larger. It appeared from beneath a dock that I'd tried and failed to skip-cast under. It was ungodly huge. Cartoonish, as if an artist had drawn it into the river. It was outside the reality of the river. Expectation didn't paint them that big. It had no intention of turning back, and I couldn't help but get lucky.

A great moment on the river: the flurry that surrounds a streamer hookup in fast water. This fine trout charged from a single isolated log in two feet of water on a freezing day in March.
GREG BEUERLE

Again with Greg. December. A gray, warm day. It was to be the best five minutes of streamer fishing of my life. Minute one involved us hooking a giant. Minute two and three was us landing it, along with photos. Minute four was spent rowing downstream. And at minute five, a fish blasted up from deep water and swiped wide at Greg's streamer and disappeared. That broad yellow flash in the tannic winter water. It was gone. Greg stripped. I stood in the drift boat to better see. The fly hovered. And then, from below it, a big white mouth hurtled upward.

Now the big water, on a day in November when the water was high but not dark, and the fish were on the inside bends. In the sand. Their chases might as well have been onstage. Greg was in the back of the boat, I in the front. The glare was such that he couldn't see the fish following his fly—a big orange male that appeared more curious than hungry. "Fish," I said. "Where?" he said. "Right behind your fly." He said he couldn't see. The rest happened nearly at my feet. The fish began to accelerate. "He's coming for it! Keep stripping!" I yelled. The fly swung down in front of me, not three feet off the bow. "Wait," I said. The fish was on plane with the fly, and without hesitation he engulfed the whole thing, two hooks and all. "Set!" I yelled. We still talk about that one, especially about how I would have yanked the fly away too early if I'd been fishing rather than dictating.

With Alex, on the North Branch. Fishing in early March, when we weren't quite certain the whole river was unthawed. Our cell phones were off to save battery in case the river was frozen solid at some point and we had to call in a rescue team. The fish were on. Oh, were they on. They chased in that early spring no-nonsense way. In the early spring, eating is a life function, like going to the bathroom. You do it now, or else. We floated into a ninety-degree bend with an artificial undercut on the far bank. At the tail-out, a large trout chased fast and ate the fly halfway to the boat. Alex hooked it. The fish stayed put and shook its head three, four, five times. Then the hook pulled out. Alex threw a cast right back in front of the fish and it charged forward and ate the fly again. This time the hook didn't pull free.

Again with Alex, and also with Kyle, above Mio Pond. It was May, and we'd thought *maybe* some hendricksons for the benefit of Kyle, a dry-fly guy. But Alex and I were thinking streamers the whole time. Kyle was at the oars, in the middle of a long soliloquy about the merits of streamer fishing for smallmouth instead of trout, which, he argued, should be caught on a dry fly. He was detailing the

It's never too cold to throw a streamer. Despite the adage that trout won't chase streamers in water under forty degrees, this brown slammed Matt's streamer in thirty-four-degree water temperatures on a day that was only eight degrees. This was the third time we'd seen this particular fish that winter, and as we approached the magic spot, hearts raced against the cold.
JOSH GREENBERG

unbridled enthusiasm of how a smallmouth attacked a swimming fly. Alex was fishing some six-inch-long white thing heavy on the schlappen and bucktail. It was kicking through the water on an inside bend. "Smallmouth just kill it," Kyle said. From nowhere, Alex's fly disappeared in a white flower of water spray from which bloomed a twenty-inch brown trout frozen two feet above the water in a perfect, head-shaking leap. "Not like that they don't!" Alex yelled.

And more. So many more. These memories of the chase may be the taglines to the pictures of us holding the actual trout. Or they may not. They may exist on the shelves of missed opportunity. Or the shelves of flat-out rejection. Those trout that chased a fly for thirty feet before turning back. Or flashed wildly, as if a sword glinting in a river shadow. The fish that levitated to sniff your fly. Or the ones that appeared, quickly, hell-bent on destruction, just as you pulled up your fly to start your next cast. As if damaging your psyche is a part of their job. There is no fish in freshwater that seems as great a personal foil as a big brown trout. We know better than to think that they are toying with us. It is us toying with them.

Right?

≈

Which is why I spend so much time in my basement tweaking some new flies, revisiting old ones, and otherwise preparing for yesterday. Which is the problem all trout anglers face. We are great at solving what stumped us in the past. We don't do as well attempting to correct the future.

This past year's streamer camp occurred in mid-November. Now that Greg and I are parents, our streamer camp date is rigid. A few years earlier, and streamer camp would have encompassed the entire month of November, and any other day that looked good. Now we had these three straight days to fish. I didn't even make it to my vise until the very last evening, and I proceeded to spend a few hours tying four perfect copper streamers. And then, over the next three days, everything was caught on black.

I shouldn't say everything. On the second day I managed a great rainbow less than ten minutes into the float on one of my copper flies.

"Looks like copper today . . . maybe," I said. It wasn't.

And it wasn't the day before either, on the Manistee. We floated a stretch that was new to me, one that Greg sniffed out. It was a clammy, cold day, with highs in the high thirties and the kind of humidity that made you feel like you were fishing in a root cellar. It was exactly the kind of day we wanted. A nasty day of weather is almost always better for streamer fishing in the fall, when the water is typically low and clear. In the spring, during thaw, a bright, sunny, warm day can actually be the best if the water is stained and high. I was shivering before we even launched the boat. The wind cut through me. Perfect.

We started with me fishing, and I turned a few trout on my copper flies. Greg told me that they'd caught a lot of surprise brook trout from this stretch. I could believe it. The river swept wide, with great gravel and rock—not at all like it was upriver. It made me wonder if there wouldn't be some dry-fly fishing here in May. I made a note to return in May, knowing full well that making a note in the winter to do something in the summer was a recipe for heartbreak. It wouldn't happen. But the new water had me excited.

We switched after an hour.

"This would be great steelhead water," I said.

"That's what Andy said," Greg replied.

And it would have been great steelhead water, with its long gravel runs and the deep turns that inevitably crashed into several decades' worth of collected timber, before shallowing out and repeating the process in the opposite direction. We fished as much as we could, though it would be better to have three anglers, two to fish and one to row. Trying to cover all this water yourself was both greedily pleasant and also exhausting. We casted at the cover. At the deep cuts. The inside bends would be wonderful if the water was a foot higher. They were shallow and unprotected now.

On a quintessential streamer run—thigh to chest deep (not bottomless) with submerged cover and a bottom of both gravel and rock—Greg caught a dandy brown. No chase involved. It was a big brown and it fought hard under the boat while I tried to get the anchor to hold. The rest was easy. The fish rolled a few times but only after the net was under it.

And that was the tale of the rest of the day. Greg moved and landed fish. I didn't.

We pulled the boat out after dark. Already we thought about tomorrow.

Matt joined us the next day, which was the day after the 2012 presidential election, an event that he stayed up all night following with patriotic attention. That night the forecast was, to our chagrin, for "plentiful sun." The next morning we woke to clouds and exchanged excited phone calls. We headed to the lower Au Sable, Greg towing my boat and Matt and I following in my truck to run the spot. We dropped off Matt and the boat at the launch, and then drove to the takeout. Greg got pulled over. I cursed, and parked behind the cop car.

The officer exited his vehicle, stared at me, and then marched over to Greg's truck. They conversed. Then the cop came over to my window.

"He says the trailer is yours."

"It is," I said.

"Where's the trailer plate?"

"It has plates," I stammered. "I think they're in my friend's car."

Meaning Matt's car, which was back at the lodge.

It sounded fishy, of course. And I envisioned our day being lost to the law. But the officer let us go, and we finished running the car spot. When we returned to the launch, we found Matt and the same officer talking fishing. Aha!

The officer smiled fondly at the sight of us.

"He says he's got the plates, so if you want to just call those in, I'll tear up the ticket."

Matt joined in, buttery smooth, "He fishes this river all the time—he already told me where to fish, so you guys are in trouble!"

It's going to be a great day, I thought. And within a half hour, a fat rainbow to hand, it seemed so. And it was. The fish were off their spawning beds and on the prowl. They attacked with abandon. Big fish. I mean, *really* big fish. One brown ate a white and olive streamer on a foot-deep flat with no cover in any direction. It was a whale of a trout, and I didn't see it sitting there. I simply saw the white of his mouth and my fly disappear. I set the hook and the fly pulled free. I threw another cast and the fish spooked—a wake going upstream.

Matt had a huge, spray-throwing blow-up on his fly.

Later, I cast a fly toward a logjam and as soon as it landed, a fish that was sitting between me and the fly chased at the fly which, being connected to me, had nowhere to go but directly back at the fish. The two raced toward each other. As the fly neared, the fish opened its mouth and the fly swam right into it. As if the fish had set a trap, somehow, and had been trapped in the process. I set the hook. It was a great, long male brown, the kind of snaky prehistoric hook-jawed fish that would have made my entire streamer camp. The entire streamer year for that matter. And then the hook pulled free. The fish disappeared.

Greg then caught another big brown, his third in the last two days. He was content to row while Matt and I flung streamers around and had more heartbreak. Fish that chased and didn't commit. Fish that flashed and never reappeared. It was all the good things about fly fishing. The pursuit of a moment becoming, in retrospect, the moment itself.

"Next year I'll have nothing but black in my box," Matt said wearily at the end of the day. "I will tie nothing but black streamers. Dozens of them. And they will all look pretty much like what Greg has on. Hopefully better."

≈

When it comes to the great variety of trout flies, there are more one-hit wonders in the streamer box than there are in all the other fly boxes combined. One of the great reasons for this is that people carry just a few of each particular kind of streamer. Most people can rustle up a half-dozen #14 Adams. But hardly anyone has six of any one style, color, and size of streamer. There are several reasons for this, each of them humorously reflective of the enigmatic nature of streamer fishing.

For one, most people don't tie bundles of any one streamer pattern. I don't think it's because a streamer is difficult to duplicate. I think a streamer takes longer to tie than the average human attention span, and so, given all that time and all that free room (streamers are *big*), improvisation is inevitable. This probably isn't a productive form of fly tying. As an example, what if that one streamer that you just lost in a tree was also the one that was working? Was that the one with the wool head, or the craft fur head? Did that one have the shot of yellow marabou in the tail? By the time you get to the vise, the exactitude of the pattern is long gone, and you're left replicating a fly that no longer exists. Which is when you begin improvising, and the killer pattern is lost forever.

Streamer fishing in itself is very unpredictable. I remember a sunny day on the South Branch where all the fish wanted was yellow. And the brighter the better. I had a blast. Fishing yellow is so wonderfully visual, and so damn ineffective, that one good day with yellow can ruin half your season. I tied a pile of yellow flies, and insisted on fishing them on every subsequent outing to the disdain of my friends. I caught nothing, of course. And I *still* have yellow flies in my box as the result of that one great day (though none of these flies are exactly the same pattern, due to the improvisation problem mentioned above).

But perhaps the greatest contributor to the one-hit wonder in streamer fishing is the fly-tying industry, which has attached itself to streamer fly tying like gum to a desk. With the explosion of synthetics, a catalog of fly-tying materials is beginning to resemble a Taco Bell menu: full of the same basic ingredients packaged in new ways. There are now about ten different types of Flashabou, from the old-school sparkly stuff that you can buy in bulk during Christmas, to the new fish-scale stuff that *you must have* in order to tie the Dalai Lama, which is taking Alaska, and the rest of the world, by storm.

Trying to keep up with this product-based innovation is both impossible and expensive. But I have to admit that some of this new stuff works better than some of the old stuff. Innovations in rubber legs alone have changed how we tie with rubber legs. They are no longer just for kicking and creating movement. They are now tied long and down the side of the fly, providing the swimming, shimmery flank of a baitfish. Hackle for dry flies is daunting enough, but there are only so many ways to grow a chicken. It's much easier to extrude plastic in fun shapes and colors, or to make a new sort of rubber leg.

So what makes a great streamer fly? I guess it's a combination of factors. I do best with flies that jig rather than swim. But this is as much a reflection of the water I normally fish (narrow, shallow) as it is a testament to the flies themselves. On small water, a jigging fly has more movement in a smaller space, which tends to equal more trout. A bucktail or other swimming fly requires more holding water because it has almost no natural movement and must be stripped vigorously in order to get it to dart around. This requires space. In other words, on a small stream there is less holding water, and if it takes two feet for your fly to attain the proper depth and movement, you may be retrieving your fly through empty water. In a big river, with greater depth, the fish could be almost anywhere, and a big fly that swims well will attract attention from a greater distance.

But color really, really matters. And three colors stand out to me on our home waters: olive, black, and copper. Because streamers are not typically monochromatic, a few good combinations are olive and white, olive and black, black and tan, black and red, and copper and olive. There are days where we'll be going through the motions, changing flies, and then suddenly tie on a fly, make one cast, and declare that *this is the one*. There's something about the fly that looks right on that particular day. It's not overtly flashy, but it stands out. In clear water, this might be a black fly. In tannic water, copper is so good. On a sunny day, olive is tough to beat.

Natural colors seem to work best in colder water temperatures, though, and in May and June, as well as September and October—when water temperatures have warmed—altering the color spectrum to include light olive, tan, white, yellow, and even chartreuse can be effective. The fish are more aggressive then, and seem to respond to attraction as much as or more so than exact imitation. I remember catching a great brown in late September on a completely chartreuse fly that I'd switched to because nothing else was working, and if I was going to catch nothing, I'd do so with a fly I could watch swim through the water.

Brook trout will chase streamers throughout much of the season, but they become positively vicious in the fall. This beautiful hump-backed male brook trout took an articulated streamer near the end of a September day. Catching such fish on large streamers is the exception rather than the rule, and typical brook trout streamers are small, colorful, and lightweight.
ADOLPH M. GREENBERG

Discussing streamer patterns is almost impossible, if only because the rate of change in streamer flies is astronomical. No sooner does a great-looking fly show up in cyberspace than the inventor himself alters it. It will then appear on another website or YouTube video, tied by a different angler, in a different way, using different materials, and presented as the *exact same fly*.

We are so far removed from the days of the Black Ghost and the Mickey Finn (not that these flies are irrelevant—they're not) that having a sit-down about streamer patterns is like discussing street art. The talk is as much about the artist as it is about the art itself. To return again to the Adams example: An Adams is an Adams. Almost every fly tyer with a year of experience knows the pattern verbatim. But the Circus Peanut in your box might not look like the Circus Peanut in mine. It may use different chenille, different flash, different legs. You may build a head out of a dubbing loop. Or yours might have wool. In the end, neither of our flies are *the* Circus Peanut. But, they're both Circus Peanuts.

It gets confusing.

≈

Which is why, amidst all this big streamer excitement, it's fun to take a day with a four-weight, a floating line, and a small classic streamer with roots dating back *centuries* rather than days, and go brook trout fishing in September and October. These are the classics: the Dace, the Mickey Finn, the Coachman, the Spruce Fly.

This is pure streamer fishing. For many, it is a wood-rod game. And while I don't know if there's a connection, a lot of these classic streamer anglers are upland bird hunters, who consider catching brook trout with streamers in the afternoon to be a fine complement to hunting grouse with bird dogs in the morning.

This is exciting fishing, and while it won't get your pulse racing like the charge of a big brown, you won't throw out your arm trying either. Going two pools without a tap means the fishing is dead. There are days where two or three different fish will attack your streamer on one retrieve. It's nothing special to have fifty fish swipe at your fly. You might only land a dozen. But if you're in need of positive reinforcement, this is the counselor to talk to.

The trout are small and beautiful. I almost said *violent*—they do attack the fly—but given their size, they don't seem violent. More like a small dog that is trying to kill you but can only manage to bite your shoe.

The average size of a brook trout in our waters is about six inches. That's not to say there aren't surprises, and after a day of catching six-inch trout, having a foot-long brookie hammer a small streamer can make you panic and lose control of your line just as easily as a twenty-inch brown could. But the draw is different. The trout are one more beautiful component of the day.

The river in late September is beautiful. The leaves are crisp and starting to turn, but they aren't falling yet. The aspens are golden and the maples are red, the ferns are brown and dying, the river is low and clear. In the morning, there are hard frosts and frozen puddles.

The streamers we fish somehow mirror this landscape. They are bright, colorful, but also slim, wispy. There is a unique pleasure in fishing classic streamers for brook trout. You almost want to say to the trout, "After all these years, you *still* get fooled by a Mickey Finn!" These flies are tied primarily with natural materials, and there are scores of streamer anglers who have boxes of beautiful flies down to a 4X long #12 streamer. In other words, small. They still pine for jungle cock and polar bear, and take true delight in a fine patch of arctic fox tail.

Many of these folks are wonderful fly tyers. Dick Shaw, a longtime lodge guest, ties the finest small streamers I've ever seen—some no larger than many of the nymphs I fish. He made the mistake of opening his box in front of me, and I was able to weasel a half-dozen flies from him. Not to use, but to frame.

≈

I waited for the perfect September conditions—alternating sun and sleet—before lashing my kayak to the top of my truck and the bike to the bike rack, and sliding several rods into my case. Such preparations preclude a full day on the water. This wasn't a pilgrimage, but it wasn't a daily wade either. I was going fishing long enough to lose focus on everything but the fishing.

The weather was perfectly nasty: localized high winds followed by an eerie stillness. I used the kayak to jet between the pools and good runs. I'd then wade downstream a few hundred yards before tromping back for the boat and pushing onward. The river was empty, as it usually is in late September. The land on this stretch of river is private, and I doubted I'd see anyone.

My first few pools produced a few small brook trout. They were sitting in their typical fall spots, around the shallow riffles of this shallow river. They sat in batches in the potholes, behind rocks, or on the deeper sides of the river where the water slowed. When I found one fish, I found three. And given their reckless nature and small stature, I pinched the barb twice to make sure it was crushed. If losing a six-inch trout causes you to blow a fuse, you should be playing golf instead, where outbursts are accepted as being part of the game.

I fished the local version of the Coachman streamer. It's a classic fly: golden pheasant tippet tail, peacock butt, orange thread midsection, peacock thorax. A beard of brown hackle and a wing of white marabou. It's easy to see in the water and easy to cast. I paused after it landed to let it sink and then began stripping as the current grabbed the line. The fly darted quickly and the trout, as diminutive and reckless as kittens, chased and pounced.

I paused for lunch, a cigar. Watched the sleet race eastward and pulled my jacket over me and sat through it, the smoke filling the hood until I choked. I realized that I enjoyed such weather in September and despised it in March. The pleasure in the fall being the cool release from the monotony of summer. And, in March, the opposite desire for that same oft-despised monotony.

When I returned to fishing, I moved little through the big pools though I fished them diligently. You fish the same river long enough, and you'll have memories attached to every logjam and bend. Instead of growing bored with a river, you become more riveted.

The light faded early, but not only because of dusk. A storm moved in and the wind whipped my kayak free of the bank where I'd stashed it. I fell running after it but didn't soak myself.

I retreated to the bank amidst lightning and immediate thunder, then hail. I pulled the kayak onto the land and walked fifty yards from the river and sat in some low trees with the hood of my jacket drawn tight. The wind bent the poplar tops and tore their golden leaves away. The leaves rode the wind to the water. The hail was blueberry-size and it came in sideways. The river was pattered and blowing in waves. The day had dissolved, quite literally, in front of me.

Then it was over—as if I'd awoken suddenly. I stood as the sun blasted through the trees and a few leaves spun down quietly. The forest glowed. The river was calm. The west sky was clear. It was, I thought, an amazing front. The kind of squall that resembled a short, intense illness. When it was over, it took the previous day with it, and I had the sense that I was fishing in the river of tomorrow.

I returned to the kayak, pushed off, and just floated, enjoying the quiet. Deer were moving now, and I spooked a number of them as they moved toward the river to do whatever deer do by the river. The birds set to singing. I pulled over at the head of a long stretch of good water where several old privately owned lodges sat on the ridge, overlooking their sprawls of land. I switched flies—changed to a lightly weighted olive Zonker, thinking it would be equally enticing to a brook trout or a brown trout.

My first fish came from an old beaver dam and it was a large brook trout, nearly twelve inches long. A male, hook-jawed, all sunset and swamp and deep space. A bonus fish. I thought to quit, of course. I always try to find a natural stopping point. Some folks take this to an extreme. One angler I know might quit halfway through a float trip if he thinks the last fish he caught will be the last fish of the day. I can't do that, I thought. The river valley was golden with a fantastic sunset. It couldn't be duplicated. I waded down the middle of it.

The next fish would be the last fish, and it took at the end of a logjam with an exciting rush. A similarly sized shark could do no better. I swore it growled. And I swear it to this day, though it could have been me that growled. I reared back. The hook-set was unnecessary, and the fish bolted hard across the river. Even with a four-weight the fight was easy, even for such a fine fish. I netted it. A surprise brown. Male. I held it in the water. There was no point in taking a picture. Like the day, nothing could be captured that hadn't been already.

Postscript

I was just e-mailing with my friend Alex, reminiscing. I asked if he remembered a particular day in 2009. And he replied:

Sure do, always wished he'd hopped in. He was a dry fly fisherman, though, and knew it could get ugly.

Just before Rusty was to begin chemotherapy (it was late March 2009), Alex and I floated from Burton's Landing to Wakeley Bridge. Rusty's illness was not yet common knowledge, but a bunch of his old friends had traveled to the lodge, in the Board Room there, to be with him and cheer him up before he began the terrible journey. I'd tied some flies, laughed at some jokes, and met Alex at Burton's so we could go fishing.

When we were teenagers, Alex was already employed at the fly shop when Rusty hired me. By 2009 Alex was at the forefront of streamer angling, and he still is. It was a pleasure to float with him on such a sad, nervous day and feel—for a moment—something familial and fishy in all the right ways.

We did really well. I don't remember quite how well, though I remember we were fishing heavy streamers on floating lines with a jigging retrieve—water temperatures were in the thirties—and in every dark spot or pool we'd move a fish. The first trout we landed was over twenty inches. I remember that.

But after the big fish, I remember the almost simultaneous, hypnotizing notion we had. We would *pick up Rusty Gates at his lodge, and float him down the river, pitching streamers at the banks.* We got so damn excited. We were fired up.

"And we won't fish. We just won't even fish. Just sit back and watch. I'll run the boat the whole way," Alex said.

"I'll just sit back here and I won't even fish," I said, repeating Alex. "He said he'd go fishing today. He said he had to with the chemo and everything coming up. He needs that one last day, you know?"

It seemed such a good idea that I couldn't wait to get down to the lodge and positively *drag* him to the river. It was the last time he'd be able to go for months. The chemo would make the rest impossible. He'd be much more comfortable in the boat, we thought. Warmer. He'd not have to wade. Not have to walk back to his truck. We'd take care of everything.

By the time we got the lodge, I was both determined and nervous. I ran up the bank and across the parking lot and up the steps. There were still a few of his friends there. Rusty looked tired, but happy.

"Well?" he said, stretching his arms.

"One like that," I said.

"Have a beer," he said, nodding at the fridge.

I grabbed a beer.

I stood by him. I waited for the conversation to go quiet. And when it did, I asked him if he'd like to join us in the best way I could, and he said no in the best way he could. I thought to push him, but I didn't. I saluted my beer, and he saluted his. I ran down the stairs, across the parking lot, down the bank, and to the boat.

"Is he coming?" Alex asked hopefully.

"No," I said. "He's tired, I guess."

We sort of stood there a moment. And then we went fishing. We killed them.

That night I got an e-mail from Rusty, who'd apparently found a half hour late in the day to go fishing:

Waded the lap. Didn't move shit. Great evening.

—*Gator*

CHAPTER EIGHT

Chrome

The drive to the Pere Marquette River took exactly two hours and twenty-one minutes, faster than normal. Along the way I crossed many trout rivers, almost all of them in the Manistee watershed. My dad, coming from Ohio, crossed many more, including the tributaries of the mighty Muskegon. On our respective journeys we saw hundreds of deer grazing on areas of exposed brown grass. There were flocks of birds now—the very first arrivals. We were looking for another recent arrival: bright spring steelhead.

The steelhead of the Pere Marquette are wild, as are the salmon, and they have been so for many generations. I do not care for catching salmon in the rivers, nor do I like fishing for spawning steelhead. Steelhead fishing for me occurs between late October and mid-March, in the pools and runs that, over the last six years, I've come to know: Burnt Cabin, Deer Lick, Spring Hole, Sand Hole, Chicago, Don King (so named for a clump of posts, each sporting an afro of grass), and many more. I have now fished here often enough to know the pools not only by name, but by memories of the steelhead hooked in them.

The history of the Pere Marquette is one of appropriately shifting identities. For many years it was a river primarily of grayling, with pike in its lower reaches. The native peoples were (and still are) the Ottawa Indians, now known as the Little River Band of Ottawa Indians.

In the mid-1600s, French Jesuit missionary Father Jacques Marquette, also known as Pere Marquette, was deployed by his superiors to the Saint Lawrence waterway. Thus began an amazing journey of manifest destiny, establishing

A day made perfect: a swinging fly stuck in the mouth of a chrome steelhead. Great Lakes Spey flies are usually very colorful and rely heavily on synthetics for color, flash, and movement.
KEVIN FEENSTRA

missions across the Great Lakes region. The local tribes were enamored with Father Marquette, who traipsed about the difficult landscape, recruiting guides who swept him around the Great Lakes over harrowing portages and difficult lake passages, leaving behind a legacy that lives on in place names today.

Marquette traveled through the Sault Sainte Marie and then to Wisconsin. He returned to the Straits of Mackinac and asked for permission from his superiors to find a rumored river: the Mississippi. From the Straits, in two canoes with five voyagers, they went to Green Bay and up the Fox River. After a two-mile portage they entered the Wisconsin River, finally reaching the Mississippi River on June 17, exactly one month after leaving the Straits. From there they traveled 435 miles to the Arkansas River before turning back. Not because they were afraid of the Indians down there, but because many of the Indians wore European trinkets, and Marquette and company feared a run-in with colonists from Spain.

Ever resourceful, trusting, and apparently cajoling, Marquette learned of an easier return route to the Great Lakes via the Illinois River, arriving at present-day

Chicago and portaging there. He and his party spent the winter of 1674 in Chicago, becoming the first Europeans to winter there. In 1675 he attempted to return to Saint Ignace, but a bout of dysentery weakened him, and he died in the modern town of Ludington, Michigan, which is at the mouth of the Pere Marquette River, which was named after him, as were many other places and landmarks in the Great Lakes region. In fact, a look at the old maps makes it seem as though nearly *everything* was named after Marquette, though most have since been renamed.

European development quickly followed on the newly named Pere Marquette River, as it did across northern Michigan, particularly in the 1800s, when two things happened, one after the other. All the trees were cut down, and new fish were imported to substitute for those lost to development and overfishing. The father of these introductions was Fred Mather, an angler and US delegate to the 1880 International Fisheries Exposition in Berlin. After meeting and fishing with Baron Von Behr, the president of the German Fishing Society, Mather arranged for a shipment of brown trout eggs. The eggs were divided between two hatcheries, one in New York and the other in Northville, Michigan. In 1884 the hatched fry were stocked in the Pere Marquette—the first stocking of brown trout in North America (it had already been stocked with brook trout a decade earlier). A year later, 2,500 rainbows from the McCloud River were released into the Pere Marquette in the spring, and by the fall they were a half-foot long and seemed to be prospering.

Anglers were particularly excited about these California fish, and waited out the winter with an expectancy familiar to all fishermen. Unfortunately, by the spring the fish were largely gone, and were soon forgotten. One can only imagine their surprise when those little rainbows returned years later as fully grown, adult steelhead. Now wise to the possibilities of these fish, fisheries managers quickly wanted more of the special trout that would head into the Great Lakes, get really big and fun to catch, and then return to the rivers.

The fishery blossomed and then stalled, apparently due to an invasion of lamprey eels into the Upper Great Lakes through the Welland Ship Canal, which opened in 1932 and allowed the eels to circumvent the Niagara Falls and enter Lake Erie, and from there, the rest of the Great Lakes. The lampreys attach to full-grown fish and bleed them out. They spread rapidly, and were considered a problem by the 1950s. In fact, native lake trout actually became extinct in Lakes Ontario, Erie, Huron, and Michigan. Much of the blame for this extinction was placed on lampreys. Lamprey control began in the 1960s, and by the 1970s return-ing steelhead counts at the weir on the Little Manistee River had increased over 500 percent from the counts of the 1950s, indicating that perhaps lampreys were the culprit.

Lamprey control was widespread across the region, most often in the form of weirs, traps, and lampricide (chemical) treatments targeting the rivers where lamprey spawned, many of which also hosted steelhead runs. The treatments continued through the latter half of the twentieth century. Many people blamed decreasing trout populations and hatches on the chemical treatments, but the US Forest Service deemed the lamprey population under control.

In 2000 the Forest Service installed an electronic grid weir and incorporated fish passage on the Pere Marquette River, near Custer. The idea was that the weak, pulsing charge would disrupt weak-swimming fish such as the lamprey, but not stronger fish such as trout and steelhead. The negative backlash, however, was immediate.

Guides and anglers said the weir was clearly disrupting normal migrations of steelhead in the Pere Marquette. With the Internet now a major conduit for scuttlebutt, the opposition to the weir developed into a virtual roar in chat rooms, forums, and fishing reports. Steve Fraley, co-owner of Baldwin Bait and Tackle, along with many other guides and anglers, lambasted the weir. Not only did the steelhead seem reluctant to head upstream through the weir, out-migrating fish—those returning to the lake after spawning—were noted to be schooled up upstream of the weir. This indicated a major hindrance to both upstream and downstream migrations of fish.

Despite the increasing uproar, the Forest Service operated the weir for nine years. Their studies showed a genuine decrease in sea lamprey larvae with the weir in place, but continued lampricide treatments were needed to effectively control the lamprey population. In 2009 the weir was removed, though the Forest Service made no mention of the unhappy steelhead anglers, nor noted any decrease in the migration of steelhead due to the weir. Guides now report that the steelhead run has been stronger the last two years, and though I've seen no official numbers indicating it has increased, it seems wise to listen to the people who are on the river the most.

≈

It was eight degrees out that night my dad and I met at the hotel, and the following day's high was forecasted to be a smidge over freezing. In my room, I began arranging clothes for the next day: two pairs of socks (one a liner, the other wool), long underwear, fleece pants, wicking shirt, polypropylene shirt, wool sweater, down vest, windbreaker, two sets of fingerless gloves, one set of waterproof mittens, and a fur hat from Mongolia with ear muffs and leather ties to secure it around my chin. You may skimp on the rod, and you may save money on waders, but there is simply no replacement for the right clothing. The hard-asses who suffer to brag do so for reasons that don't interest me. When I dress for the cold, I stick to these materials: 100 percent polyester or polypropylene, wool, down, and Gore-Tex. I'm particularly fond of wool for everything—socks, underwear, sweaters, gloves, and hats. We have not yet improved upon wool and down. They are evolution's coats.

Many of these clothes have been with me for years, earning their stripes in New Zealand when I was outside nearly every day, wet wading through snowstorms, and with nothing to return to at night but a fire and a sleeping bag. They are burnt, ripped, stained, and warm as hell. More than that, I *trust* them.

I only brought one rod because I knew Jeff Hubbard, our guide, would have a boat full. It was a ten-foot seven-weight—an excellent indicator rod. The reel was a golden Fin-Nor, a classic beauty used by the previous owner for bonefish and small tarpon. I figured any reel with those credentials could handle even the brightest, biggest steelhead—and so far this had been true, though it did have a tendency to turn into a block of ice on cold days.

My line was a steelhead indicator line, which meant it didn't become fence wire in the cold. A good steelhead indicator line has a heavy head, which allows it turn over a large indicator, several split shot, and two flies. A good steelhead line also has a long handling line, which allows you to mend the entire line. There are a number of single-handed Spey lines on the market, and they're wonderful for streamers and wets, but because of their long running lines, they don't mend as well as those lines with a specific handling section once you get into the running line portion, which is usually thirty feet into the line itself.

My waders were breathable boot-foot waders. Some folks swear by neoprene in cold weather, which is the same stuff that wetsuits are made from. Neoprene *is* warm, but it is also very clammy once you start sweating, and I also find it tight and uncomfortable. Breathable waders let some moisture escape, and they are also supple, and very comfortable, even if you have to wear more layers of clothing underneath them. The one thing that everybody agrees on is that boot-foot waders are far warmer than stocking-foot waders and are a must for spending cold days waist-deep in cold rivers.

I knew I wouldn't sleep well that night—the anticipation was too great. Not only for myself, but for my dad, who had yet to catch a steelhead. Steelhead caught in the winter are always trophies—every single one of them, but wild ones especially so. The stigma with steelhead, at least around here, is that they are like salmon, and therefore crudely caught on big flies while they are spawning. In fact, steelhead can be caught on simple indicator rigs and by swinging streamers and wet flies that are no heavier than those used for trout. And while steelhead are in the river primarily to spawn, they feed along the way, holding in dark pools, beneath cover, and in random pockets.

Some steelhead have journeyed in the fall, following up the salmon, gorging on eggs and flesh. Others have entered throughout the winter, during small thaws, under the cover of overcast skies. And, now that it was March, the spring fish were adding to the ranks, magnetically drawn to the mouth of the Pere Marquette at Ludington and journeying up this historic river.

Tomorrow morning I hoped to touch one of these fish and briefly connect myself to its journey.

The day was cloudy and cold, and the wind cut through the river valley and us. Thankfully the Pere Marquette is a small river, and is surrounded by hillsides. We slid the boat down an ice slick, and then slid ourselves down after it, me tearing the crotch of my waders—something I didn't notice until later in the day. Jeff rowed us down to the first run, and we set up slowly and deliberately against the cold. It was fifteen degrees. The wind chill was much colder. This day would be a day of indicator fishing. We used ice-fishing bobbers for indicators. Our leaders were straight fifteen-pound monofilament attached to a swivel. My swivel was gold. Jeff grimaced.

"Does it make a difference?" I asked.

"It might," he said with a shrug, and handed me a black swivel.

When it comes to eggs, quantity trumps quality. These eggs are both numerous and well-tied, and represent a variety of colors, any of which might have their day.
ADOLPH M. GREENBERG

From the swivel we attached 3X fluorocarbon, leaving the tag end on the knot unclipped. The split shot (almost always two and large, the AAA size) were attached to this tag end. An overhand knot at the end of the tag prevented the split shot from sliding off.

We fished two flies. Dad had a pair of eggs. I had a bead-head nymph, with an egg behind it. There were roughly twenty inches from swivel to first fly, and from first fly to second fly.

Yarn eggs are comically simple and colorful—nothing more than yarn on a hook. A steelhead probably doesn't eat a bunch of eggs while in the Great Lakes, or the ocean for that matter. But these fish had co-evolved with salmon, and the egg seemed ingrained in their pea brains, similar to how bacon seems ingrained in ours. Fly tyers being fly tyers, there were now a zillion different eggs—clown eggs, nuke eggs, bead-head eggs, cheese eggs, raspberry eggs, sucker eggs, egg clusters, and so on—present in every box of every guide on every coast in Michigan. Most of these would be made with Mcfly Foam and heavy thread, but there would be some eggs made of Antron and others made of ice dub or sparkly chenille. The way Jeff explained the rules, it seemed simple: If the water was dirty, fish a big egg. If the water was clear, fish a small egg. The color of the egg seemed to matter, but it was hard to say exactly how much.

The cast was upstream from my position in the river, toward the head of the run. This was always a roll cast and never an overhead cast. A switch rod would make roll-casting the cumbersome rig surprisingly easy, but the single-hand ten-foot rod wasn't bad.

After the cast landed, Dad and I were instructed to immediately throw a stack mend. Perhaps *mend* is a misnomer, as it implies a lifting of the line with a rod tip. In fact, the stack mend is a very bad roll cast that moves the line and indicator upstream of the flies. The indicator could and should leave the water with the stack mend. The flies should not. Relocating the indicator upstream allows the flies a moment to sink straight through the slower bottom currents. On the short, deep trenches of the Pere Marquette, the quicker the flies reaches the correct depth, the better.

And what is the correct depth? Answers vary. Perhaps there isn't one right one. But it's probably not as deep as most people think. Steelhead and trout usually move up in the water column to feed, not down. In a pinch I err on the side of fishing extra split shot to get to the appropriate depth quickly, but not necessarily fishing deeper. I usually try to match the depth of the pool with the distance between my indicator and weight, and then add to the distance and number of split shot as I see fit.

The water temperature, Jeff announced, was thirty-three degrees. In other words, cold. There was a bit of uh-oh in his voice. There was less uh-oh in his voice when I hooked a dark male from the top of the run. The fish ran hard but it had been in the river since the fall, and much of the fight had drained from him. We landed him quickly—a nice five-pound fish, the golden nymph in the corner of his hooked jaw.

A fish from the first pool. It seemed an omen.

It was indeed an omen, but I feared it was the wrong kind. I caught it from water my dad had already worked. In the next pool—a lazy bend beneath several towering pines—I switched places with my dad and immediately hooked a fish. It ran quickly across the pool and then down, and I followed it like every trout fisherman does, while every steelhead guide like Jeff admonishes me for allowing this to happen. The handle of the Fin-Nor thumped my left palm and I did the low rod thing, running down the bank, while Jeff ran ahead of me with the net and the old man trotted behind with the camera. It was cold—below twenty degrees—but I was sweating, trying hard to land the fish all the wrong ways. By panicking. Holding the rod in one position. Watching the fish without reacting to it.

"Fresh hen," Jeff said, as it fled the net. "Real fresh hen."

Like the first, this steelhead didn't jump, but it pulled hard, with an unrelenting power that reminded me of a saltwater fish, which in genetic fact it kind of was. There were trout that had fought hard. The trout on the San Juan that tore off on amazingly long-winded runs. A brown on the Au Sable that took me into my backing in the big water so quickly, it seemed impossible. There were fish in New Zealand that were very quick and acrobatic. But there was nothing in freshwater that I'd hooked that compared to a steelhead. Even in these near-freezing water temperatures they seemed too much to handle. Perhaps this was why steelhead anglers spoke in terms of percentages, as in *I went one for five today,* meaning they'd hooked five, but only landed one. Meaning also that the loss of a steelhead was built into the nomenclature. It was an expected part of your day on the river. A coping mechanism, sure, but it worked.

It helped, of course, to have a guide with a big, long-handled net standing below you. Jeff scooped the fish and we spoke in workmanlike whispers as the flies were removed, and the little fish-holding glove was produced. The water numbed the fingers instantly, and crawled up my shirt cuffs. We took pictures against an ambiguous backdrop so no one would know where the fish was caught.

Afterward, Dad fished the head of the run, then Jeff—at our urging—went through the whole pool with a Spey fly and we watched him work around the bend. The snow was deep on the banks still, but there was exposed ground away from the river, particularly around the cedar and hemlock stands, where the snow was captured in the branches and lost back to the sky. This river was far different from the Au Sable, I thought. There was little winter ground-cover in the forest, and the banks were solid and high, and though the area was sandy, it was not nearly to the same magnitude as the headwaters of the Au Sable or Manistee.

Jeff moved nothing, so we moved on.

In steelheading—at least on the smaller rivers—the boat serves as both base camp and vehicle, so we rarely fished from it. On busy days, this river can be full of drift boats like ours, push rowing, sliding around each other, trying to stay out of other people's water. The Pere Marquette is a narrow river, and every year a drift boat or two is swept into a jam and flips. On a float with Jeff the year before, I spotted a silver reel trapped on the bottom of the river. He pulled over and reached up to his shoulder for it, thinking it was a Tibor. It wasn't.

The next pool was a famous steelhead pool, and where I caught my first steelhead ever a few years earlier. The pool is really two deep chutes separated by a small gravel bar. The first chute is the kind of standing blue chop that is tailor-made for an indicator rig. The bottom chute is deep and slow, with an undercut wood structure on the far bank. Below that, the river pinches deeply between two sweeping cedars.

I sat on the edge of the boat and watched my dad work the top of the pool. The second drift was right, the indicator standing on end, and Jeff said, "That should be it," and it was. The bobber dove, the old man set sharply, and a big steelhead boiled the surface and then dug hard for the other side of the river. I ran around with my camera, taking a series of blurred pictures. The secret, niggling motivation behind this trip was for him to finally land a steelhead, which is atop his bucket list of fish, and I was determined to photograph the whole thing, in focus or not.

Then the tippet broke. There is nothing like the loss of a fish that is desperately wanted, and the initial urge is to dive into the water after it. It didn't help that, after the fight was over, the fish leapt to free the hook.

"That's what we call giving you the fin," Jeff said.

I went into my *it's-all-part-of-the-game* speech. Then, within minutes, Dad hooked another from the downstream chute, from that deep pinch between the cedars. I looked up to Jeff's wild yelling in time to see a bright steelhead suspended between the cedars in a silver crescent. Dad fought it well. When the fish headed downstream, he coerced it upstream. When it was upstream, he turned it back toward Jeff. The fish avoided the net and ran toward the near bank, and there was some cussing. Then, with a mad scoop, the fish was netted.

It was a small, perfect buck. Light green on top, with big black spots and a quick streak of blush across its flank. They told me all about it. About how the drift started along the far cover and Dad started walking it down, letting the float extend farther than others do (Jeff's words) and then, at the last second, when it was either tree or fish ("and I thought it was the tree," Jeff admitted), it was fish. The relief was transparent. We shook hands and pantomimed the fight with the fish still in the net. We hoisted it for quick pictures—now in focus—and then released it to the river.

Except for a few populations of summer-run steelhead, most Michigan steelhead fishing begins in the fall, near the tail end of the salmon runs. Some strains of fish run in fall, others don't. During low-water years, there are usually less fall-run steelhead than in high-water years. A single flood can make the difference between a good steelhead winter and a bad one.

In October and November, the upper rivers are filled with fish. There are a few remaining king salmon, the flesh literally rotting from their skeletons, and many dead ones drifting in the backwaters and settling among the silt and leaves on the bottom. There are fewer, but fresher, coho salmon. The brown trout are either spawning or thinking about it. They are aggressive and dark in their spawning colors, and fat with eggs. The lively rainbows and steelhead smolts are also feasting on eggs, jockeying for position behind salmon redds. And among all these trout and salmon, ghostly and rare, are the first fall steelhead of the year.

While the salmon are around, most steelhead are caught on small egg imitations. The water is clear and low in the fall, and pressure is heavy on the river from the many wading anglers trying for salmon. The first cast into a pool is the best cast, and the next cast, and those thereafter, offer diminishing chances of a take. Thin tippets—3X and 4X fluorocarbon—and small indicators are the name of the game. This is the best time of the year to sight fish to steelhead, and though I have

Using a switch rod for indicator fishing for steelhead allows the angler to control the line over multiple currents. This is particularly important on rivers that have small, churning pools, such as the Pere Marquette. Here, Kevin works the obvious seam while guide Jeff Hubbard coaches.
JOSH GREENBERG

done this successfully only a few times, there are guides who catch good numbers of steelhead this way, along with many handsome trout.

As the salmon are flushed from the river, and the brown trout conclude spawning, the rivers empty of people. There are around five months between the end of the salmon run and the beginning of the steelhead spawning season. It's at this point that a growing number of anglers happily string up their Spey rods in preparation for their favorite five months of the year.

Spey fishing hit the country like a fad, but now, half a decade later, the fad appears to be sticking. There were many Great Lakes pioneers who developed the flies and techniques to catch these unique steelhead on the swing. They worked the big waters of the Muskegon and the Manistee, and then went to work solving the riddles of the smaller rivers. The flies they developed are colorful creations heavy on sparkling synthetics and swimmy natural materials like rabbit strips and marabou, yet many rely on traditional materials as well: wood duck and feather wings and jungle cock.

Spey fishing—or streamer fishing for steelhead in general—is not a game of instant gratification or great returns. There are days, Jeff says, where five or six steelhead are hooked on the swing, and there are other days where nothing at all is hooked. To me, an outsider to this game, the charm of Spey fishing is not its utility, or even the odds against its success. Instead, it's the pleasure of the tool, the method of the technique, and its simplicity. Unlike an indicator rig, the Spey angler need only carry a spool of tippet, a small box of flies, and a long rod. There are a variety of casts one can make with a Spey rod. The best Spey anglers in the world can throw casts beyond imagination, some which require many steps. But a few simple casts will suffice.

Up until last year, "the swing," as the gurus call it, wasn't my thing. Years of indicator fishing demonstrated to me that I'm one of those aesthetically devoid people who likes watching the bobber go under. Jeff pushed me both as a guide and then as a friend, taking a day when he should have been fishing alone to fish with me, though he rowed the whole day and made me fish every pool first. And that day we went zero for zero. The big strike-out.

All told, until last year, I'd had exactly one strike on the swing. I'd flipped my fly to the far bank with a simple roll cast, and within a second my line went from a lazy bow to taut, snapped from the water as if by a train. The pull went into my shoulder. I didn't strike—which is *exactly* what you're supposed to not do. But then, why wasn't there a steelhead attached to me?

My second "pull"—to borrow the nomenclature of the real Spey anglers—occurred in the lower, flies-only water of the Pere Marquette. My dad and I had returned for another year of fishing with Jeff and we were on our first day of two. It was a beautiful, dank, late February steelhead day. Cold and just barely above freezing. We'd awoken to an ice storm and the trees were still heavy with it. Dad nymphed the top end while I swung flies through the middle and tail-out. I worked diligently. My snap-T had improved.

The depths of winter aren't hopeless for the angler with designs on catching a steelhead on the swing. It is simple fishing: rod, reel, one fly box, a pair of gloves, and as many good clothes as possible. But the intricacies of swinging flies go beyond the old heave-and-hope stereotype, and the best anglers are the ones that seem to always catch the fish when no one else does.
KEVIN FEENSTRA

Dad and Jeff laughed behind me, and I turned my head. As I did, I *heard* the sizzle of my line leaving the water. It snapped taut with a twang. It felt nothing like the pull of any fish. It wasn't a nibble. It wasn't a wet-fly swinging take. Not the dead stop of a stripping streamer take. It was sharply electric. One good jolt. I struck so hard and quickly that I didn't realize what I'd done until I'd done it.

"Did you just set the hook?" Jeff said.

"Yeah." I would have dug my toe in the sand if I hadn't been standing in the river.

"Greenberg," Jeff moaned. "Steelhead?"

"Yeah," I replied.

"Oh man," he said.

Oh man.

≈

But that wasn't when I became addicted to the swing. And it wasn't the next day either, when, at the eleventh hour of our last day of steelhead fishing for the season, I somehow managed to do everything passably right and land an enormous double-striped male on the swing. It was a glorious fish, and I fought it like a buffoon: "Oh no . . . no, no, no . . . it's . . . don't roll baby, don't roll . . ." We got several pictures. It is a great awe-striking fish. And if my wife ever asks me if there's a fish I'd like a reproduction mount of, it'll be that one. But she won't ask.

No, it wasn't until this past fall that I finally had a day that convinced me that the swing is my thing. On the second day of another annual float I do with Jeff—this time with my friend and former client Kevin Kanger—all three fish we hooked came on swung flies. And here I began to realize why many people are coming to prefer this method. Even after a month and a half, I can still remember

My first steelhead on the swing took a year, but the wait was worth it.
ADOLPH M. GREENBERG

each take. And not just the take, but my thoughts, the surroundings, the river, the lighting. It is not the same with the indicator until after the fish is hooked.

The first pull was on a long, lazy right bend. The river has been scalloped by years of spawning salmon, and the bottom rises onto gravel shelves before dropping into small pothole pockets, each the size of a small garage. Kevin was indicator fishing the lowest drop, where it straightens into a nice, deep pool. I was casting toward the base of the uppermost cedar out of a clump of them, the water deep and dark beneath them. Jeff was kneeling on the bank.

"If I were a cold winter steelhead, that's where I'd be sitting," he said.

And it was. The first swing produced three successive taps, like I'd thrown three quick jabs toward the river.

The second swing produced a tap, and then an empty jolt.

"I didn't strike," I said. "I dunno."

"Cast again," Jeff whispered.

This time, right through the meat of the swing, when the line was bowed like the far flick of an angry cat's tail, the fish took and stayed on. I lifted the hook after a second, and the fish twisted wildly in the depths. It was not much of a fight—a dark fish for November. And the water temperature had dropped eight degrees in the past two days, and that had slowed it down as well. Still it was a great, long male fish, with a mercurial side which, in the new year, would begin to stain red.

The second pull came from a big deep hole named the Frog Pond—a pool with several trenches and gravel bars. Near the end of the pool, casting toward the base of a cedar, the fly got ripped immediately after it hit the water. I tried a different fly and snagged up. At my insistence, Jeff tried as well. Nothing.

The third pull of the day was near the end, in a well known run, where a big house overlooks a long skinny run that crashes into a logjam. I'd fished through the top half of the run which, in low water, is the best. And I just kept fishing. I fished through the jam and was feeling the swinging-for-steelhead vibe so much, I was ready to fish down to the launch and right on through morning. In fact, I was already planning future trips this winter, carefully replacing my intended trap lines with Skagit lines instead.

As the river pinched, I turned to go, and the line went twang and held solid. I set the hook, felt a moment of twist, and the fish was gone. Gone!

≈

It's understandable that more and more trout fly fishers are discovering the joy of swinging flies for steelhead. It's difficult. It's pleasing. It's a purist's pursuit, right down to the need for so little gear. Contrast this with the virtual tackle box that indicator fishing requires, and you have the makings of something that's difficult to master and easy to pursue. In fact, compared to most fly fishing, it's downright cheap.

While I'm certain the high-end switch and Spey rods are worth every penny, I chose a more modest rod that I picked up on sale from Hardy. It's a nice rod, perhaps a bit stiffer than it should be for a small river like the Pere Marquette. I've not swung flies on too many of the larger rivers, but I suppose a more traditional Spey rod of thirteen or so feet might be better. Especially if you know how to use the thing.

Because steelhead are big, powerful fish, most anglers will benefit from a reel with a top-end drag system. There are, of course, dissenters. And many of the more accomplished Spey anglers are using traditional click-and-pawl reels, in which the reel is palmed to apply extra tension to a running fish. Fine. But I enjoy the drag mechanism. The same as I enjoy switching gears on a bike. Expensive rods are nice and I have accumulated too many of them, but the reel is the signature piece in angling. Or should be. These are actual machines that do something. A nice reel—be it with a drag or without—is a beautiful, non-failing device. And whatever reel you choose for steelhead fishing should probably cost as much as or more than the fly rod it's attached to.

Rods and reels are easy. So are tippets. Even the flies are easy if you're just getting started. But the lines are not. Scandi, Skagit, and all those tips! It's a daunting list, and even the most sage advice is really an opinion. On the small rivers, I've more or less copied Hubbard with my rig: running line, Skagit head with an intermediate terminus, and a T-14 tip that sinks very quickly. The goal on a small river is for quick, easy turnover and for the fly to sink very fast so it works the small pothole pools that steelhead like to sit in. But other than that one combination of lines, I'm clueless, and my best advice would be to hire a guide and learn every single thing you can. And *then* hit the Internet and forums and chat rooms and slowly accumulate the right stuff. There is no silver bullet all-in-one *cheap* system out there. Even the Rio "Complete Set" costs $500. To the beginner, having all that gear is probably more harmful than helpful. Rio does offer a basic Spey set, with a nice Scandi head and four tips. And for a person who figures to go once or twice a year, or fish a variety of rivers, it's an inexpensive way to get started.

Jeff enjoying a midwinter afternoon on the Pere Marquette River. A few hours on a cold day are plenty.
JEFF HUBBARD

Swinging flies are fun to tie. From what I can tell, the classic ones are harder and don't work as well. This isn't fact, or really an honest observation. But I've seen a fair number of guide boxes, and they are heavy on flash and light on the married wings.

While I'd never claim fly tying to be as enjoyable as fly fishing, tying the flies that are becoming popular on Midwestern steelhead streams is great fun. Forget sizing hackle and the ten shades of CDC, the magnifying glasses and the feeling, while straining over a #24, that you'd like nothing more than to stand up and punch a hole in the drywall. You are now tying flies for fish that *like* gaudy, outrageous flies.

For a dedicated tyer of trout flies, liberation isn't always immediate. We are a conservative bunch—a rowdy fly provokes in us the same disdain as living in sin does the moral police. It may take several tying sessions and a reassuring friend before you finally push through the barrier between representation and attraction. It did for me. But the end result is complete freedom. A sense that your tying bench is not only no longer safe, but will never be the same again.

After several failed attempts at tying good Spey flies, I realized that I was tying flies as if they'd be stripped through the water instead of swung. A good Spey fly must move with the soft movements of the river, not the rapid jerk of a streamer strip. Many streamers focus on the head shape to produce a kick and flutter during the retrieve—two elements that are impossible to produce under the constant pressure of a fly swinging slowly through the current. The way a fly swims relates to the materials behind the head, which is why Flashabou, aside from its shimmery colors, works so well. It swims. As does rabbit, which undulates in even a slow current. For winter steelhead, it's a tough pattern to top.

The gear for swinging resembles nothing to me if not that of the small-stream angler, and yet they are opposites. One uses a long rod, the other a short rod. One wears sandals and shorts, the other every kind of wool and fleece and Gore-Tex imaginable. One heads to a creek, and one to the river. But the basics are there. A yin for a yang. Travel light. Fuss little. Fish hard.

Last week I traveled to a river known for its lake-run rainbows—what we all call steelhead. Maybe they are, maybe they aren't. To me, they are steelhead. In late fall, a portion of the lake fish run into the river. They are big—the size of steelhead—and I'm told they fight like them as well. I wouldn't know, having never caught one. Which means, for me at least, they are hard to catch. Which sure makes them seem like steelhead.

This is-it-a-steelhead-or-not business is a national phenomenon, something that hasn't made it into the presidential race yet but may one day. There are some anglers on the West Coast who figure that a true steelhead is one that runs out of the ocean and into a freshwater river to spawn. In other words, all the steelhead in the Midwest are nothing but giant lost rainbows. And while no one in the Midwest would argue that the fish on the West Coast *aren't* steelhead, they wouldn't mind recognition of not only the great runs of fish in the Midwest, but also the enormous number of *wild* fish that we have here. In fact, wild steelhead are everywhere in Michigan, as well as Canada and the other Great Lake states.

Who knows what a West Coast angler would think of me calling these inland lake-run rainbows steelhead! But call them that I shall.

I came with my friend Paul, who we call PB, and met another friend, Lance, there. We met on the river actually, Lance and his dog Drake arriving to stand above the pool I was working. We held a terrible conversation involving a lot of yelling, river noise, and me continuously putting my hand behind my ear.

Then I finished working the pool and we spent a few minutes shooting the shit on the bank before Lance invited PB upstream to some promising water. He then instructed me to work downstream to "the old gas line" and then head upriver to fish with them. They left. I started downstream. This river is narrow, swift, and deep. It is difficult to wade, and difficult to fish. It is flashy. It floods. Compared to the Au Sable, it is sterile. The rocks are not slick with algae. There are few water weeds waving in the current or on the sides of the banks. The hatches here in the summer are passable, but not prolific. After trying standard steelhead fare (eggs and nymphs) on previous trips to this river, I brought my new passion for the swung fly to the river with a theory, which pretty much goes something like this: If there aren't a lot of small things in the river, try something big.

This is a fishery with several unknowns, the first being: How many fish come in from the lake? Perhaps this is the golden question. At a recent Christmas party, I cornered the resident DNR fisheries biologist and asked him.

"I don't know," he said.

Well, okay.

But after a few empty swings through a few (maybe) empty pools, the mind begins to contemplate the odds that there's even a steelhead in any of the pools. I mean, if a thousand fish come in from the lake, how many fish is that per pool? It's a long river, one notorious for its serpentine route and the power of the fast water to cut pools everywhere and anywhere. Instead of having too little holding water, it seems to have too much. This hurts morale. Or PFA (Positive Fishing Attitude), as my friend Matt says. What if it is only a hundred fish? In that case, there would only be ten fish per mile, and that number may be skewed by the few basketball-court-size holes around where maybe four or five might take up residence. This would leave me five or six fish per mile, of which I'd be lucky to find one that isn't a yard under the many cut banks and logjams.

I love this river, which is why I return. It is, in spots, nearly as wide as the Pere Marquette. The banks can be high, the river shaded by hemlocks. There are actual standing-water rapids here, and long troughs with good depth and big rocks that seem perfect for swinging flies. The river seems untamed and wild in a way the Au Sable or Pere Marquette is not, in a way that any of the big rivers below the dams can't be.

I worked into a short tight bend, one that seemed to require me to stand well into the middle of the river to hold my fly over the depth. This is the same tactic we use on the PM. I'd originally pictured swinging flies while standing in ankle-deep water on the shallow side of the river. But on a small river, where the depth of a pool may only be a couple yards across, a long swing like that will move the fly too quickly through the holding water. So you stand almost directly above the pocket, and let the line slowly work across the pool below you. It is cold work, standing up to your nuts in a winter river, but that day the air temperature was above freezing, and the water temperature wasn't too bad either.

I began to like the pool—that creeping feeling of confidence. It had a nice, easy riffle feeding it instead of a rapid. There was a bush on the top of it, and some under-water cover there, and what looked to be a clay shelf on the far bank, underneath which I could actually present a fly. The line moved very slowly across the river, ticking bottom only when it hit the still water on the inside of the bend. I stood above the pool and worked down it not by wading, but by making longer casts, switching from a roll cast to the more powerful snap-T, enjoying the spray of the line leaving the water as I started the rod in its final motion back, up, and forward.

Below the bush, I had a pull. A good one.

I cast again, several more times, and I vowed to work back through the run with the indicator rig. Then, several feet down, another pull, then another less than a second later. I thought the fish was hooked, and I raised the rod to nothing.

I cursed.

I tromped over to the bank and grabbed my indicator rod and almost immediately lost my rig. I re-rigged. I lowered my indicator. Nothing.

I returned to the switch rod and a new fly. Nothing.

There was nothing to do but continue. I could feel the short winter day growing shorter. I knew I should head upstream, meet up with PB and Lance, and share a few pools. But I didn't.

I fished through two more pools and skipped two others as the trail went high up on a bluff and then returned to the river, where a small feeder stream entered the run, and here I waded across the easy current. I switched back to the original sculpin, the one that had fooled the fish upstream, and I began swinging down the fast chute where the river met the high bank and had eaten away beneath the clay there.

To my inexperienced eyes, it seemed a good swinging pool. It was three times the size of the small pool upriver where the other fish had been, and the deep tail-out, where the river moved evenly yet slowly between narrowing banks, seemed right. Instead of daydreaming, as I had when I began swinging flies for steelhead, I found the force of experiences past—the electric, ripping jolt; the feel of it in the joints—so tactile even in memory that my focus stayed riveted on the mundane sight of a lime-green line wiggling in the water.

And there it was. Again. That sudden jolt. The yank of the river. And already the fish was trying to run. I lifted the rod with the motion of a man throwing a log over his shoulder. Too hard. Far too hard. My overwrought strike an uncool reaction to the fierceness of the action. The leader broke at some weak point, where it had frayed against the countless logs both above and below the water I'd touched on the small river.

I wasn't excited so much as terrified by my sudden need to properly hook one of these fish. Instead of sitting on the bank to meditate, I charged farther down-river almost immediately. Slipping. Flailing. Rushing toward the gas-line pool that Lance had promised me was "just downriver." I didn't see it. I saw nothing but one great pool after another, and I thought: *This time*. With each pool. Each swing. The banks closed in and night did, too. It began to sleet.

Finally the frenzy didn't wear off so much as I *knew* I had to get the hell back upriver before dark.

I stumbled around the woods, losing the trail and getting momentarily con-fused by two small beaver ponds. I stopped to fish any pool I came to. My confidence was off the charts. I made terrific, blind crossings, nearly losing my footing just so I could stand on the opposite side of the river, to try a swing there because I thought the currents might move the fly better. My mind flew with future plans to return. With flies that needed to be tied and tried. I ran through the woods looking for PB and Lance. Stopped to fish. Ran upriver. Stopped to fish. One cast. Two. Time to move.

They call it the pull of the river.

I know what they mean.

CHAPTER NINE

Fun Not Trout

Eivind Bjorke is from Norway. He is six feet tall, with long blond hair, a full red beard, and a Buddha belly. We call him Bjorke (Bee-york-ee). I knew all about him before I first met him at an airport in New Zealand. Bjorke had brought another guy with him, who's name sounded a lot like ESPN pronounced as a word. The guy didn't speak English and spent the first week giggling to himself. Then one day he caught a train and left to travel New Zealand on his own.

"Who was that guy?" I asked.

"Don't know," Bjorke said. "Some guy who wanted to come to New Zealand. I told him I would take him. He's from Norway. It's fine."

Bjorke is a carpenter and a philosopher, and together he and our mutual friend Kyle, as well as Katy and myself, traveled New Zealand in a series of cars that we bought and subsequently drove to death. We hiked deep into the mountains, and lived beneath tarps, and fished great rivers, and ate instant mashed potatoes.

By the time Bjorke left, we were fast friends. So I was excited when, a few years later back in Michigan, Kyle, who was at the time living in the attic of our pole barn, yelled across the parking lot that Bjorke was coming.

"When?" I yelled back through the open kitchen window.

"August—for the wedding!" Kyle was engaged, though his fiancée didn't live in the attic of the barn with him.

"Great!"

"Well, we better come up with something to do fishing-wise!"

We decided to float the lower Au Sable for smallmouth—figuring the Norwegian might as well see something new—and then motor across the lake to the takeout. I'd been contemplating buying a drift boat for several years, and when one came up for sale with a small outboard, I jumped on it. I guess it's not prudent to buy the first boat that pops up in order to float for a day or two with an old friend, but prudence only goes so far as permission in a marriage, and Katy, who did our taxes, thought it wouldn't be such a bad idea to accrue some business expenses while we could still afford it. So I bought the boat, and Kyle and I hatched a plan that involved a float, an overnight stay at a hotel, and a repeat float the next day.

We should have been more prepared, but Kyle had bought a Ping-Pong table for the pole barn, as well as a stereo system, and so we spent most nights playing Ping-Pong and drinking instead of testing the motor, tying flies, arranging car spots, or booking hotel rooms. By the time Bjorke arrived, we were classically unprepared, and we ended up testing the motor in a garbage can full of water.

"It works fine!" Bjorke announced. We were in no state to know better.

So we went fishing.

We got a hotel room and car spot—each of which took longer than it should have. It wasn't until three in the afternoon that we were rolling the boat down the launch with PVC pipes; this was the same way, Bjorke announced, that the pyramids were built. There were at least fifty people swimming and drinking by the put-in, including one drunk fellow that ended up cutting his leg on a zebra mussel while executing an underwater somersault. The guy clearly needed stitches but he didn't seem to care, and neither did his crew, and frankly, neither did I.

We launched into a warm, humid, hazy summer day. I was on the sticks, Kyle in the back. Bjorke looked ten feet tall up front. The river was wide and clear, flowing over large oval stones, some a striking orange. It is a real river, and simply floating down the middle is not close enough to either bank for two to adequately cover everything. It's best to pick a side and work it. We cast at the trout-looking spots, but also far back into the stagnant backwaters, along the weed edges and the big, dead insides of bends. When I'm fishing a smallmouth river, I have to remind myself often that I'm not fishing for trout, and working hard, fast shelves for smallmouth might catch a fish or two, but it's much better to cast in the slow water below them or along the bank.

I kicked off my sandals and let the old boat water slosh over my bare feet. Shades. Shorts. A fishing shirt. Lanyard. Ball cap. Perfect.

I was orating on the merits of smallmouth when Bjorke hooked a fish. Then *he* began orating on the merits of smallmouth.

"This is a glorious fish," he said, as the bass bucked and skipped across the current. "It pulls *hard*. This is a great game fish, Josh. Junker [Kyle's last name], look at it jump! Camera!"

Kyle fumbled with the video camera as the tall body of the bass caught the current and Bjorke's rod bent.

"They pull *very* hard," he said.

We netted the fish—a plump fifteen-inch bass, slightly better than average for this water, though the average seems to change from year to year. We took several minutes of film with the bass in the water. This was for posterity. To a fly-fishing Norwegian, a smallmouth bass is on the bucket list. Just as an Atlantic salmon is on mine. Never mind that a bass will eat practically everything it can, while the other—while it's in the river, anyway—is meant to eat nothing at all.

This midsummer smallmouth fishing is part of what is known as the WarmWater Tour. Tom Buhr, president of the Au Sable Big Water Preservation Association (ASBWPA), coined the phrase. Tom also began the 70-Degree Pledge, the purpose of which is to encourage catch-and-release anglers from fishing the river when the water temperature is over seventy degrees.

The river below Mio Dam will hold its temperature for days on end. Meaning, if it's seventy degrees at noon, it will likely stay seventy degrees for at least a day, or even a month, depending on the air temperature. This is in stark contrast to the upper Au Sable, which is diurnal and will routinely hit near or at seventy degrees during the heat of the day, only to drop into the low sixties by the next morning. The upper Au Sable—meaning almost anywhere above Mio Pond—also benefits from numerous springs and seeps that offer a buffer of cold water along the banks. It is rarely too warm to fish.

The problem the lower Au Sable faces is the same problem that plagues almost every major trout river in the country. Dams. The Au Sable's dams are not bottom-release dams. Our tailwaters aren't the kind with the mysis shrimp and the ten thousand trout per mile. Instead, these are very fertile rivers that are of marginal trout habitat. There is some natural reproduction—more than originally suspected—but not a lot.

The 70-Degree Pledge is in place to help anglers do what's right for the fishery they love. But Tom took it a step further. You can't have all these big-river devotees just standing around with nothing to do all summer! So he began promoting the WarmWater Tour on the ASBWPA website. It helped introduce scores of anglers to the idea that smallmouth aren't simply the second option. In the heat of summer, the bass leave the lakes and head up the cooler rivers to hang out, eat, and otherwise enjoy life. In other words, the dog days of summer are smallmouth days, as opposed to can't-fish-for-trout days, for big-water aficionados.

As a species, smallmouth bass are more foolish than trout. They will chase a streamer to the boat and, most of the time, they'll eat it. They fight very hard, especially the big ones. A big, river smallmouth will double over an eight-weight and give you a sore forearm as fast as a steelhead that weighs twice as much. Their pugnacity alone gives them an audience. They are not great drag pullers, like steelhead. Smallmouth don't have that build. But they are bulldogs, often leaping several times before fighting in a series of careening circles that are both non-threatening and exciting. People curse while fighting steelhead. They laugh when they're fighting smallmouth.

Smallmouth reside in almost every river in Michigan that doesn't have trout. Rather than detail all of them, suffice it to say if you put your finger on a map anywhere in Michigan, you're really close to a good smallmouth river. And that's just the rivers. Michigan is full of lakes, and many of the lakes have smallmouth, including, of course, the Great Lakes and Lake Saint Clair.

Earlier this year I took a trip with noted muskie fly-fishing guide Brian Meszaros on Lake Saint Clair, which may be the best muskie lake in the world. The muskie fishing was so bad, he cut us a half-day rate (we saw only one fish, and it was headed the other way). He said the smallmouth fishing was bad as well, but I thought it was pretty damn good. At times they followed my huge muskie fly on every cast, and some even had the guts to attack it.

Clearly their availability is an explanation for their growing popularity. But it's also their affability. Smallmouth are so affable, even a trout snob can't help but love them.

The smallmouth bass is a popular quarry that, while often willing, has moments of moodiness. Their pluck, along with their ability to thrive in a variety of water types, has raised their stature among fly anglers. Even trout purists seem to enjoy a day "just spent bassin'."
MIKE SCHULTZ

They like cloudy days, but they don't mind sunny ones. They will eat a top-water in the daytime, but not nearly as well as they will at dusk. They will rise to a hatch of flies, but when they do, it's usually not with the selectivity of trout. Smallmouth fishing is a breath of fresh air, as well as a relaxing one. Trout anglers will take great pleasure in throwing streamers at bass rising to an evening spinner fall . . . and catching them. One after another. In a sense, a trout is a stubborn child who only wants *one* thing, and a bass more like an adult who may be working on a book, but is easily tempted by friends to go fishing instead.

Even after saying all that, little things do matter in bass fishing. Tom Buhr and I take an annual float down the lower Au Sable with guide Mike Bachelder. We fish several dams downstream, where the bass population is much greater and the average size smaller.

We began around 3 p.m., when it was just too damn hot for anything other than fishing. We stood in bare feet and cast sinking lines and small flies to the banks and stripped them in quickly with short strips, like tapping in a nail. Favorite flies are the Trick-or-Treat, Zonkers, and Wet Skunks (a traditional Michigan pattern with white legs, white tail, deer-hair wing, and black chenille . . . with a little lead on the body to sink them). It was hot, sweaty fishing. Finally the heat got to us, and Bachelder fired up the jet motor and we just cruised up and down the river to have some wind in our face. Steelhead anglers will grumble—most despise jet boats—but there was no one fishing, or boating for that matter. And the speed and wind felt great.

After dinner we switched to floating lines with heavy heads and began fishing unweighted or slightly weighted streamers retrieved with a long, slow strip that ended with an inch or two of acceleration, as if the fly was about to flee. We used bigger streamers for this type of fishing, up to five inches long, and they were minnow-type flies, Deceivers and Murdich Minnows in white and chartreuse being the most effective.

And at dusk, someone tried a popper. Popper fishing is addictive enough that once the first fish blows up, the other angler has to try popper fishing, too. We used standard balsa-headed poppers with rubber legs and feather tails. Last year the Gurgler, fished with a quick twitch-twitch retrieve, worked as well as the popper, and after dark even managed to catch a surprise walleye ("What the hell is *that*?" I said when it came into the light, eyes like cue balls).

It was a tiring day of fishing. Over the last two years we've landed well over a hundred smallmouth. I once asked Bachelder if anyone ever did this two days in a row, and he shook his head no. I wasn't surprised. It stops just short of boring, at that place where you begin to wonder what *won't* catch a bass.

Still, there have been moments when the fish became selective. Where one angler would start catching all the fish, and the other nothing. The fish have switched to copper. So the other angler switches to copper, and the fishing is back on. These small changes will continue throughout the day, and we exchange little notes—"the last three have been on white"—and change repeatedly to keep up with the smallmouth's whims. In fact, Terry Warrington described a day with Bachelder on this lower water when a huge cloud of mating flying ants hit the river, and the fish were all over them. The bass would not touch a popper, or even a big dry. They wanted ants. Terry happened to have a box of trout flies, and they tied on some flying ants and proceeded to straighten the hook on every single one they had.

It's not exactly Swisher and Richards, but it's something.

It was no different on my float with Junker and Bjorke. That day it was small black streamers. And we tried *everything*. But no. Small black streamers, fished with short strips, which always seems the best retrieve for smallmouth. We caught fish on nothing but. And if we hadn't had a handful of flies, the fishing would have been slower than it was. But it was slow. Around dinnertime we actually pulled over and took a nap on the bank to "wait for the fishing to get better." It was a decidedly New Zealand thing to do.

≈

I have not traveled far for smallmouth in Michigan, but some have. In fact, it is possible to hop in a plane and fly over the flats around Beaver Island—a small but developed island off the northwest shore of the Lower Peninsula, with a year-round population of 650 inhabitants—spooking carp and smallmouth, before settling down and walking unpopulated sand flats. It sounds pristine and somewhat dangerous, not unlike a trip to Central America for permit, minus the permit.

If the stories are to be believed, some of these smallmouth run up to eight pounds, putting them within spitting distance of the nine-and-a-quarter-pound state record.

That's a lot of smallmouth.

The smallmouth is ubiquitous. Certainly there are places where you stop, stare, and declare: "Now this looks like smallmouth water." But there are many others where the fish just exist, whether they are appreciated or not. More and more, they *are* appreciated. If anything, having a fly shop or guide service spring up around a heretofore unknown river is a type of validation. It says, *not only are there smallmouth in this river (or lake), but we think they're worth something*. In the politics of Michigan conservation, the value of a fish isn't its ability to conjure poetry. It's money. And this is hard to quantify. What is a Michigan smallmouth worth? What is a Michigan trout worth? More to the point, what is a smallmouth worth in *this* river (say, a beautiful undeveloped river in the Upper Peninsula) versus *that* river (a river flowing through a business district)? For a threatened smallmouth river, their ubiquity puts individual fisheries at risk. After all, smallmouth are everywhere, right?

To me, the development and promotion of these fisheries is important in establishing measures to protect them, even if those measures aren't yet in existence. It's one more step in the direction of trying to keep freshwater fresh. To some, the Huron River in southeastern Michigan is a polluted ditch. To others, it's their home waters, a place where the white flies hatch in August and the smallmouth rise. Not like trout, but like smallmouth, dammit.

There are now a growing number of anglers who travel around Michigan in search of great smallmouth bass fishing. They might not all go to Beaver Island, but they travel to a river or lake, often hire guides, and otherwise explore a new fishery. The fact that it may be within an hour of their house somehow adds pleasure to the experience, as if they'd discovered a patch of morels in their backyard.

One of my favorite streams is a small little creek about forty-five minutes from my house. It is a dirty little ditch, the banks strewn with canoe trash, the swamps swarming with mosquitoes and deerflies. It is hell to wade so we float it in our Au Sable riverboats. It is possible, in August, to catch a hundred fish during a long day of fishing: smallmouth, largemouth, rock bass, bluegill, and pike.

I "discovered" this creek while following a rumor that there were big rainbows in it. Well, there weren't. But I saw plenty of smallmouth that first trip rising to brown drake duns in the middle of the day (they ate our #2 Gurglers just fine). Since then, I've learned its seasons and patterns just enough to know where I'd like to be if I go there in July, or August, or early September. I know that by mid-September, the fish drop back to their parent lake and the creek is empty. I know, also, that other people know about the creek. And I know some of the people. They don't talk about the creek. And neither do I.

It's become a place, like the lower Au Sable, that I journey to three or four times a year to fish. As I've done this, my fly selection has grown to the point that I now have a separate "smallmouth box" that has a dozen or so flies that I think of as smallmouth flies, my favorite being a fly that Matt tied for me. He'd read about it in a magazine—something about a hot new smallmouth fly. You know the deal. It's nothing but marabou, Krystal Flash, body fur, and a single red hackle at the head.

"Guy probably never even fished it," I said.

Well, the fly works like hell for the smallmouth. And it's been a pretty good night fly for trout also.

The rest of my box is pretty standard. I'm from the easy-is-more school of smallmouth bass flies. Clousers in white and chartreuse, a few rubber leg Woolly Buggers in copper, brown, olive, and black, Matt's fly, some poppers, some Gurglers. Deceivers made of craft fur. Some folks really get into smallmouth flies, and I know that the flies make a difference. If they didn't, the same people wouldn't always win the B.A.S.S. tournaments on ESPN. Picket Pin—a die-hard smallmouth angler—has boxes of smallmouth flies. I mean, suitcases of them. Go to any fly show in the Midwest and you'll see entire businesses for whom the smallmouth is, if not king, a worthy knight. Visit any tying consortium and there'll be folks who are tying flies for smallmouth. Who are talking smallmouth.

Where did this smallmouth craze come from exactly?

While it may be academic, I'd take my consideration of the influence of *Modern Streamers for Trophy Trout* one step further. Not only did the book get a bunch of people fishing streamers for trout, it also got a bunch of people fishing streamers for other fish, namely smallmouth, pike, and muskie. I think this happened for two reasons. The first is logistical: More people had streamer gear and less time to use it on trout streams, so began using it on their local waters. The second reason is experiential: These other fish will knock the stuffing out of a streamer.

Smallmouth fishing became very big around the Midwest. And now fly fishing for muskie is at a sort of high point in popularity. I know it's not *all* because of Bob Linsenman and Kelly Galloup, and there were people fishing for warm-water species with a fly rod long before I was born, but the popularity of it seems directly related to the sudden increase in streamer anglers in the last six years, which seems directly related to *the book*.

These other fish will chase a streamer. And for streamer anglers, it's the chase that counts.

Which is why, along with the boom in synthetic materials, I think the encyclopedia of smallmouth flies, once it's written, could be many hundred pages long, and out of date before it hits the press.

Companies have jumped on the bandwagon, though fly-fishing companies are a little more true in their intent than are, say, the manufacturers of soda pop and kids' toys. When someone builds a fly rod designed specifically for bass, they are not only filling a niche and making some dough, they are also getting a lot of time on the water in the name of "field-testing." I don't own one of these bass rods if only because I have to draw a line somewhere when it comes to fly-rod ownership. For bass, I like medium-action rods in a six- or seven-weight. The slower action allows for better feel on the pick-up or for throwing wind-resistant poppers, which requires a slower casting stroke.

There are only a few bass-specific fly rods, but there are a ton of bass-specific fly lines. In fact, every major line manufacturer offers at least a warm-water-specific taper, and usually a bass taper, or even a smallmouth bass taper. Some of this is good old-fashioned marketing hogwash. But there are some very good bass tapers out there. For big, fast water, I use the Cortland Precision 250-grain sinking line. It is a thicker line, and it doesn't seem to kink up as often as thinner sinking lines do. It is also easier to manage a fat line. For slower water and subsurface presentations, I've copied what the real smallmouth guys use and gone with a Rio Outbound line with a clear, intermediate head. Rio also makes an Outbound Short floating line, which I like best for fishing poppers and Gurglers and other surface flies. The Scientific Anglers Titan taper and the Rio Clouser line are also popular lines for popper fishing.

I prefer fluorocarbon tippets and rarely use anything less than 2X. A short leader is fine for river fishing, though lake fishing may require a leader up to ten feet if the water is clear and the fish flighty.

Every river and lake is different. There are places where indicator fishing with nymphs works, and others where casting baitfish imitations at old docks pilings works, and places where you have to count to twenty with a Type V full-sinking line if you want to catch a bass. I've not fished all these places. I've only read of them, or viewed them on the Internet, or watched a video. It's clear that to someone, this is smallmouth fishing. It's home. And it kicks ass.

Michigan has the distinction of being both a state and a peninsula. Two peninsulas, actually. It has more coastline than any other political subdivision in the world, and is surrounded by Great Lakes on nearly every side (it borders four of the five Great Lakes—only Lake Ontario is excluded). With these credentials, one would expect the state to have a rich history of fly fishing the coastline. It does not. In order to understand the disparity between available coastline and folks fishing the coastline, I think of New Zealand's Lake Taupo.

New Zealand is river rich: There are rivers everywhere, and almost all of them except for the most northerly rivers have excellent trout fishing. But the most famous and most photographed fly-fishing location in all of New Zealand is Lake Taupo, particularly where the diminutive but swift Waitahanui River enters the lake. There anglers from around the world line the incoming current, forming the famous Picket Fence. The Lake Taupo fishery is the backbone of New Zealand's fly-fishing heritage.

But New Zealand's fly-fishing history is intricately tied with that of Great Britain, where loch-style fly fishing has deep roots. America's fly-fishing history is far different. Here the fly was synonymous with the streams of New England, and as the sport spread westward, America's fascination with fly fishing remained overwhelmingly centered on catching trout in streams—particularly in Michigan.

First we fished with wet flies and streamers, then dry flies, then more specific dry flies, then nymphs, then once again streamers, and now with Czech nymph techniques. It's not that any one of these techniques supplanted the others so much as added to them. Michigan anglers became diverse. And as the fruits of that diversity were enjoyed in the form of better fishing memories and longer fishing seasons (for many years the "fly-fishing season" was the last weekend in April through early summer . . . what hell!), the want for even more experimentation led anglers in search of new experiences. It was inevitable that they'd eventually come to what is known affectionately as the Third Coast.

A friend shared this with me, and in memory the image has grown stronger, though perhaps exaggerated. He was standing on a remote shoreline near the Saint Marys Rapids: the home to what Ernest Hemingway declared "the greatest rainbow trout fishing in the world." Well . . . probably not. Anyway, mere miles from the rapids, in the big lake, a rocky point extended far into the water and created a break in the lake currents. My friend was there in late June. Here the waves didn't crash so much as stand on end—a thick, sloppy meeting of currents where bubbles and flotsam gathered. It was an alleyway in the city. A drunk tank in a farm town. The water was turquoise and cold and clear. The clouds were dark yet tattered, some heavy enough to drop small, quick-passing showers.

He said that the water below the cliff appeared bottomless.

Then he looked past the rock point, in all the bubbles and flotsam, and noticed that there were fish rising. In the big lake.

"I couldn't believe it at first," he said.

The fish were fifty yards away and their rises, in the small standing waves, were vicious. They were silver fish and the distance and the height of the vantage didn't detract from their size or speed. Listening to him, I could see the fish. Silver. Moving quickly in small hunting schools, as predatory lake fish do.

A man approached from the house behind my friend. It was the old house among the nicer, newer ones. The old house with the old rowboat upside down on sawhorses. The old man had overalls hanging from one shoulder, and not by way of fashion statement. Rather, a missing latch. His hands comfortably found the overalls and hung by thumbs.

"Cohos," he said. "Oh, it's like that every June out there."

"It is?" my friend asked.

"Well, sometimes it's steelhead," the old man said. He paused, then nodded. "But mostly cohos. When it gets like that, you can't catch them on a spinner. All they want are those goddamn flies."

Even when you're lucky enough to live within a minute of your favorite trout stream, the possibility of new water and new fish cause in me a chain reaction that always seems to begin at the tying vise. On a cool September night with autumn in the wind, it was 2/0 stinger-style hooks and enough Puglisi fibers and Flashabou to dress up a drag queen for Mardi Gras. The flies were three to five inches and tied primarily in white, olive, green, and chartreuse, with nice polished heads and glued-on eyes. They sat on the drying corks looking resplendent and without fail. Each fly increased anticipation. It was the opposite of the sensation experienced by a plane-fearing human the night before an overseas flight.

By the time the flies were finished and the gear was packed in the truck, I needed four fingers of scotch and a cheap cigar to transition to sleep. Vacations for me are short in the summer, and within the next twenty-four hours I'd drive across the state before dawn, spend all morning casting into the backlight of the rising sun, return home, ready my gear, and meet my clients for a night-fishing trip. It wouldn't be poetry in motion, but with enough coffee I probably wouldn't fall asleep either.

The Michigan coho salmon is a fish with both a long and short history. The first coho, or silver, salmon were stocked in the Great Lakes in 1873, but it wasn't until 1966 that this fine sport fish really took hold in the lakes. While they spawn successfully in a number of rivers, according to the Michigan DNR website, there aren't enough streams to produce the number of coho salmon the Great Lakes can handle. In other words, the fishery is managed not by the carrying capacity of their natal streams, but by the carrying capacity of the Great Lakes themselves. To me, this is a backward way of managing a fishery—even a non-native one. To the captain of a charter boat, it's perfect.

The average Great Lakes coho salmon is purported to be eight pounds, though the few I've caught have been a little less than that. In the rivers, they color up nicely, turning a faint red color. At times they can even resemble a steelhead. In the lakes, they are a sleek silver fish that hunts in packs. In September, they crowd the bays near the mouths of their natal rivers, and at that time, with a strong north wind and waves crashing, they are an excellent and reliable fly-rod fish.

The next morning I drove in the dark exhausted, the coffee burning away the taste of scotch and cigar. It was a longer drive than I expected, and by the time I parked near the river, it was a green dawn. As I walked to the river mouth, I passed two spin anglers *leaving* with their morning catch of two cohos and a huge, late silver king hanging from a string hoisted over a shoulder.

"Gotta go to work," the man holding the fish said.

"I don't work 'til later," I said.

"Could get 'em on flies if you got something that looks like a purple squid," the other man said. He shined a light on his lure: a silver spoon with a purple rubber skirt. "They hit this real nice. Or glow stuff works, too, but it hasn't been too good yet. Don't know why."

"Hmm," I said.

"Well . . . they should still be biting for a little longer anyway," the fish-man said.

We parted ways and I slogged through the sand and saw, in the half-light, a dozen anglers already in position, lining the mouth of the stream in classic picket-fence style, though none appeared to be fly fishing. Farther down the beach a few anglers had bait rods standing up, their cork grips buried in the sand.

Being new, a fly fisher, and unfamiliar with the protocol, I crossed the river to the less populated side and walked down the beach fifty or so yards. The waves were two feet high. The bottom was firm, even sand. I walked out into the water and started to cast. It went well at first, and so I waded in a bit deeper. The sky behind me was pale yellow. There were still a few stars out. The water was warmer than the air. I was only thigh deep in the lake, but the taller waves hit me in the chest. It wasn't long before a wave broke over my waders and I remembered the hard way not to put my waders *over* my rain jacket. I was soaked.

I waded back to the beach, removed my rain jacket, and put it on over my waders.

"Dumb, dumb, dumb," I whispered.

I looked around in the growing light. The other anglers. The big lake. It seemed almost impossible that I was doing it right. I cast as far as I could, stripped at a medium pace. Occasionally my line caught in a layer of collected weeds about ten yards from me and I strip-set as if it were a fish. The water was cobalt blue and frothy. Double haul. Wait a few seconds. Strip, strip, strip.

I'd only been fishing a half hour when a silver fish leapt from the top of one of the crests. In the faint light it appeared very much like a surfer bailing on a wave. I lifted and cast at the point where the fish leapt and almost instantly a fish was on. Whether or not it was the same fish I didn't know. It pulled hard and took line, but I didn't let it get away with much. I was using fifteen-pound fluorocarbon, and the combination of stout tippet, seven-weight rod, and tight drag limited the fight's drama to the point that it was just plain fun. I backed out of the water and beached the fish and stooped to examine it.

It was a little silver missile, about twenty-four inches long, with a bright iridescence that was lacking from the taxonomic paintings I'd seen on the Internet. The eyes seemed lifeless to me. I wasn't disappointed by this, but curious. I wondered if the fact of their impending death by spawning had begun to alter the look of even this bright, firm-fleshed fish. Or if the salmon was simply a fish with lifeless eyes, a larger version of a goby or shad or smelt. Or if I wasn't projecting on the fish my personal opinion of what a Pacific salmon was: a single-spawning fish born to die within the confines of the aquatic hourglass. Or all three.

"That's luck. Or easy," I said to myself. "I should drive home right now."

Of course, I didn't.

The rest of the morning was both spellbinding and revelatory. As the sun climbed in the east, its light cut deep into the now-green waves, and I saw the packs of salmon moving through them quickly, so quickly, and more than once I ran several yards while casting in an attempt to put a fly in front of them. Here and there salmon flung themselves into the air as the first fish had. The lake swarmed with salmon. It was unlike anything I'd seen, and I was amazed to still be the only person fly fishing. Several times salmon followed the fly to me and then skipped away. To the north, up the coast, I made out Sleeping Bear Dunes National Lakeshore. Dozens of small boats moved through the waves a hundred yards out, and beyond them, the larger charter boats. It was spectacular.

I changed flies, went with a small bucktail that Bjorke had given me in New Zealand. It was a fly he used for sea trout. It was less than three inches long and composed completely of white and blue bucktail. I tied it on and began casting. After a half hour I changed retrieves, speeding it up to the point that I quickly tired. And that's when a fish much larger than a coho—a huge steelhead or, more likely, a king salmon—appeared in one wave heading toward me, disappeared, and then the line twanged taut and I strip-set.

This was a huge fish and it leapt, though I couldn't see what it was, except big. Over fifteen pounds. Almost certainly a chinook. It ran directly away from me quite unlike the coho. It ran right through my fly line and into my backing, and the big reel churned spray. It ran seemingly beneath the closest boats. I thought to myself, *you will not forget this*. And I haven't.

Then the line went slack and I stripped in, thinking I'd lost the fish, though I hadn't. It was swimming *toward* the shallow water, and though I wanted the fish back on the reel, I had no choice but to keep stripping and stripping. The fish swam within *yards* of me and shook its head and the fly came free. I had gone from 20 feet to 120 feet to 10 feet in under a minute. There was slack piled around me, snagged around my legs, drifting in the sand. I stood there letting it wash into me—the waves, the line, the lost fish.

It was nearly noon before I hooked another fish. The sun was now high and the shore was crowded and the lake had gone flat. The magic wind had died. The air temperature was in the high sixties. I'd since crossed the river once again and was now on the more populated side, standing in line with a dozen other dudes trying not to feel like we were all pissing in a giant urinal.

I didn't know why I'd crossed the river. There were fish over there. In fact, once I stood on the opposite side of the river mouth, I spent my time looking longingly at the peaceful spot I'd left. But I stayed put.

The tone on this north side was jocular and conversational. I didn't speak but I listened and laughed at what I hoped were appropriate times to what I assumed— hoped—were inappropriate jokes. No one made fun of me for fly fishing, except to say, in a helpful tone of voice, that "that sure looks like a lot of work." Most of the guys threw spoons. Some stood there holding their rod, and I assumed they were fishing spawn. No one caught a thing.

And then, after more than an hour on the north side, I caught one. It ate unseen, deep in a pocket off the incoming river current. I'd let the fly sink for what I thought too long, and retrieved it at a pace I thought too slow. The fish ate and I struck. It came twisting out of the dark water. It didn't fight as hard as the first coho, and not nearly as hard as the big fish I'd lost. Still, I was glad for the salmon. I played it as quietly as possible, but the rest of the gang noticed and began clapping with the same sort of that-was-inspirational cadence that you typically hear at sporting events. Even the guys in the boats started pointing and a few clapped as well. It was a surreal end to a surreal day that was, for me, simply a morning before a day of work.

Great Lakes fish are big and pull hard, and they carry the spirit of the Great Lakes in them: cold, defiant, strong. They behave as any other big predatory fish does in big water, with a predilection toward killing and eating other fish. This is thrilling stuff to a trout angler who rarely has the opportunity to see such widespread fish-eating pandemonium occur in freshwater. Racing after seagulls. Running along a beach. Or laying a cast twenty feet in front of a school of silvers that are swimming so fast, it seems no cast leads them too far. These events which are innocuous to the local anglers are something exotic to the rest of us inlanders.

Big water, high wind, and strong fish necessitate the use of big rods, heavy lines, and big reels. These aren't tarpon and don't run like bonefish, but you still want a setup that can put the brakes on a hard-pulling fish, and you also want a reel that doesn't free-spool or lock up when frozen. To me, this does eliminate some of the fine cork-drag systems on the market, at least for cold-weather angling. For midsummer carp fishing or late summer/fall king, coho, or steelhead fishing, this last requirement is unimportant. But for the many cold-weather coastal opportunities—primarily brown trout, steelhead, and lake trout—there is a good chance that you'll be fishing in subfreezing temperatures, and a nice, dependable sealed-drag reel will be worth exactly what it cost you when you finally do hook a fish.

Either by convenience or by choice, I prefer a nine-foot seven-weight rod for the surf. Some prefer an eight-weight. Some a ten-foot rod, or a switch rod. There are worthy arguments for each of these tools. Most would agree, however, that a six-weight is just not enough rod for handling the big fish the Great Lakes are capable of producing. Or for throwing the big flies and heavy lines, or for battling the wind, or any of the many challenges one faces when fishing the coast.

My first foray to the coast involved me wading in far too deep and then proceeding to smack the water on my backcast with almost every attempt. I learned later that you wade to a point where you can comfortably cast and no farther. Wading in deeper will invariably result in a shorter cast, as you simply can't hold as much line off the land and water behind you. Find a spot where you can cast as far as you'd like, comfortably. And then get in a rhythm. For me, this is a roll cast to break the surface tension and work out some slack, followed by a backcast that shoots line and a double haul on my forward cast, followed by me doing my best impression of the Echo Rods logo (picture man spearing invisible mastodon with invisible sword) in the hopes of shooting all my original line out, or even a little extra.

In fact, part of the fun of surf casting is just casting. It's the best kind of practice—better even than casting in the yard. Not only are you casting as far as you can, but you might also catch a fish. My best days on the coast are nothing more than a progressive improvement of casting efficiency and results. There's nothing better than nailing a cast and sending all the line shooting through the guides with such force that it pulls a turn of line from the reel against a tight drag. That's how you know you could have gone farther. So you pull out a few feet, and spend a half hour in search of *that* one cast. And so on.

Almost all surf casting in the Great Lakes involves sinking lines. I prefer the Scientific Anglers Streamer Express line in a 250 or 300 grain. It has a rapidly sinking head and an intermediate running line. Because you're wade fishing, you're presumably standing in shallower water than what you are casting to. The sinking head gets you down deep where you want to be, but the intermediate floating line allows the fly to parallel the bottom on the retrieve. In other words, you're not stripping your fly into the sand toward the end of every retrieve.

The exception to all of this is carp. And despite the fact that carp fishing is at its best when the trout fishing on the Au Sable is at *its* best, I have something of a fetish for carp. It's the southern Ohio in me.

Though, to be fair, the carp in the Great Lakes have little in common with the carp that used to roll in the mud flats of Acton Lake just outside my hometown of Oxford, Ohio. It's not the fish, I guess, but the lake itself. Acton Lake is a gross little lake filled with carp and endlessly circled by vultures. Lake Michigan is a grand blue lake that is one of the largest in the world.

Stepping onto a Lake Michigan carp flat in June *seems* like it should cost you money. As if you are stepping into a remote Bahamian flat, or at least the Keys (not that I've been to either of these places). But the quantity of fish—at times overwhelming—coupled with the relative lack of people, along with the challenge of it and the comfortableness of it (sandals and shorts, two spools of tippet, one box of flies, shades, hat, sunscreen), seems exotic. Put another way, if these were bonefish, there wouldn't be a square foot of sand to stand on.

Carp fishing has been around for years, and its growth in popularity in Michigan has trudged along in the decade and a half that I've lived here. Which is fine with me—I like empty beaches. There are places around the country and even within the state where the carp rise and they can be caught on dry flies imitating everything from mayflies to berries. But in the Traverse City bays they seem to feed almost completely under the surface—at least in my limited experience. The flies I've used range from Hex nymphs to crayfish imitations, to straight-up bonefish flies given to me by friends fortunate enough to have used them.

Because I'm a carp neophyte, I enjoy going to the Traverse City fly shops and playing the part of customer. I end up not only learning something about carp fishing, but I also remember what it feels like to be on the other side of the counter in a fly shop, wondering if you sound stupid asking "How do you know when to set the hook?" and "What sort of leader should I use?"

The fly shop folks have been helpful. In fact, I'd probably be without a carp if I hadn't gone in and asked questions. Being a non-retired working stiff, I get one or

A day on the freshwater flats is one of solitude and what I believe to be a world-class experience. Sure, they are only carp. But they are carp: big, golden, powerful, stingy, and, to my eye, beautiful. Hours go by fast, and often I puzzle at my sudden inability to see into the water only to realize that the sun is setting and the day is done.
JON RAY

two carp trips per season, and usually these come after a full day of work. All told, I probably had four hours on the carp flats this past summer. At that rate, I'd be dead before I learned how to catch them on my own. Your local fly shop survives because the staff helps you catch fish on their watersheds. A box store survives because you didn't buy something from your local fly shop.

It was late May when I sprang free of my local fly shop at lunchtime and headed west. Phone off. Music on. I'd called ahead to the Traverse City shop to get the word, and the word was: a few carp around.

"Enough to make the drive?" I asked. An unfair question.

"Hey, you think there are enough carp around for this guy to drive an hour?" yelled the guy I was talking to.

"Hell yes," said another guy in the background.

"We think so," the first guy said.

Perfect answer.

So I drove. And drove. And then, when I was within five minutes of my target, I decided to head up Mission Peninsula—the long finger of land that divides East Bay and West Bay. My thought was that the turn for Mission Peninsula was *right there,* and I'd be fishing in no time. I knew that there was a lighthouse at the end of the peninsula, and I'd heard there were some nice carp flats there. So I took a turn and headed up the peninsula and drove, and drove, and drove. Well, it turned out that Mission Peninsula was one long middle finger to my carp day. It was beautiful. Vineyards and all that. But I was ready for some carp fishing and I'd grossly underestimated the detour I was taking.

By the time I arrived I had a headache, and was strangely exhausted and panicked. I ran to the lake, crashed into the flats, walked a mile in knee-deep water, saw nothing, literally ran back through the lake, got in my truck, and sped away. I looked like a man who was looking for a bomb, found it, failed to deactivate it, and fled. In trout gear.

It was terrible.

There was no fishing for me that day. The hour and a half my detour had cost me drained the rest of the spotting light from the sky. I drove between several spots I'd seen carp before, but there was nothing to see. It was a miserable afternoon compounded by the Memorial Day weekend traffic, and I was only too glad to escape and make plans to return the following week.

Which I did.

Under the guise of a family trip, my wife, son, and I went to Traverse on a beautiful day in early June. The "word" now was that the carp were in thick, and I couldn't miss seeing them. We stopped at the deli for a sandwich, and the adjoining fly shop for some flies, and then we headed up the coast to a spot where the year before I'd literally been surrounded by carp. It was amazing, like wading in a magnified koi pond, and as we ate our sandwiches at a picnic table overlooking the lake, I could see the carp all over the flats. I played it cool. Took my time. But once I grabbed my fishing crap, I was *gone.*

There is nothing quite like standing in knee-deep water when the carp are in thick. These are big fish, and to my eye, beautiful. There are the dark ones, the golden ones, the tan ones. There are the little ones, and the humongous ones. All of them are chubby and kind of cute, cartoonish and huge. They are the Homer Simpsons of the fish world. But they are smart. These are a fish that can sniff out a bread ball a quarter mile away. They won't play the fool to your hook and feathers, even if you do everything right. A trout has a hard mouth, a carp a soft one. You can pick up broken glass with a glove on and not know the difference.

And to the new carp convert, of which I am one, they do things that are inexplicable, awesome, and frustrating.

There are the ones swimming in the deep water, and the ones swimming in the shallows behind you. There are the slow ones and the fast ones. Some seem to sit motionless despite the fact that you've been plunking your fly on top of them for the last five minutes, thinking that *this* time the bastard will eat it.

Great Lakes carp will come into very shallow water in June and July.
BRIAN PITSER

Carp often travel in schools, and can cover a lot of ground when not actively feeding. Carp are not difficult to see, but polarized shades are still necessary to read the body language of the fish.
JON RAY

That bastard will not.

I stopped to look up and wave to Katy and Holden. She waved back. He appeared to be crying. I didn't have long.

The bottom of the flat is a mixture of sand and a few large rocks. I found a large rock to stand on and waited for a carp to come into range. It wasn't long before they did.

Five of them, coming in hot. The carp in this open water can swim quickly, and I hurriedly arranged myself and tried to fire out a cast. The fish swam past my fly. I picked up and tried again. Two bolted to deeper water. Three kept swimming. I cast again, straight over their backs, and the other three bolted.

It was a familiar situation.

The problem I'd had with carp was twofold. The first was knowing what I should be doing to attract them. Should I strip, or let my fly lay on the bottom? These fish were not swimming on the bottom. Nor were they stopping to feed. They appeared to simply be swimming. If they were feeding, they were feeding on things in the middle of the water column. Which was precisely *not* what any of the carp flies I had were designed to do. In fact, all carp literature I'd read involved tailing carp. Gary LaFontaine had even designed the Bristle Leech, which created a plume of sand on the bottom—a clear sign of a living, edible thing. Perfect carp fodder for carp acting like carp. These carp were acting like cohos.

It was the same situation I'd been in last year, a year where I'd pricked two but had failed to land a carp. I'd stood on a big rock—perhaps this very same rock—and thrown casts to carp that were swimming very quickly and without pause, coming into my radar and leaving it within ten seconds. Sure, there were a few moments of interest, a few follows. There were times where I'd be casting forty feet in front of me, and turn and see a carp less than ten feet behind me.

It was one of those recurring problems that *must* be solved. I stepped off the rock and left the water completely, and stood on the beach and stared out over the flat. I stared and stared and stared. I looked as far to the south as I could, as far to the north as I could. I wasn't sure exactly what I was looking for, just a nonspecific solution to a specific problem.

And then I found it. Far to the north, way up the coast, I saw a black rock. The black rock was moving. Then a second black rock appeared. And another. A tail. Another tail. Those rocks were carp. And those carp were doing something all the others weren't: feeding.

I moved deliberately in that direction, ignoring the urge to cast at the schools of carp swimming past me. I ducked under a low boat dock and then I began to sneak, hunched at the waist, heart ticking in my ears. I got to within forty feet and I waited, still hunched. I tied on the small fly with the little dumbbell eyes because it just seemed like a small-fly day. These were feeding fish, I thought, they'd want a small fly. Whereas I'd spent most of my time up to my thighs in water, now I was only up to my shins. And the fish were shallower than that, in less than a foot of water, swimming very slowly, or stopping, or tipping down, tails up. They were moving just slightly away from me—three of them—and I fired a cast that was about ten feet short. One of the three carp broke free of its pack, came over, and stopped. I stripped my fly once. The fish accelerated, tipped down. I waited. I strip-set.

Hookup!

A carp fights with power instead of speed. I had no choice but to let it take some line. It ran back toward the other two carp, and the other two wanted nothing to do with the hooked fish. They bolted. Which made my fish bolt toward them. Which made my reel purr.

It was no great fight, but I wasn't disappointed. And while it wasn't humane, I did walk the fish during the fight back to Katy and Holden, who had come down to get their feet wet. I could still hear Holden crying and I wondered if the runny nose that had started on the drive over wasn't manifesting itself into something worse. But as soon as he saw the fish, he forgot all about crying. I walked the carp up the beach and then I hand-landed it in shallow water while Holden yelled "ish, ish, ish," pointing, patting the fish once I subdued it, and even kissing its cute golden forehead.

"He's sick," Katy said.

I looked at the boy: red-faced, runny nose, pale eye sockets, big smile.

"Looks fine," I said, thinking of the other black rocks. My carp epiphany.

We took some pictures and released the fish.

I wordlessly began to walk back to the tailing carp, and the boy coughed and began crying. I stood on new ground. I knew it. I looked at the boy. He looked sick. I looked up the bay. The carp were still there. More of them. Dozens of fish in a foot of water feeding. This would be my last carp trip of the summer. The first few Hex had been spotted at the street lights in Grayling. The whole mad dash was about to begin, a season lived in the space of two weeks. By the time the Hex were done, the carp would be gone from the flats for the summer, having spawned and retreated to cooler offshore waters.

I swooped up the kid. And we left.

While there are great pike lakes and rivers in Michigan, pike just get overlooked as a fly-fishing foe. For one, muskie are both en vogue and, well, cooler. Muskie are recalcitrant. They are bigger. Meaner. They are fewer and farther between and far harder to catch. Most pike lakes are filled with "hammer handles"—pike under twenty-four inches. These small fish attack savagely but fight poorly or often not at all, allowing themselves to be retrieved like a clump of weeds hanging from a streamer. The pike is cool. But it's not as cool as a muskie. And given Michigan's stature as one of the better muskie states, the muskie has understandably received top-shelf treatment among Michigan's growing legion of big-fish fly fishers.

I have chased muskie on the fly exactly twice and failed both times. One because I tried to fly fish for muskie out of a tippy canoe, which is something like trying to walk a tightrope on one leg. The other was with Captain Brian, and he was as put off with the poor conditions (sunny, no wind, *dead*) as were the muskie. Muskie anglers use big rods, even ten-weights, and throw big flies on big lines. I would love to catch a muskie on a fly. Though I think that in order to do this, I'll

A day casting for muskie is often a day spent casting. Lake Saint Claire is one of the finest fly-fishing lakes in the country, and even on this unproductive day, we had dozens of smallmouth chase or eat our muskie flies.
ADOLPH M. GREENBERG

have to go many more times than twice! The problem is that there aren't a lot of muskie lakes within an hour of my house. But there are some pike around. And while it's true that a small pike fights as well as a cornstalk might, a big pike—especially a big, river pike—has a bit of a freight train in it.

When the regulations changed on the Au Sable back in the spring of 2011 to allow for year-round fishing on almost its entire length, it opened up a wealth of trout opportunities . . . but also a wealth of pike opportunities. These pike seem to spend much of their time in the lakes and floodings and deep water, but in the cold months they move up into the slower sections of the rivers to eat everything they can. Or, it could simply be that the resident pike simply bite better in the colder water. Either way, we catch them when it's cold out.

Some trout anglers are very anti-pike and I understand that. A pike does eat a lot of fish. I'm sure they eat some trout. But the places where I see the most pike are also places where the whitefish and suckers far exceed the trout population. I doubt this is a coincidence.

My first experience with winter river pike was with my neighbor Tim, and it came in the middle of a pretty good trout day. We were throwing small black streamers, and it seemed we were moving a decent trout every hundred yards. And then I moved a pike. Followed by a larger one. Around the bend, in a big muck flat, a pike came and bit me off. Instead of returning to the small black streamer, I switched to a big olive and white fly. Pike fishing suddenly seemed like a good idea.

Along a deep, dying weed bed a giant pike—the biggest fish of any kind I've seen in the Au Sable—followed lazily behind the fly. I tried to figure eight (in which the fly is kept a foot or so off the rod tip, and the rod tip inscribes a figure eight in the water) but I did a poor job of it. The big fellow slid across the sand and then scooted upriver. A trout moves quickly through the water, to be sure. But a pike, shaped as it is, merely wags its tail and disappears.

In fact, it's odd that pike have this stigma of being lethargic, especially on the end of the line. A big pike has speed characteristics very similar to a steelhead. They can go from zero to nearly twenty miles per hour in under a second. That's a lot of speed.

After Tim and I had our first pike experience, we, along with a few other friends, began to seek out the pike and trout in these lower reaches of the Au Sable using streamers that were small enough to interest trout, but big enough

Pike are more than just violent fish. They are beautiful. They are particular. And despite stereotypes to the contrary, they pull plenty hard. They also have a fondness for bright colors, which makes actively fishing a streamer to them as visual as streamer fishing gets.
JOSH GREENBERG

to interest pike. These were mostly five- and six-inch-long flies, most with two hooks. We fished these flies on fifteen-pound Maxima Ultragreen or 0X fluorocarbon, which would make true pike anglers cringe. But that's what we had, so that's what we used.

Our best day of the season came on a snowy afternoon in late February. Matt and I launched the boat and hardly moved a fish for the first hour. And then, at a slow corner with a series of logjams, he moved two pike, landed a twenty-inch trout, flashed another trout, and then a pike. We switched, and I had a pike of over thirty inches chase my fly to the boat. Only a half-dozen casts later, I caught a twenty-two-inch brown trout. Followed by a nineteen-inch brown trout. Along a piece of backwater cover, I moved a *huge* trout, and set, and hooked it . . . and then it was gone.

"That was a pike, right?" I said.

"Looked yellow to me," Matt replied.

"That was a trout, wasn't it?" I said.

"That was a whale," Matt said.

"That was a whale," I repeated.

We switched again. The sun was setting as we rowed into the last deep bend and we shared a few memories of Hex fishing. Matt clipped off his fly and tied on the biggest thing he could find, some huge wool-headed fly with two serious hooks, a whole chicken's worth of schlappen off the back, and Flashabou and rubber legs and anything else that was lying around the vise. He grunted melodramatically as he began to cast toward the left bank—a couple hundred yards of weed and wood. This wasn't trout country. It was pike country. Well, we didn't know what kind of country it was. The day—a short afternoon, really—had been a series of surprises, an aquatic Jurassic Park. Trout in the pike spots. Pike in the trout spots.

We were talking about dinner, as we often do during the end of a nice, cold float on the winter river. Matt describing the steps he'd take in preparing ribs, the way he'd eat the ribs sitting on his couch, watching some garbage television, the house heat saturating him.

I knew that I'd return to a fire that I built before I left. I knew Katy would politely ask how we'd done without caring one way or the other. I'd eat, talk to her visiting parents, hold the baby, and then disappear to my sanctum to exorcise some fly ideas from my winter skull with the oil heater warming my feet.

The way it happened—the comic seriousness of it—is classic Matt. It wasn't a big pike to most pike anglers. But it was huge to us. While we'd been chatting, Matt had been firing casts toward the left bank. On one of those casts, on about his third strip, a mortar exploded beneath his fly. In retrospect, it was the sort of swirl a pike of that size should produce. But familiarity breeds context. In the context of this river that we'd fished for so many years, had seen live within certain bounds, it was an exceptional water event.

Matt's jaw dropped. I don't mean this as a cliché. He set the hook and whiffed, and his jaw dropped open. The huge fly fluttered behind the boat. The slack draped over him. He stood hunched, his rod dangling, his jaw still dropped, a soft cooing sound blowing from deep in his chest. He looked very much like Jack Nicholson at the end of *One Flew Over the Cuckoo's Nest*, after one too many electroshock therapy sessions.

"Jesus Christ, cast back over there!" I yelled.

Without gathering line, he levered the rod forward. The huge fly fluttered weakly over his head and landed atop forty feet of slack, about twenty feet from the boat. As soon as the fly hit, a wake appeared in hot pursuit. That's when fly-fishing-all-his-life Matt returned. He quickly gathered in the slack. The first strip, and the fish took with a huge, water-humping turn. He set, and the fish fled upriver. Nothing that I've hooked in freshwater could have done better. It was a single, straight-line, furious run, the slack sinking line snapping and whipping as it went through the guides. Then the reel screamed. I followed the fish with the boat, which was probably unnecessary, but it seemed in the spirit of the spectacle (possible Dorf on Fishing movie: *Two Dry-Fly Anglers Go Fishing for Pike*). I ended up netting the pike with my trout net and holding it in place with my free hand.

That night, I proudly served pike fritters to my in-laws, before grabbing a phone and calling Matt.

"How's my pike taste?" he said.

"How's that taste?" Junker yelled, setting the hook. It was dark now, and he and Bjorke and I were not even close to the end of our float. We were popper fishing, which, as far as I know, is the best way to catch smallmouth at night. We cast, and waited, and waited, and the boat moved slowly down the river. And then *pop*. Wait. Ten seconds anyway. *Pop*. The fish took with a sound not unlike the popper made. We caught some big bass. Not many. The fishing was slow. But over a few dark hours we caught a handful of fish over fifteen inches, including one near nineteen inches, and a surprise largemouth—evidence that we were nearing the lake—almost the same size.

We didn't know, at that moment, that the motor wasn't going to work. That we should have drained the gas out of it and put new gas in. That the gas in the motor had likely been in there for *years*. That we would row halfway across the lake with me yanking the pull-start until my sore shoulder was sorer than a day of casting had already made it. That, once the motor lurched uncertainly to life, we would hit a submerged tree. That I'd get a leech on my foot. That we'd get lost down every single bay, thinking we were at the dam. That we wouldn't arrive at the ramp until nearly three in the morning. That we would be looking for something to watch on television and Bjorke would say, "Yes, *The Breakfast Club*, this is a great movie!" And we would watch *The Breakfast Club* together.

We didn't know that yet. We simply knew that we were fishing poppers and occasionally a bass would eat one of them. The motor was a niggling doubt, but apparently only to me. I'm the kind of guy that, when I'm on my day off, is always saying things like "We really should be going now, fellas, shouldn't we?" But why should we? Out there with the universe spread around us and the big, open river sweeping us downstream, and the sound of fly line, the pops of the poppers, the louder pops of the smallmouth. I felt something of *the New Zealand way* in the night. The way, after a few tight-assed months of worrying about things, I loosened up. There was literally nothing else for us to be doing. Our motto was, *Let's get ready to get ready to do something,* and then we'd go on doing what we were doing. Fishing in the day. Drinking tea and smoking hand-rolled cigarettes at night. Hoisting our packs and hiking up a river just to hike up the river. Setting camp. Hooting at the morepork owls. Once, hearing the rare whistles of the kiwi birds. Playing cards. Reading books. Ten straight days was nothing. Fifteen. Twenty. I remember sitting on a huge round rock in the middle of a thrashing river and reading a book on day twenty. And then going fishing in one of the best rivers on earth.

We talked about New Zealand as we threw poppers, floating through the dark. We talked about other places. Bjorke of Finnmark. Kyle of Pennsylvania. Me of Michigan. Time is said to be that which keeps everything from happening at once. But it seemed to me that it was happening at once, and that we were, in fact, momentarily timeless. That we were casting on several rivers, to several species of fish, with several different rods, starring in several different memories. We were on the Crow and we were boiling eggs while watching a trout eat yellow mayfly duns. We were on the South Branch and the hendricksons couldn't fly in the snow. We were in a riverboat with stars flashing between clouds and fireflies flashing between cattails and the Hex spinners were down and Kyle was kneeling in the front of the riverboat working a fish. Or I was with my wife Katy on the Black and we were catching brook trout. With Greg in big water. With Matt, in winter, sneaking on fish in sand. *It is endless,* I thought.

Only the river's slow push reminded me otherwise.

INDEX

towels, 44
Trico hatches, 83–85, 87–92, 96–98

waders, 44–45, 171–72
wading, 32–33, 133, 205–6
WarmWater Tour, 191, 192
Warrington, Terry, 88–89, 91–92, 94, 194–95

water, reading the, 31
weed beds, 33
winter fishing, 43–60
   clothing, 44–45
   fishing, 51–60
   gear, 45
   indicator fishing, 45–50